Women Builders & Designers
Making Ourselves at Home

Other Books
by Janice Goldfrank

The Boston Bicycle Book (with David R. Godine)

Women Builders & Designers

Making Ourselves at Home

Janice Goldfrank

Papier-Mache Press
Watsonville, CA

00 99 98 97 96 95   5 4 3 2 1

ISBN: 0-918949-26-2 Softcover

Cover design by Cynthia Heier
Cover photograph and author photograph by Edward Goldfrank
Interior Design by Julia Hamblin
Typography by Deborah Karas

Grateful acknowledgements:
Photograph and drawing credits: pages 69, 71, 73 by Samantha
Morse; page 78 by Gwen Demeter; pages 84, 85, 88, 89 by Leona
Walden; pages 97 and 98 by Robert Schlosser; pages 102, 106, 109,
110, 190 by Raine De MuLouise; page 151 by Bachrach; pages 155,
156, 158, 159, 160 from Special Collections Division, University of
Washington Libraries.

All other photographs by Janice Goldfrank and
the women profiled here.

Library of Congress Cataloging-in-Publication Data
Making ourselves at home : women builders & designers
edited by Janice Goldfrank.
        p.   cm.
    Includes bibliographical references and index.
    ISBN 0-918949-26-2
    1. Women architects—United States.
    2. Women construction workers—United States
I. Goldfrank, Janice, 1946- .
  NA1997.M35 1995   95-7215
  728'.082—dc20   CIP

Acknowledgments

I wish to express my gratitude to the many people who helped build this book. My parents, first of all, laid the foundation. Later influences prompting me to notice women's accomplishments came first from Bettina Aptheker whom I interviewed for a women's radio program in 1982. Her ideas and personal outlook have been a source of inspiration ever since. I particularly recall her admonition to document women's experiences—not only to set the record straight, but also to make us "visible to ourselves."

Karla Kavanaugh helped me gather the first set of interviews with women builders and, with encouragement from Carole Furman, think about writing a book. There were many other women—building, designing, dreaming, and struggling with many of the issues touched on here—with whom I have had lengthy conversations that contributed to my ideas on the subject of women and building. Donna Lilborn is one of my favorite sounding boards.

I am heavily indebted to the women whose stories I collected but eventually left out for lack of space. They generously provided the materials and the framework for this book by telling me about their lives and their work as they put up with the intrusion of microphone, camera, and probing personal questions.

My most critical structural support has come from my husband, Edward Goldfrank, to whom I am deeply grateful. He helped me in a variety of ways—financial, emotional, editorial—and at all the critical moments, he sharpened my focus on what I've wanted to say.

Eric and Betsy Handley put me up in Boston and gave me the run of their darkroom to print most of the photographs. Thanks also go to the women in this book who loaned me their personal photographs and to the photographers credited in the front of the book. Nelda Patton and Suzanne French Black gave me valuable background information on Elizabeth Ayer. Phyllis Guthrie rescued me by generously pitching in with eleventh hour editorial assistance.

As for the nuts and bolts—and for believing in this project from the beginning—I extend heartfelt thanks to my publisher, Sandra Martz. She guided me through the production process, including revisions and rewrites that would try the patience of a saint. Without her backing, this book would never have been written. Editors Shirley Coe, Laurie Neighbors, and Kim VanDyke also worked hard to make the book coherent. Leslie Austin, production manager, Julia Hamblin, designer, and Deborah Karas, compositor, did the finish work.

Contents

Introduction

I don't remember exactly when I first became interested in designing houses. My father had a workshop in the basement, and as a child I was allowed to play with his scrap wood. Although he taught me how to use some basic tools, he didn't promote my education in the mechanical arts. I'm sure he didn't think I would need to know more than how to hammer a nail and operate a screwdriver. On the other hand, I wasn't discouraged from learning how to do things. When I was quite young, my folks bought an island and eventually built a cabin there. The whole family helped, but it was pretty much a case of grunt labor organized by the foreman, my Dad, who was the only one who needed to know what was going on. I didn't look at the blueprints or understand how the cabin was all put together. I did, though, learn quite a bit just witnessing the process, and I saw that a person could build a house without professional help.

All during my childhood, I was constantly making things—a Halloween costume, a rabbit cage, even a wooden raft (it sank). However, most of what I created

"My father had a workshop in the basement, and as a child I was allowed to play with his scrap wood."

would probably be considered arts-and-crafts projects. I certainly never thought I was heading toward a career as a carpenter. My proficiency with tools was considered harmless recreation, perhaps a convenient capability, but not a necessary skill.

When I entered high school, I found even less support for nontraditional activities. I recall taking an aptitude test, the results of which the guidance counselor discussed with each student. About that time, my art class was learning about architecture, and I had been drawing a design for the "perfect" house. I never thought I would build my own house, but I was fascinated with the idea of controlling my living space. My guidance counselor, who knew nothing of my enthusiasm for designing, told me my profile was pretty typical, except that I had a remarkably high score in the mechanical area—especially for a girl. Then he said, "But don't worry about it." This was in the early 1960s before the women's movement provided a political model for understanding the insult this represented. I was, however, vaguely offended and never forgot his words. I knew that he was defining limits for me.

Yet my design interests continued through college, where I majored in art history and took several courses in architectural design and history. I whittled away many hours in the library doodling floor plans when I should have been studying. Not only did the aesthetic elements intrigue me, but also the challenge of devising a plan that offered everything you wanted in a house. Somehow I could never get all the elements—traffic patterns, sunlight, efficient use of space—right at the same time. The design always resisted a satisfying solution. I didn't take it seriously; it was just a puzzle I enjoyed. It never occurred to me to pursue this as a career. Eventually, however, circumstances put me in a position to design and build my own house.

"There were moments when I would have quit if I could have. There were also glorious moments—it was a creative process and was very engrossing."

In 1975, my husband and I joined his brother in a fledgling cabinetmaking business near Kingston, New York. Without hesitation I took up a "man's" occupation. After a few years, my husband and I decided to strike out on our own, and we moved to Columbia County, a few miles southeast of Albany, New York. We searched for months for a house to rent or buy, but we couldn't find one we could afford. So we bought a piece of land and began building a house and a woodworking shop. We really didn't know what we were getting into, but our friends assured us we could do it. After all, we had all the tools we would need, and we knew how to use them. We hired an architect to help us plan the basic layout, then we asked everyone we knew for advice on how to proceed.

We bought a small trailer to live in, moved onto our land, and worked from dawn to dusk nearly every day for a year. There were moments when I would have quit if I could have. There were also glorious moments—it was a creative process and was very engrossing. Unfortunately the trailer had no heat or running water, and the roof leaked. In effect, we spent a

year outdoors. Even though it was unpleasant at times (most of January and February, as I recall), I was physically healthier than at any other time in my life. It was harder than we expected, it cost more, and it took much longer than we thought it would. But we built our own house. And the experience had a profound impact on my life. It was simply the biggest tangible thing I had ever done.

We moved in as soon as we could, then got to work reestablishing ourselves in the cabinetmaking business. I met a few other women in the area who had done some carpentry or who were furniture makers. After being surrounded by men in the business, as well as having been trained by men, it was a treat to talk to other women about work. I realized I wanted to experience working alongside other women. One of the cabinetmakers I met felt much the same way, and we decided to do a joint project. In no time, we had enlisted four or five women and did a small remodeling job and a few repairs for neighbors. We had a good time, and we decided to make a business of it. In 1982, we formed an all-woman carpentry company called Octagon.

I had learned from building my own house that I could do more than I felt capable of doing, and this realization extended to my experiences with the business. We were hired for jobs that stretched our skills and knowledge. This caused some anxiety, but somehow we forged ahead, found out how to do whatever we were called upon to do, and succeeded.

By the beginning of 1985, my business partner, Karla Kavanaugh, and I decided to shut down our operation for a couple of months and travel together. We wanted to meet other women in construction—to find out what other women builders were doing and how they approached their work. Carole Furman, a mutual friend, expressed an interest in our plan; she hoped to learn whether women design differently than men. She suggested we formally interview the women we met on our trip and write a book defining these differences.

Karla and I met and interviewed several women who had designed and built houses, but the material we gathered wasn't enough to answer the question of how gender influences design. We collected some wonderful stories, though, and other fascinating questions were raised in the process. Upon returning from our trip, running our construction business took top priority, and the interview tapes gathered dust for almost five years. In the meantime we divided the partnership, and I continued to do remodeling and construction on my own as Octagon Custom Builders, Inc. Yet I kept remembering what I had seen and heard from other women builders and wanted to explore the subject further. I held onto the hope that someday I would be able to write about women's experiences building houses.

In the years since that trip, many women have told me they want to build a house. Several women asked if I would be willing to teach them carpentry. For some, this was the first step toward being able to build a house. For others, it was a way to increase their independence and self-sufficiency. I have since taught introductory carpentry to many women in workshops and to apprentices in my own business, and I watched the women change in the process. Building seems to have many layers of meaning for women—issues of control, self-esteem, identity, ambition, and their place in society. I began to realize that housebuilding is not an unusual fantasy for women. However, unlike men, who call their building fantasies plans, women are more apt to refer to these aspirations by another word: Women call them dreams. And most women don't expect to actually carry out those dreams.

Yet there are women all over the country building houses, communes, apartment buildings, and cabins in

> *"However, unlike men, who call their building fantasies plans, women are more apt to refer to these aspirations by another word: Women call them dreams."*

the woods. Most of them are inventing their actions as they go; they have no one to model as they begin their projects. They have probably never seen other women build houses: women did not build the houses in their neighborhoods; their female relatives are rarely builders; and it is unlikely that their women friends have done anything remotely similar. My firsthand encounter with the isolation of being a tradeswoman

*"It's a powerful experience—
it stretches and bends,
challenges and frustrates,
and sometimes reveals profound insights to women."*

and a builder has led me to wonder how other women build and what it means to them.

Over and over, I heard women who built their own homes say the experience changed their lives. It's a powerful experience—it stretches and bends, challenges and frustrates, and sometimes reveals profound insights to women. This is a part of women's culture and contemporary history that is scantily documented. In fact, I have been unable to find a single book on the subject of women who build houses. I decided that it was important to look more closely at what was going on with these women and to share what I learned.

By 1990, when I finally tackled the job of writing this book, the topic had evolved from its original emphasis on design to encompass the much broader question of the importance to women's lives of engaging in the building and design process. I contacted some of the women Karla and I had interviewed in 1985 to learn about the changes and progress they had made in the intervening years. Then I interviewed several additional women in 1990 and 1991. As in 1985, I was amazed at what I saw women accomplishing. The structures they were building, the design issues they were addressing, and the persistence they were showing in spite of the challenges were and continue to be impressive.

In 1992, I taught an eight-week class for women who had been victims of domestic violence. The program was designed to boost their self-esteem and enable them to become more self-reliant. I taught them how to change the locks on their doors, make minor repairs, and tackle common household emergencies. The results were spectacular, and I was deeply moved by seeing the transformation that acquiring those simple skills allowed. So two years later, I designed a job training program to help women enter nontraditional occupations such as carpentry, plumbing, painting, and equipment repair. I obtained funding for the program, put my contracting business on hold, and became program director of Training for the Trades. Having launched the training program, I was finally able to complete the manuscript for this book. I hope that it encourages more women to realize their dreams of building or designing houses, note their accomplishments, and think about what houses mean to all of us.

In this book, I describe the buildings the women profiled have built or designed. I convey their attitudes about their work and explore the design elements that intrigue them. In some cases I suggest what enables these women to realize their dreams when so many other women do not. I probe their backgrounds and personalities and their perspectives on their lives and work. I attempt to determine what these women brought to building and what they took away from it. As is typical in such an endeavor, more questions were raised than answered. But I hope the answers and the questions stimulate further thinking about women builders, their motivations, and what can be learned from them.

*"The structures they were
building, the design issues
they were addressing, and
the persistence they were
showing in spite of the
challenges were and con-
tinue to be impressive."*

My sample is not random, and it doesn't necessarily represent the experiences or the thinking of the majority of women building and designing houses in America at this time or in the recent past. The selection presented here represents women who came to my attention through informal contacts and word of mouth. Inevitably, my own focus and time limitations narrowed the scope of the project. Most of my contacts came from middle-class and white communities, but this was unintentional. I don't know if most women who build and design houses are middle class, or white.

The women profiled in this book encountered diverse phenomena and faced a variety of decisions—from women who built their homes with their own hands and those who built houses for other people, to architects and designers. Their reasons for choosing to build or design houses also varied widely. Some had no prior carpentry experience; some were professional contractors. Their houses are elegant, employing state-of-the-art technology, and extremely modest, humble cabins built with salvaged materials. Some women found joy and liberation in building their own homes, while for others it was an ordeal.

The first part of this book documents the projects and careers of the women I interviewed. I explore their backgrounds and what led them to housebuilding, their various design processes, and their feelings after actually building or designing a house. In Part Two, I share what these monumental endeavors mean to women, combining comments from the women profiled in Part One with my own experiences and observations.

Part One

Part One

In some ways these women are remarkable. But largely they are ordinary women who have a little extra self-confidence, determination, or who needed houses they couldn't afford to buy (so had to build). In looking for a common thread among them, I did not find one in the kinds of houses they designed or built or in their attitudes toward their work. I became intrigued as to how these women became who they are and how they decided to build in the first place. I wondered if there was something in their backgrounds that made it possible for them to dare—often without training, preparation, or social support—to undertake building a house or trespass in the male domain of architecture.

As women, we are socialized to believe building and designing are things we cannot and should not do. We're untrained, we lack role models, and we sometimes have to overcome resistance from family, friends, teachers, and employers. The distinction between men's and women's roles starts very early. Little boys are encouraged to be physically active. Climbing trees is excellent preparation for climbing ladders and scaffolding. But little girls are praised more often for being cute than for being competent, daring, or mechanically inclined. While boys are learning to fix their bicycles, girls are learning how to assemble a wardrobe. Later still, girls are warned (in many subtle ways) not to be *too* smart or *too* ambitious. So for a woman to overcome these limitations and build a house or become an architect takes a lot of personal strength.

Although most of the builders described here took on their projects with little or no carpentry experience, they usually had something in their backgrounds that prepared them in some way for the demands they would face. Many were already familiar with handling responsibilities as children—they cared for younger siblings, had jobs, or came from families where self-sufficiency was a necessary survival skill. The architects came from families in which women had careers. So they knew what it meant to be resourceful, and they approached the task with the idea that they could find out what they needed to know.

For some of the women, doing nontraditional work was an act of resistance. They take pride in doing "men's work," or they believe that women should have equal say in how homes and communities are structured. Several of them said they wanted to avoid being like their traditional-minded mothers. They wanted more control over their lives and objected to the passive role they were expected to fulfill. Others did not see themselves as rebels in any way. They knew that what they were doing was unusual for women, but in other respects they considered themselves entirely conventional and properly "feminine."

The women whose stories are recounted here had a variety of backgrounds, personalities, and reasons for building and designing houses. But they all had in common high degrees of self-determination. This does not necessarily mean they had a lot of self-confidence. Many had periods of doubt and uncertainty over what they were doing. But they all persisted because of a strong drive to be authentic—to be themselves, in some very profound way.

These women produced a variety of styles—modest cabins, elegant town houses, sprawling mansions—to accommodate diverse living arrangements. The structures aren't limited to houses, either; they include a dormitory, a conference center, hospital buildings, and high-rise apartment complexes. Those who did building primarily by themselves found out it is an enormous amount of work. Collaborative ventures sometimes went smoothly, sometimes not. Women who hired professional help had the easiest times, but they also found that the role of construction manager requires its own set of skills and knowledge to perform well. The architects, trying to establish themselves in a traditionally male profession, had to struggle to be taken seriously.

In combination, these stories reveal something not just about how women's houses are structured, but also how our lives are structured, and about what happens when we take such matters literally into our own hands.

Karen Terry

Karen Terry grew up in upstate New York and later moved to the Southwest with her family. She married and worked as a secretary for many years. Following a divorce, she quit her job, went back to school, then went to Alaska to work on a fishing boat. When she came back to the Southwest five years later, she built a solar adobe house. She went on to build numerous adobe houses in the Santa Fe, New Mexico, area and was a pioneer in passive solar design.

Santa Fe Solar

Karen Terry has been building houses in and around Santa Fe, New Mexico, since 1974. She didn't plan her career as a builder; it came about through a chain of circumstances that took her from Denver to Alaska and finally back to Santa Fe, where she had lived years earlier. She had worked for fifteen years as a secretary in order to support herself and her young son. Raising a child alone was emotionally and financially draining. She was bored and unfulfilled. Her job felt stultifying, and eventually she became seriously depressed.

I was in a high-rise office building in Denver. It was a pressurized building, and you couldn't open the windows. Everybody had terrible headaches and sinus problems. It was because of the air—the pressure was ruining us. I tried to jump off the roof. I went up there, but I couldn't get out. They had the door locked. So I took the elevator down, and I walked out, and I said, "I don't care what happens. I don't care what I have to do. That's it. No more." I had to do something utterly different.

Fortunately, about that time Karen inherited some money, which allowed her to step back and look at her life. Her teenage son went off to boarding school, and she returned to college to study art. This wasn't enough of a change, however, so when she saw an opportunity to do something radically different, she jumped at the chance.

A friend of mine went up to Alaska and took up with a fisherman. I said, "Can you get me a job?" She said, "Yeah, I know a boat that would be just right for you." So I went. I got a job on a salmon fishing boat. I was there for five years.
Was it hard? You bet.

While working on the fishing boat, Karen gained a lot of self-confidence as she learned she could do many things for herself that she hadn't tried before. When she returned to New Mexico, she was ready to settle down. But she didn't want to just buy a house—she wanted to design and build her own home. Karen isn't sure why building the house herself was so important other than that she remembers feeling the need to have complete control over her life.

I wanted to build a house. I just decided I wanted to do it, though I had absolutely no idea how to do it. So I thought, well, I'll go to work for somebody and learn how. But then it became apparent that nobody would hire me.

"There were no other women builders at that time."

There were no other women builders at that time. So then I thought, I'll hire somebody to teach me. That's much smarter. So I hired Tom. We built the first house together. I'd guess I did about 75 or 80 percent of the work. It turned out to be a gorgeous house.

Tom taught Karen the basic construction skills she needed. Like the fisherman Karen had worked for in Alaska, Tom was an independent jack-of-all-trades. But he was also a careful craftsman. Karen learned to pay attention to detail and to work with precision. Together they made a great team. She'd supply the idea and the vision, and he'd figure out how they could make it work on the ground.

Karen had been interested in solar houses for some time. She had the good fortune to connect with David Wright, an excellent architect who had already made a name for himself in the emerging specialty of practical solar designs and had an expert command of the technology. With his help, Karen plunged right in, even though she had no background in construction or design.

In keeping with the traditional building style of the Southwest, Karen built her first house of adobe bricks and covered the floors with tile. Her design perspective had been influenced by organic shapes. When she studied art in school, she had enjoyed working with clay. She was struck by how familiar it felt to be building with adobe.

It was really exciting to build a big pot like that. I had been doing a lot of pottery, but here was this whole big house.

The roof was mostly glass, slanted to catch the sunlight and direct it into the house, and was equipped with louvers that covered the glass in the summer when heat gain was not desirable. For cloudy winter days, Karen installed a backup wood stove, but the house was designed to depend primarily on solar heat. The heat absorbed during sunny days was released gradually from the adobe mass, generally delaying the need for additional heat for several days.

Passive solar houses were very rare in 1974, so this one made a big splash. News reports, magazine articles, and a tremendous amount of attention were showered on Karen. The idea was considered very futuristic. Besides the technological aspect, the shape and layout of the house was highly unconventional. The combination was irresistible to the media and fascinating to the architectural community.

It was exciting. There were conferences and television and all this stuff. Then I got a wild idea that I should build another one. I had five or six thousand dollars left. I bought land, then I went into a savings and loan with all the articles about the first house. We built it. We had an open house. Three thousand people came, and we had six buyers the next day. We started to feel swell, you know.

The second house—a sinuously curving adobe with hardly a right angle anywhere—is one of the best examples of early passive solar design. Retaining walls surrounded a patio in front and the wall extensions that formed partitions at the front of the house sloped gently to the ground. The edges of the adobe walls were softly curved as well.

Part of what made the second house so successful was that it was set into a hillside with the front at grade-level and the back completely underground. Thick concrete provided retaining walls and formed the back and sides of the house. The floors exposed to sunlight were made of brick for added heat storage, and the front of the house was mostly glass, set in two tiers. The first tier was floor to ceiling; the second tier formed a clerestory set back from the front wall at the depth of the front rooms. This way, the rooms at the back of the house got natural light. There was also a skylight over the dining area.

A side door, made possible by a retaining wall that opened the buried portion of the house to the lower grade level, provided light and ventilation to the back of the house. The house was relatively small with about 1,500 square feet of living space, but it seemed roomy with two bedrooms, two baths, a kitchen, a dining room, and a living room.

Because of the incredible amount of exposed mass, the house was calculated to need no backup heat for seven days without solar gain. In spite of architects' and engineers' assurances, however, the bank that financed the house insisted on the installation of a backup electrical heating system.

The first few houses I built created quite a stir. It's all integrated into the system now. Everybody builds passive solar. But at that time, there were only four or five examples to show of the whole incredible idea, and I had two of them, so . . .

Then I started to make mistakes. I built another one that was a disaster. It was a much too ambitious house. It was on a mountainside, and we had to carry every adobe brick up the hill. I think I had eight guys working on it. I didn't know anything about that kind of an operation. It was a nightmare. I had to borrow money to finish it. It went way over budget. I had no idea about budgets and stuff. And then it wasn't so salable because it was pretty expensive.

I didn't know what to do. I just took two thousand dollars that I had left, and I went to Europe, trying to run away from it. I was crazy all the time I was in Europe. I

"I've built almost one house a year since then."

called the Realtor from the post office in Nice. He said, "Get your ass home—it's sold." I just started screaming (in French), "I sold my house! I'm going home!" Everybody sort of smiled.

I've built almost one house a year since then.

The house Karen was working on when she was interviewed in 1985 was one of the last spec houses she did. She did most of the work herself. The front of the house's long curve, which was repeated in the matching line of the stone retaining wall that enclosed the patio, earned this house its name—the Curved House. The interior rooms were laid out along the back wall and separated by dividing walls but were mostly open on the front side. Though it was a small house, the open plan and the large windows made the interior seem much larger. A gently undulating side wall at the west end and the curved dividing wall between the bedroom and bathroom added an overall feeling of softness.

While she worked on completing the Curved House, Karen began developing plans for the Pyramid House, which was built in 1988, where she now lives. A small, square building with a pyramidal metal roof, it has 1,200 square feet of living space. The long-range plan is to double its size with an addition (also with a pyramidal roof) connected to the first section by a greenhouse-entryway. Currently, it has a Trombe wall

backed by an adobe wall on the south side which acts as a heat sink, and the roof has a dormer on one side that will match the dormer planned for the addition. Inside there is a loft covering half of the downstairs space. Oddly enough, this house is stud-frame construction (unusual for Karen, who generally builds with adobe bricks). However, she did mud the exterior surfaces so the house has a traditional adobe look.

The land surrounding the Pyramid House is beautiful. Her property has several large trees and two small hills at the back of it. In the desert, finding an interesting building site with water, road access, appropriate zoning, and reasonable pricing is quite a chal-

---

"The hills made me think of the design for this house."

lenge. Karen walked the land for a long time before deciding on the exact location for her house. This was no easy feat; she had injured her knee and was on crutches the entire time. Getting around over soft sand and uneven ground was exhausting, but Karen was determined to site her house very carefully.

The hills made me think of the design for this house. This was the place. This little hill, right here. It's wonderful because the wind can be howling up the valley and through that tree so loud that you can hardly hear yourself think. And it's totally still right here where the house is. The wind just goes up over it—aerodynamics.

Karen built and designed ten new houses, reconstructed and added on to three, and remodeled three others. She did some of the work herself and hired a crew or subcontracted the rest. Doing her own work was not easy, but on the other hand, being a general contractor and having to oversee the work of other people also took a great deal of time and energy—and patience.

Karen managed to make enough money from each house to secure financing for her next project. She found herself becoming something of a land speculator and developer. But even in the height of the building boom in Santa Fe, spec building was no sure ticket to prosperity. She had to work hard, take risks, and keep her eye on the bottom line. Her success seems to derive from a combination of ambition and excellent design sense.

Karen's primary goals in designing a house are making spaces that are the right size and shape for their functions and creating the right balance between indoor and outdoor activities. Every house she built was an adventure for her. Even though it was hard, she loved the work. Karen said that the later houses had fewer problems than the earlier ones because her designs were better, she made fewer mistakes, and she was able to plan more realistically.

Of all the houses she has built, Karen likes Pyramid House the best. Its symmetry and church-like, pyramidal space is very appealing. The simplicity and refinement of the design make it really stand out. It was well engineered, and construction went more smoothly than on any other house she has built.

Karen decided to stop building when she finished her last house. It has been difficult to make money in the current economy, and the physical demands are intense. However, there never seems to be a "last" house. There's always just one more project that has to get done, one more idea to capture her imagination.

I discovered, after I'd been to college, that I didn't want to work for anybody else. I guess that's where I got it, going to art school. Because you learn to think in creative patterns, and you learn that if something doesn't work out one way, you know, you learn to turn it around. I don't know. I'm just maturing, I guess. Learning how to make it better.

I really would like to not do this, but . . . on the other hand, I keep thinking—my goal, I guess everybody's goal, is to have a house that you like, free and clear, on land that's free and clear, and enough money to live on that you can invest it and not work. Hell, I'm close, but I'm not there yet.

When I asked her where her ambition came from, she attributed it to her personality and the admiration she felt for her father. Her mother's goal was only to "do right and be good," which meant to be a proper wife and mother.

My father wasn't like that. My father was great. He was a self-made man. He was ambitious, but not manipulative. I must have got my messages from him. I'm just different, I guess, from all the rest—my cousins and my sister. I've always just wanted to be like my father. I don't know. I like to do things. I like to make things.

Jane Dexter

Jane Dexter grew up in Vermont on a dairy farm, where she loved to work outdoors and operate farm machinery. She married at twenty but left the marriage four years later, seeking independence. She found a job at a sawmill and later bought some adjacent land on which she built a house from trees she cut herself, and almost entirely without power tools. After building her home, she built a barn and then a cabin for her elderly aunt and uncle. She has since remarried. In 1994 Jane, who had become co-owner of the sawmill, sold her share of the operation and opened an independent sawmilll service business with her husband. They plan to build a new house on nearby property.

Sawmill House

Jane Dexter moved to Sutton, Vermont, in 1974 after a divorce, to establish a life of her own. She wanted to build a house as soon as she could save enough money. While looking for work, she happened on a part-time position at a local sawmill. The job was originally intended to be temporary, but she discovered she liked the work. The part-time job became full-time, then a partnership, with Jane as co-owner of the mill (originally Fox Sawmill, now called Calendar Brook Lumber).

I was just fascinated by the whole activity of making logs into lumber. Something intrigued me. I don't know what. But it still does. Every log is different and every piece of lumber is different. It's a challenge to imagine where each piece of lumber is going to go in a building structure.

Three years after arriving in Sutton, Jane bought some wooded land on the side of the mountain above the saw mill and set out to build a house on it.

It was part of my need for independence. I had a need to establish something of my own. Hands on. Create for myself. I also really wanted to experience the process of building from start to finish. I thought it was possible, and it turned out it was.

Jane took great care in selecting the location for her house and would not be rushed into picking a spot until she knew every inch of the land surrounding it.

I spent a year skiing on it and looking at it in different seasons. It was hard to pick the exact spot for the house. I traipsed around through the woods a lot. I kept going there and having picnics. And I tried to imagine what it would be like without trees.

I tried to take as many things into consideration as possible. Partly the lay of the land. Partly the size of the trees—how much lumber I could get out of the area I needed to clear for the building.

Jane's friends also offered suggestions. They pointed out that the farther off the road she built, the more difficult it would be for firefighters and other emergency workers to reach her, and the higher her insurance rates would be. She didn't want the location of her house to be based on an insurance perspective, but there was also the question of safety. In the end, she

"I had a need to establish something of my own."

scratched her first-choice location deep in the woods in favor of a site closer to the road.

Once the site was chosen, Jane began to design the house, incorporating a little of everything in her design process. She thought about the proportions of classical Greek architecture to create a pleasing facade. On a more practical level, she wanted a house that would be easy to heat during cold Vermont winters. Her plan was to build another, better house someday and convert the first building into a woodworking shop, so she was really designing two buildings. She thought that as a workshop the building could get by with only an outhouse, but she eventually decided to put in a bathroom.

To Jane, including a lot of windows on the south side was one of the building's most important features. She wanted plenty of light for both a workshop and a house. She also included plenty of storage space in her design. She planned to use the attic for lumber storage, so she made it easily accessible.

The building's orientation was another fundamental consideration. Jane placed the house, located on a mountainside, so the ridge of the roof would run east and west to get as much heat and light into the building as possible. The sun is high enough in midsummer that the house doesn't overheat, and in the winter, when the sun is low, it is bright and sunny. She put her bedroom on the east end to get the morning light.

Jane's friend Peter Moore, a builder and architect, helped her design the house and drew up plans for her. He taught her a lot of basic construction techniques (such as how to lay out window headers) and showed her standard building practices, explaining why things were done a certain way.

Once the plans were drawn, Jane made very few changes. Peter also was among the several people who came on weekends to help Jane build. The friend who helped her the most was Eileen Riley, who lived with her on the land that summer. They basically built the house together.

Actual construction began in the summer of 1977. It was an exciting, though not easy, time. Jane started by clearing trees for the building site and skidding logs down the hill to the mill. She worked full-time at the mill during the day, then built at night and on weekends. Jane's boss at the sawmill, Warren Fox, helped her by sawing logs and offering advice on construction details.

The building was twenty-four feet wide, thirty feet long, and one-and-a-half stories tall. Since it was not intended to remain a house forever, the structure had a somewhat rustic style and was constructed mostly with rough-sawn lumber. The total cost (in 1977) was around $2,500, which included the spring and waterline. Fortunately there were almost enough trees in the area being cleared for the house to provide the lumber for construction. Also, Jane was able to use the mill's bulldozer and grade the site herself. She couldn't afford electricity at the site until several years after the house was built, so trimming the rough boards to size was done with a chain saw or a handsaw.

Jane and Eileen dug four-foot-deep holes for piers, put footings in the bottom, and built tapered forms (held together with metal strips of lumber banding from the mill). They filled these with concrete, forming the piers to support the body of the house. The piers were spaced every ten feet around the perimeter of the building.

The first floor was built with an uninsulated crawl space beneath it. Since Jane couldn't afford insulation for all parts of the house, she planned to leave the crawl space uninsulated and bank the house with straw in the winter. (This technique works. The ground never freezes under the floor, and it stays dry.) She did, however, put 3 1/2 inches of fiberglass insulation in the walls with a vapor barrier on the inside. Inside, the walls were covered with whatever boards she could scrounge, mostly planer rejects from the mill. The exterior siding was vertical, shiplap pine, with no underlying exterior sheathing. To have something to attach the siding to without sheathing behind it, Jane and Eileen nailed blocking between the studs (a time-consuming and frustrating chore).

The subfloor on both the downstairs and the bedroom upstairs was made of hemlock boards that were only three to five inches wide. That was what was available cheap. They took a lot of time to lay. Especially since we ran them diagonally.

Jane got windows for her living room for a dollar apiece at a veneer mill that was being torn down in North Troy. She repaired the broken glass and built frames for them. She chose these windows for their large size and traditional shape. Although they are fixed-glass windows that don't open, windows on the second floor, which do open, provide plenty of ventilation. All things considered, it was quite an accomplishment for a summer's spare-time work.

"That September it rained for twenty-nine days straight."

I cut down the first tree on my birthday, June 12. The house was closed in enough to use by mid-October. There was no insulation in the walls yet, but the wood stove was hooked up. We were working day and night, living in a tent. It was hard. That September it rained for twenty-nine days straight. We were soggy and miserable a lot of the time.

Jane admits she didn't know what she was getting into when she started building. She didn't realize how much work it would be or know what to expect. Friends occasionally showed up for weekend work parties, but mostly she and Eileen struggled alone.

We made parties out of it. It was depressing and fun at the same time. We ate a lot of pizza. I just remember night after dismal night trying to warm up and dry our clothes off at the local pizza parlor. And this was Eileen's very first experience pounding nails anywhere. I can remember some teary nights toenailing the blocking for the siding.

Although she is pleased with her house, there are some things Jane would do differently, such as using wider floor joists to eliminate the springiness in the floor. The 2-by-8s she used meet code, but they aren't stiff enough and flex a little when you walk on them. She would also think harder about how to handle the insulation. It is a dilemma for her, as both an environmental and practical consideration. She doesn't think fiberglass is entirely safe, but she thinks it is the best thing currently on the market.

Her next project, in 1979, was to build a barn.

I still had the farm in me. I really wanted a few animals around me. So I built a barn and got a cow. And I raised up some pigs in the summertime.

Originally Jane had wanted to build a combination house and barn . She wanted to have a few animals, especially a cow, near her in her new home. Fortunately, friends convinced her it would be a good idea to keep the cow in a separate building.

By this time Jane was on her own, and the 24-by-40 foot barn was pretty much her handiwork. Again, she used a chain saw and a handsaw, although she did have a gasoline-powered generator to power a circular saw, which she used for some of the rafter cuts and studs.

Before she started the barn, Jane cleared more land around her house. She hired a man with a team of horses to do some logging, and she sold some of the logs and the pulp from others in order to pay him. She kept the low-grade logs, which had a low sale value, for her own use. The wood was mostly tamarack, a very strong wood. Since the wood was going into a barn, Jane didn't care if some of the logs were a bit twisted.

Eventually Jane bought more land to provide a pasture for her cow and a site for a second house. (She now has a forty-acre plot, with mixed hard and soft woods, a clearing, and a meadow.)

Since Jane's first project, her uncle and aunt had enjoyed visiting from Concord, New Hampshire, to watch her progress. In 1984, Jane decided to build a little cabin for them. In return, they paid to have electricity run to the property.

Unlike the house and the barn, the cabin was constructed entirely of "store bought" lumber. The sawmill had burned down the previous year and had not yet been rebuilt. After the fire, the sawmill owner retired, and Jane and three others formed a partnership and bought the business. They rebuilt the mill and reopened it as Calendar Brook Lumber. The new mill hadn't started operating when Jane started building the cabin, so she was left without any way to saw the lumber herself.

The cabin began as a one-room building; it was built on two large beams and was well braced. Someday, when her aunt and uncle no longer needed the cabin, Jane planned to bring the skidder up from the mill,

move the cabin near the house, and attach it as an addition. (Her garden shed was also designed to be movable—she can just pick it up with a forklift and move it to a different spot if she wants to.)

Jane originally planned to build the cabin way off in the woods, to fulfill her aunt's fantasy of owning a "little cabin in the woods." Again, however, practical considerations—like access to electricity and the driveway—won out, and the cabin was built in the same clearing as the house.

A few years later, Jane remarried. She and her new husband, Bruce, added a downstairs bedroom to the back of the cabin; Jane's aunt and uncle had been using a foldout couch in the main room, because the finished upstairs floor was accessible only by a pull-down staircase. The addition was built entirely of wood Jane sawed at her mill, which makes the place very special to her and to her aunt and uncle. When Jane sees the familiar pieces of wood, she remembers the individual logs and how she decided which logs to cut for which size lumber.

Jane and Bruce covered the lower half of the bedroom walls with wainscoting made of twelve-inch-wide pine boards. And, as in the main part of the cabin, Jane ran a bead by hand along the edge of each board and placed a cherry wood rail at the top of the wainscoting

"When Jane sees the familiar pieces of wood, she remembers the individual logs and how she decided which logs to cut for which size lumber."

to match the floor and the door and window trim. She also hand-plastered the walls above the wainscoting and used pine boards for the ceiling.

I didn't think it would take as long as it did. I am still surprised at how long it takes to do some parts of a job. Finish work, especially. To do a nice job, you just have to take some time with it. It always takes about twice what I expect it's going to.

Despite her farm background, Jane hadn't done much actual carpentry before she started her own house. As a child she had regular responsibilities, in the house and on the farm. She loved machinery and field work. She helped with the haying and couldn't wait until she was old enough to drive the tractors. Her parents were very supportive of her interests and projects.

Although she had helped some of her friends with their building projects, and she had some experience doing minor repairs, Jane wasn't as familiar with tools as she was with large machinery. And she didn't really get acquainted with lumber until she moved to Sutton. But she does remember one special carpentry project.

I was maybe eight or nine years old. It was to surprise my dad on his birthday. Some of our cows were big old Holsteins. When a Holstein gets big and old, so do their bags—their udders. If they stood in the gutter (which they tended to do), then their udders dragged on the cement. So I built a wooden platform that would fit right down in the gutter that the cow could stand on so that she wouldn't ever get to the point where her bag was dragging.

I had to sneak that project—work on it after school without my dad knowing. I went out in the middle of the night before his birthday. He used to get up at a quarter to four to start milking, so I had to get out there before that and have it in the barn behind that cow with a bow on it. I was so proud.

Jane's original plan was to turn her house into a workshop and build a new house on the meadow at the top of her property. Instead, she and Bruce found a spectacular piece of property about three miles away which they purchased and on which they intend to build a new house. In the meantime, they have built a workshop there, where they manufacture the patented "Dexter File Guide," a tool she and Bruce invented to sharpen the huge saw blades at local mills. They also repair saws and consult on production and operation problems for mills in the area.

Jane has sold her share in Calendar Brook Lumber and plans to sell the old house—a "horrifying" idea at first. However, she's excited about the new house and plans to start construction this summer. She also wants to move her aunt and uncle's cabin to the new site.

When she and Bruce designed the new house, they paid a great deal of attention to exterior aesthetic details. Jane remains attracted to maintaining square or rectangular shapes in the overall design of a building. The pitch of the roof is critical to her. She feels that the entire roof, including the cornice work and the window trim tied into it, can make or break a design, and she places a great deal of importance on window placement.

When I was a kid and in school and doodled, I always doodled houses. You know, this house and that. Different roof pitches and different additions and ells and so forth. My sense of building is that a house should be beautiful from both the inside and the outside. When you're driving and looking at different houses, there are some houses that just feel warm, and they fit. They're right. And there are certain design features that make them that way.

"I love wood. I'm always coming home with a piece of wood under my arm or on the rack up on the truck."

Jane looked forward to building the new house as an opportunity to use some of the special pieces of lumber that she set aside at the sawmill, then moved to her attic to slowly dry. She has an impressive collection of prime boards—clear spruce, clear cedar, and some twenty-inch-wide pine.

I love wood. Bruce teases me. I'm always coming home with a piece of wood under my arm or on the rack up on the truck—just can't let this one go by. That's going to be a fun aspect of finishing off the new house—doing the different gleanings justice. The treasures. There's going to be no holding back on this; this is the place where I say, "What have you been keeping this butternut for, any-

way?" It's no more, "I'm saving that for the house." This is going to be the house. It's time.

Like some of the other women in these profiles, Jane believes the rewards of building go beyond owner-ship. Her sense of control over her surroundings and intimacy with the house she created are deeply satisfy-ing. Clearing the land, shaping the contours of the site, and building the house, barn, and cabin herself have had a profound, if subtle, influence on what it feels like to be "home." The house and the land are in some way an extension of herself. So in a sense, that which is "Jane" in the world takes up a much larger space than it would if she lived in someone else's house (regardless of whether or not she was the legal owner). By building her house, by creating what she calls the "settlement," she enlarged the boundary between herself and the rest of the world. Jane also thinks about how long-term a housebuilding enterprise is. What she put into it extends her "self" in time and in space.

It feels really good. There is less and less construction going on with that consideration in mind. Most of the peo-ple who come here to buy lumber want the smallest, cheap-est stick they can get, just to get themselves by. When I built the cabin, I put my name, a newspaper clipping, a coin, and a few little things in the cornice return. For posterity.

Dale McCormick

Dale McCormick grew up in New York City and Iowa. She was the first woman in the country to enter and complete a union apprenticeship in carpentry, then she started her own carpentry business and taught carpentry at an owner-builder school in Maine. She built her first house with the help of students at the school, and she designed and built a second house, partly with hired labor. She wrote the books, Against the Grain: A Carpentry Manual for Women *and* Housemending: Home Repair for the Rest of Us. *She now administers a preapprenticeship training program for women in construction trades, and she is a state senator.*

A Long View

Unlike many of the women interviewed, Dale McCormick was a professional carpenter prior to building her own house. She is part of that special group of women who broke the trail for women entering union construction work.

Dale was first exposed to carpentry in shop class in second and third grade in New York City's progressive Downtown Community School, where both girls and boys took art and shop.

I cannot remember not being able to use tools. I knew how to saw, hammer, and use a chisel. I remember I made a boat out of a 2-by-4. I chiseled out the center and put a mast on it, a dowel mast. I also made a planter box. Those are major things for a kid that age to do. I have adult students making things like that as their first projects.

I think it had an amazing effect on my later life. It's like when you learn how to tie your shoe or ride a bike.

"I cannot remember not being able to use tools."

You just don't forget it—it's that kind of motor skill. And I cannot remember not being able to do that, which is quite something for a woman of my generation to say

Unfortunately, when Dale and her family moved to Iowa she wasn't allowed to take shop there, because it was against the rules. But with the support of her parents, she participated in 4-H, where she refurbished an old shed on her parents' property for her lamb and built a chicken coop.

Dale was involved in a variety of group projects, such as putting on puppet shows with other children in her neighborhood. She recalls being a sort of foreman on these projects, doing much of the stage and set building and directing.

Dale feels that her take-charge attitude is a result in large part of having great expectations put on her as a child. Although these expectations weren't necessarily explicit, she feels there was substantial pressure on her to make up for the chaos and mayhem of a dysfunctional family life.

Like most other tradeswomen pioneers, Dale has a great deal of determination. In the early seventies, she decided to apply for an apprenticeship program and asked a male friend to pick up the application at the union hall. She used her own name, which could be read as a man's name, on the forms, and her friend submitted them and made an appointment for her—being careful to avoid referring to Dale with a pronoun. Then Dale kept the appointment in person.

The business agent couldn't believe that it was me. It took him five minutes, literally, of double takes and saying, "This is for your brother, right?" "No. It's for me," I said.

"This is your husband sent you down here, didn't he?" "No," I said, "this is for me." And then he said, "Who sent you? Somebody sent you. The government sent you, didn't they?" I said, "No. The government didn't send me." "They're trying to get us, aren't they?" I said, "No. I really want to be a carpenter."

Finally he said, "Well, they could have been smarter. They should have sent a black woman." He just never got it. I said, "Fine, whatever you say, just let me take the test." So I took the test, and I got the highest score. Then they were in a pickle.

Although they did enroll Dale in the union apprenticeship program, the president of the union wrote a letter to the business agent, saying, "Heavy construction is no place for a woman."

Dale received her journey-level card in 1975 and was hired immediately by a private contractor to work as a carpenter. But with a slowdown in construction, she was laid off in less than a year. She made good use of the time, however, by writing *Against the Grain: A Carpentry Manual for Women*, published by the Iowa City Women's Press in 1977.

After finishing the book, Dale decided to start her own construction business, specializing in energy-efficient buildings, greenhouses, and solar additions. She later accepted a job at Cornerstones, a school in Brunswick, Maine, for amateur builders, hobbyist woodworkers, and people who wanted to learn to design or build their own homes. She expanded their hands-on program, supervised a new in-house contracting arm, and developed a housebuilding class for women.

In 1983, Dale decided to build her own house, a small post-and-beam structure on the edge of a blue-berry field in Yarmouth, Maine. She chose the land mainly because of the view: a 60-acre blueberry field behind the house site, and beyond that a border of timber. Having a long view was one of her highest priorities, influenced, she felt, by having grown up in the Midwest.

She did much of the work alone, but she received a lot of help from the students and instructors at Cornerstones. Raising the structural frame became a class project for a timber-frame course, and her women's carpentry class helped with the finish work.

Dale's house combined the best features of old-fashioned framing methods with the latest in superinsulated construction technology. It was tiny by most standards—600 square feet—but Dale thought of it as a starter house. She designed it so future additions would not disrupt the basic function or design of the house.

Living in Maine, Dale first and foremost wanted a house that was going to be warm, so her design centered on the heating system. She carefully calculated the amount of south-facing glass she would need for passive solar gain (15 percent of the floor area is considered ideal), and she made sure all of the joints and seams in the house were sealed tightly to eliminate infiltration of cold air.

She put drywall on the outside of the wood framework of posts and beams, stapled vapor barrier over it, and attached Larson trusses to the outside. The outermost layer was 1-by-12 clapboard siding. The Larson trusses were 2-by-2 wood strips separated by a series of $3/8$-inch plywood panels about eight inches wide. The trusses were attached vertically and at right angles to the outside of the wall at two-foot intervals.

The 2-by-2s on one side were nailed to furring strips on the wall, and sheathing was attached to the outside 2-by-2s. The plywood in the Larson trusses spaced the sheathing out from the wall and formed the sides of cells, which were filled with fiberglass insulation.

There's a great deal of satisfaction and ease of living that happens when you live in a house that works. I can remember living in apartments where I had to wear my down jacket in the living room because it was so cold, because air was coming in at such a rate that nothing could be done. That didn't happen in my house. Now when I go to people's houses, I get annoyed if they're not warm and cozy houses. And sunny. And pleasant. It's possible to do.

The house had a kitchen, bathroom, cathedral-ceilinged living room, and a loft bedroom. The loft, nestled under the ceiling with a view through the dormer windows of the blueberry fields, was Dale's sanctuary. The most impressive part of the house was

"There's a great deal of satisfaction and ease of living that happens when you live in a house that works."

the living room, with its huge hammer-beam trusses. The tall, open space, white-walled with exposed dark wood beams, made the small room seem spacious. The oak beams served as heat sinks as well as structural support. If the house was cold, it took a long time to heat it up, but once it warmed up, it held the heat well.

A few design elements didn't work the way Dale had envisioned. For example, the kitchen window should have been lower so she could see out easily while she ate. She briefly considered building up the floor in the kitchen but in the end decided to just accept it.

Although the kitchen, situated under the bedroom loft, was small and cozy, the house didn't have the diversity of spaces Dale would have liked. Additionally, the living room had a high ceiling (seventeen feet at the peak) that made the room feel almost too big. The effect was very dramatic—the tall space, along with the cathedral-like beams—but it was a little grand for such a small house.

By fall 1985, Dale had finished the Yarmouth house and had begun to write a book on remodeling and home maintenance, *Housemending: Home Repair for the Rest of Us,* published by E.P. Dutton in 1987. Two years later, Dale started construction on a second house in Monmouth, Maine.

When Dale began to design a second house, she employed concepts she learned from Steve Oransky's architectural design class at Cornerstones. The course was based on the theory of thinking first about what kinds of spaces you wanted in a house—defined by how they "feel," the textures they have, the kind of light they should have, and what goes on inside them—then fitting the house around those spaces.

It entailed using bubble diagrams to show the relationships among spaces, but not how the spaces would be shaped, constructed, or sized. Large bubbles indicate more important rooms, and smaller bubbles represent less important rooms. Houses are laid out to get the desired light and flow from one room to another. For example, to have east light in the kitchen and the ability to walk directly from the kitchen to the dining room or living room, one bubble was drawn for the kitchen on the east side with two adjacent bubbles for the living and dining room.

Exactly how the rooms would be constructed—how the parts of the house would be physically connected—was not decided until it was known how the rooms connected experientially. A privacy gradient was used to rate how public or private each space was to be. She marked these ratings on her sketches, which helped determine traffic flow between adjacent rooms. The bubble diagram was transformed into a floor plan as the rooms took final shape.

When Dale began her design project, she was living alone, but she was in the early stages of a new relationship with a woman named Betsy Sweet. Later, as she began to contemplate sharing her house with someone, she realized that not only was her original design too small for two people, but it didn't reflect the needs of the other person. It was *Dale's* house. So she had to start all over again and come up with a design for the two of them.

What you realize is that designing a house makes you ask very large life questions. Like where do you want to live, who do you want to live with, who is in your life, do you want children, how much private space do you want, how many people are going to cook at the same time?

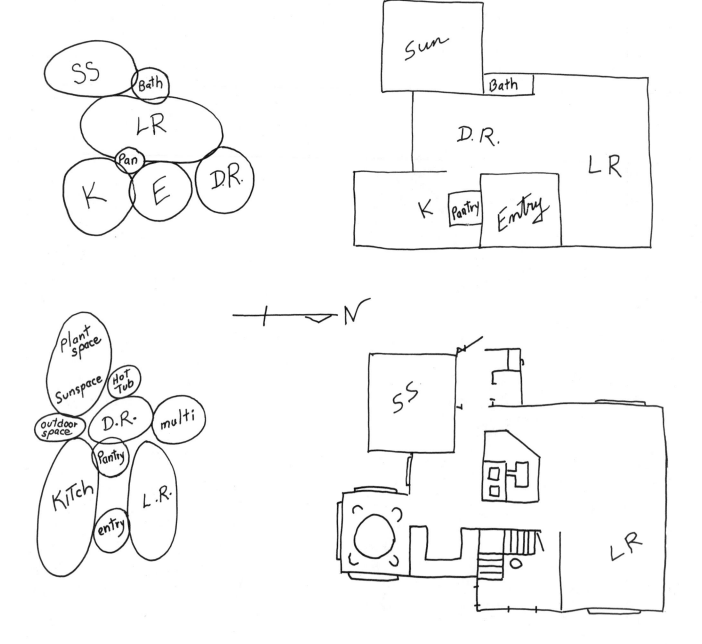

Dale and Betsy sat down and made a list of all the activities they expected their house to accommodate: How much square footage did they think each activity would take? What time of day would each room get used the most? Which rooms did they want to be bright, airy, and open? Which ones should be small, cozy, closed in?

They traded drawings back and forth as they worked through the design process. Step by step, Dale transformed their drawings into plans, plotting how the

> *"What you realize is that designing a house makes you ask very large life questions."*

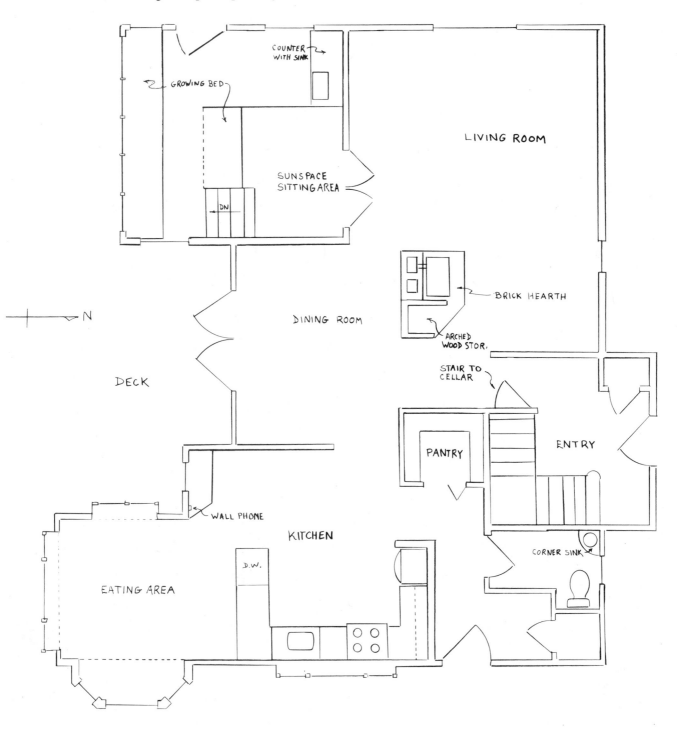

rooms would connect, where the stairs would go, how the second floor would relate to the first. Problems came up and were worked out as Dale started figuring the framing plan around the functions.

One of the more important design problems they encountered was dealing with different living habits— not to accommodate different room arrangements, but to account for their polar-opposite standards of tidiness. The challenge was to design a house that allowed them to live together without getting on each other's nerves. Could they confine messiness to part of the house and designate the rest of the house as neat space? Should they maximize the separate, private space of each person and deal with incompatibilities only in common areas?

Dale was convinced there was a solution to most of their differences, and that it's harder to change one's personality than it is to change one's physical environment. She knew that people can adapt to what they have, but why miss the opportunity to anticipate and address the known problems?

The solutions lay partially in designing a house that would be easy to keep clean, with lots of well-organized and intelligently placed storage space. The kitchen turned out to be the focal point for dealing with the issue of clutter. Both Dale and Betsy are politically active and very social, so they designed a dining room big enough to accommodate a large number of people and to hold meetings comfortably. They also included an informal sitting area in the kitchen where they could be social and cook meals at the same time. Since Dale spends a great deal of time on the phone, she needed a

place in the kitchen for a phone and for desk space where papers could accumulate without interfering with food preparation.

They designed an alcove at the side of the kitchen as an office nook, with a long phone cord so Dale could keep an eye on the stove while paying bills or talking on the phone. It would provide a communications center for the house and keep paper confined to one area.

Of course, to some extent that stuff takes over the whole house. But that is not a design flaw. That is a life flaw. I mean, paper is the bane of my existence. What to do with it. Where to put it. You're going to laugh at this, but I've always believed that if we have physical structures around us that are efficient, then our lives will be more efficient. That theory is what led us to put a "paper space" in the kitchen. I still labor under the illusion that if we can

*"But that is not a design
flaw. That is a life flaw."*

*just get the right combination of little mailboxes to put on
top of the bookcase in the kitchen, that the table will not be
cluttered all the time and that we will be more organized.*

Dale and Betsy worked well together, agreeing on
most issues. The only major design contention concerned window placement in the bedroom. One of
Dale's goals was to get light from two directions in each
room. However, for the bedroom she wanted west light,
and Betsy wanted east light. Eventually, they solved the
problem by putting the bedroom over the sitting area in
the kitchen, which had three outside walls providing
eastern, southern, and western exposure.

Dale also tried to consider disability issues—not
an easy task—during design and construction. To make

the entire house wheelchair accessible, it would have
had to be a one-story dwelling, but single-story houses
incur greater construction costs and are less energy efficient than multistory houses. They did provide an
accessible downstairs bathroom, and planned to eventually make the entire ground floor accessible for people with disabilities.

Another priority for both Dale and Betsy was a
multipurpose greenhouse. A small pressure-treated
deck at the back of the greenhouse was planned as a
three-season sitting area. Raised above the level of the
greenhouse floor and furnished with a stuffed chair and
a table, the deck provided a clean space in which to sit,
eat, or read, leaving the lower level as a gardener's work-
space. Since they wanted the greenhouse to provide
both heat and fresh vegetables, that required a sloping
glass roof. Some heat is gained from a vertical-walled
greenhouse with a solid roof, but to grow plants the
glass had to be tilted toward the sun—otherwise the
light would pass through at too much of an angle to
allow the full spectrum that plants need. Designing the
roof and building it properly so there would be no leaks
was a major undertaking.

For heating, the greenhouse also included a water tank for preheating hot water to use in the house. Also, connecting it to the house by a second-floor window allowed heat from the greenhouse to flow up into the house. If the downstairs door was also opened, a convective loop was created that evened out the temperature of the house. The heat in the greenhouse rose, flowed through the window at the top into the second floor, moved downstairs as it cooled, flowed across the floor, and was drawn back into the greenhouse through the open door by the vacuum created when the heated air passed out the upper window.

Dale also included "positive outside space" in her design, with a small quadrangle on the south side of the house, next to the dining room. The space is sheltered by the two projecting ells of the greenhouse and the kitchen's sitting area; it catches the sunlight and stays warm from early spring to late fall. A deck is also planned for this space.

Dale chose a Victorian arrangement of gables that made the roof framing somewhat complicated. Since this design is relatively labor intensive, the roof was rather expensive. But Dale felt it was worth the extra expense to achieve the look she wanted.

An entryway was also part of the Victorian motif. She wanted to provide gradual access to the house, rather than being dumped in the middle of the living room upon entering. A true Victorian entryway would have been much bigger, but the house was getting very large already, so they settled for a small entry that contained the stairwell and a hall to the living room, dining room, and kitchen.

Groundbreaking for the Monmouth house was in the spring of 1987, and construction took about a year. During that time, Dale was also writing grant applications to fund her preapprenticeship trades-training program for women, as well as paving the way for her election campaign, which would win her a seat in the State Senate in 1990. Dale wanted to do the wiring and other parts of the project, but she had begun to run out of time. So she did some of the work—the greenhouse, almost all the plumbing, and with Betsy's help, the siding—but contracted out the rest.

Even though much of the physical work was done by others, Dale continued to oversee and supervise the job. A carpenter-contractor was hired to erect the frame and do most of the carpentry, and an electrician did the wiring.

The drywall and insulation were also contracted out, in a relationship that proved to be difficult. Dale was very particular about leaving no gaps in the insulation—she wanted to do an infrared scan to make sure. (Holes in a superinsulated house make it un-superinsulated.) It took a lot of assertiveness on her part to get the contractor to comply with her directions.

The finish carpentry presented another tough situation: The carpenter thought of himself as an artist. Dale found she had to be around most of the time to

"The chimney was constructed of two-hundred-year-old brick."

ensure that the trim and the flooring were done to *her* design, not his.

Dale always looked for ways to simplify and reduce the amount of work involved in the project. She chose to build exterior walls into the skin of the house on the outside of the skeleton. This way she eliminated both having to build stud walls to fill in the spaces between the bays and the time-consuming process of cutting drywall to fit the irregular surface of each post and beam. For the ceilings, Dale even painted her stress-skinned panels before putting them on top of the roof timbers, so she didn't have to build scaffolding to paint the ceiling afterward.

Dale also hunted for bargains in materials. One of her better finds was the trim work from a house slated for demolition that belonged to Bath Iron Works. Dale used the turn-of-the-century, four-inch-wide molded cypress with fan-shaped corner pieces for some of the door and window casings.

The chimney, which Dale designed herself, was constructed of two-hundred-year-old brick from a house that had been torn down in Litchfield. The brick was too old to reuse in an exterior application, so the mason sold it to Dale for her interior chimney. She liked the old brick, which has softer edges and creates a warm effect.

On the inside, door and window trim added to the lushness of the design. Dale and Betsy decided to use hardwood for the baseboards and door trim in the living room. Although the effect of the rich, reddish cherry is beautiful, Dale discovered hardwood trim entails a massive amount of work.

They cut a round molding into the trim boards as an added touch, which gave texture to the trim and looks very old-fashioned, reminiscent of the casings in many of the older houses in Maine. The trim boards are 3/4-inch thick, and they used one-inch blocks at the top and bottom of the side casings around the doors.

These blocks serve two functions: the effect is elegant, and the installation is easier. The finish carpenter can make all the trim pieces with straight cuts and butt joints, which are more forgiving than flush joints. And it is less time-consuming than doing miters (forty-five degree angles, picture-frame style). The blocks project a

little from the boards, adding depth and texture to the trim work.

Dale and Betsy moved into the house as soon as the interior was substantially complete, leaving some of the outside work to be finished when they could afford the time and money. But, as people who move in before everything is complete often discover, it's very hard to get around to the final touches.

During construction, Dale had worried about the overall proportions of the house; it seemed tall and imposing. But the final grading raised the ground level next to the house about two feet. Once the deck is built, the house will seem lower, since the deck would spread the footprint of the house at the bottom, lowering the apparent center of gravity.

The siding would also affect the appearance of the house. At the back the exterior sheathing is still covered with vapor barrier—creating a large, white mass that is cold and aggressive-looking. When the siding is finished (a combination of wood shingle and clapboard with a twelve-inch-wide trim board run horizontally around the house), the house will appear lower and more settled, as it now does on the north side.

I think, in general, that if houses work, then your life works better. If you move into another person's house, unless you can knock down a few walls or move things around, that space isn't going to help your life work better. I think that belief drove me to want to design and build this house. Of course, that's completely optimistic. It's just the essence of a Pollyanna.

In this instance her optimism seems justified. The house continues to function the way it was intended and gives them a lot of satisfaction. And from her office aerie on the third floor, Dale can take a moment from her work to look out over the woods and fields and enjoy a long view from her own home.

Is this my dream house? Yeah, I would say so. It would be more dreamy if it were done. But that's not a function of the dream. That's a function of reality.

"I think that belief drove me to want to design and build this house. Of course, that's completely optimistic. It's just the essence of a Pollyanna."

Rosa Lane

Rosa Lane is the daughter of a Maine lobsterman. She built her first "house," a tiny cabin in the woods behind her parents' home, at age eleven. When she was twenty-five, she built a real house for herself. That structure later became the kitchen and dining hall for Hardscrabble Hill, a conference and workshop center for women that she helped found. Rosa is a poet, an activist, and a builder. In 1991, she graduated from the University of California at Berkeley with a degree in architecture and is now a licensed architect. She is the author of a book of poetry, Roots and Reckonings.

Hardscrabble Hill

Rosa Lane grew up in New Harbor, Maine. Her family never had much money, and she credits her background for her self-confidence, resourcefulness, and general competence. As a child, in addition to doing endless odd jobs around the house, she helped her father repair and build lobster pots. She learned how to use tools, and she watched buildings under construction. In Rosa's case, poverty made for self-sufficiency.

When you're poor and in Maine, you can't afford to pay a plumber or any specialized labor. You just can't afford to pay for it. So then you just do it yourself. I guess it really comes back to that sense of being a survivor. Surviving was the greatest achievement.

The house Rosa grew up in was originally a boathouse. When the boat her father built was launched, he partitioned the inside of the boathouse and converted it into a home for his family. Over the next few years, he made improvements as they could afford them, with young Rosa and her mother as his helpers. She and her mother spent many hours side by

> *"I grew up with, really, a hammer in one hand and a doll in the other."*

side pounding nails. Rosa picked up some carpentry skills in the process and, quite naturally, learned something about how a house is put together.

I grew up with, really, a hammer in one hand and a doll in the other. I would be downstairs hammering on Dad's pots, you know, his lobster traps, from the time I was six or seven going on 'til I got out of high school. I helped him paint his boat, pot buoys, and build traps, and I'd go lobstering with him.

My father really believed in me. There wasn't anything, ever, that man didn't think I could do. Nothing. Ever. One of my uncles told my father, "Oh, you got just girls. They won't amount to much." My father never told me, until recently, he had lived with that, what my uncle had said, and the pain it always had for him. But he said he always knew underneath that his girls could do anything.

Rosa responded to that encouragement in a big way by building her first "house" when she was eleven years old. She was sharing a small bedroom with her two younger sisters at the time, and the walk area was simply a path between beds. Every day the bedroom was a potential battleground.

Rosa wanted privacy more than anything else in the world. So when her father left out some extra lumber from a new cellar he had just built, Rosa couldn't resist the neatly stacked pile. She found a secluded spot in the woods at the back of the yard and started to build herself a house.

I would take some boards—every day I would haul a few more down so he wouldn't notice. No one knew about it 'cause they went out fishing. It was in the summer. It was only forty or fifty yards from the house, but you couldn't see it. But pretty soon Dad said to my mother, "That lumber pile. Something's happening to my lumber, Marie." I just kind of hid in the living room behind a chair. But Mom came in and said, "Do you know any-

thing about what your father just asked me?" It was time to tell them, and I told them I'd built a house that I was moving to. At first my parents were pretty upset. They were more mad that I was going to move out of the house than at my taking the lumber.

Rosa's camp, as she called it, was solid and well built. The little 12-by-12 cabin was set on rocks for a foundation, and had sills, plates, studs, and rafters—all of the basic elements of stud-frame construction. The rafter cuts were amazingly precise, and the windows and doorway were framed out correctly. The rafters even had the proper bird's-mouth notches so they would sit flat on top of the wall. The cabin contained furniture she had built: a table and chairs and a set of shelves. She had even constructed a loft with its own stairs. Also in the cabin were some of Rosa's toys, which she had carefully sneaked from her parents' house. She hung a devil mask on the door to keep everyone away.

I never got to live there. The family wouldn't allow it. But I went down and stayed there daily. It became, really, a phenomenon in the town. And eventually my father was proud of me. He would show people what his eleven-year-old daughter had done.

That little cabin allowed Rosa to develop her sense of self as separate from others. Still standing in 1985, twenty years after it was built, it had a caved-in roof and sagging walls, but otherwise was remarkably intact.

After spending years sharing living quarters with other people—sharing a bedroom with her sisters, living in a college dormitory, living in rented apartments with roommates—Rosa wanted a place of her own.

She found four acres of land in Orland, Maine, on a ridge overlooking Penobscot Bay, and on June 16, 1975, Rosa stood on her very own property—with $257 in her savings account. She invested $250 to install a driveway and bought $450 worth of lumber on credit, which the lumberyard allowed her to pay for in $50 installments. Over the next two weeks, Rosa worked from five o'clock in the morning until she left for work, and again after work, from five-fifteen until dark.

When she began construction, there was no electricity at the building site, so Rosa worked only with hand tools. She laid out the perimeter of her new home, making sure she picked a high spot so rainwater would drain away from the house. Her house was to be 16-by-20, one story with a loft. For a foundation, she stripped the bark from cedar posts, applied several coats of used car oil, and dug eight holes (by hand) four feet deep. The main carrying beams (6 by 6 by 20 feet) were laid parallel to the long dimension of the house and spiked into the posts. The joists (2 by 6 by 16 feet) were laid crosswise to the beams and toenailed into place. She laid one-inch-thick rough-sawn boards on top of the

"My father was proud of me. He would show people what his eleven-year-old daughter had done."

joists and beams as a subfloor. Then she was ready to frame the walls.

First, however, she needed to know how large to make the openings for the windows. For $100 she bought odd-sized and secondhand windows from a local dealer. Then she walked around the platform, picturing activities that would take place within each space and positioning the windows accordingly. She made a rough sketch of the framing plan for the walls, then assembled the walls, using the subfloor as a platform, sliding each wall off the edge to make room for the next. When she was done, each wall was on the ground next to the appropriate side of the house. All that was left to do was to tilt the wall up and lift it onto the platform.

Then it was time for a work party. Rosa invited all her friends, cooked a feast, and had her own "barn raising." In one day, they raised all four walls; plumbed, braced, and nailed them into place; and installed the joists for the loft above. The next step was to complete the second-floor loft and build the roof rafters. Rosa felt

"I nailed the last bit of roofing, braced myself against the ladder to the loft, and wept deeper than I had ever wept up until then or since."

that getting the roof framed in was an exceptionally thrilling moment. It was like a three-dimensional line drawing thrown up into space.

In a matter of hours, the house is released from the earth and connected to the sky. I fantasize that I am inside a whale with its wide rib cage towering above me.

Sister Lucy Poulin, who Rosa knew from her part-time job at Homeworkers Organized for More Employment (HOME), helped her build the rafters. Together they figured out the angle of the rafter cuts, based on how much headroom Rosa wanted in the loft. They also built a dormer into the roof to increase the usable space there. They completed the job in two days. Then Rosa closed in the walls, applied the tar paper, installed the windows, and made and hung a door. Though the house was far from finished, she couldn't wait to move in.

This was the first time in over twenty-five years that I had a place I could call my own. On August 18, 1975, I nailed the last bit of roofing, braced myself against the ladder to the loft, and wept deeper than I had ever wept up until then or since. I was finally safe. I slept my first night in my own home I built myself.

Rosa lived her first year in her new home without electricity or plumbing. The walls glistened with uncovered foil-backed insulation, and tools and lumber piles decorated her living room. But it was home, and it was warm.

Rosa's little house became the seed for a much larger project—Hardscrabble Hill, a retreat and workshop center for women. Rosa and two other women, Margaret Pavel and Gayle Dawn Price, began building the center in 1975. Rosa's house was converted into a kitchen and dining hall, and eventually seven other buildings, including meeting rooms, a staff house, a bath/shower house, and dormitories were built. Some of the work was done with the help of friends and workshop participants, sometimes as part of a workshop on carpentry or house building. But Rosa did the bulk of it herself.

Hardscrabble Hill's builders shared a dream to provide women a safe place to gather and take whatever steps they felt necessary for personal, professional, or social change. Margaret led workshops on personal and professional growth, Gayle Dawn led wilderness expeditions, and Rosa taught poetry and carpentry. Hardscrabble Hill's vision encompassed concepts such as self-sufficiency, harmony with nature, feminist process, creative expression, and spirituality. These women also felt that collaborative effort was itself a potentially rich field for exploration.

Operating the center and constructing the buildings for Hardscrabble Hill were mutually inclusive activities for Rosa, both in terms of timing and in the nature of the undertaking. Each carpentry workshop focused on whatever building was under construction at the time. Along with this hands-on experience, each student was given the option to design her own house. Many women took these workshops because they anticipated building their own homes and were taking the first enabling step.

"Each carpentry workshop focused on whatever building was under construction at the time."

It was very important to me that each woman design her house and experience the confidence to build it before she left the workshop. Each woman was at a different place with respect to building construction. Some women had never held a hammer before, others knew how to operate power tools. No matter the level of previous experience, the carpentry workshops focused upon the place of confidence each woman had experienced before. Whether she was a massage therapist (who knew touch and pressure) or a business analyst (who knew project management), these skills were transferable to construction and could provide beginning places of success from which to launch into the unknown.

Rosa helped support the building activity at Hardscrabble Hill by working the midnight shift at the paper mill in Bucksport for two years. She used the credit union for short-term loans, borrowing money to buy enough materials to get started, then, after paying that back, immediately borrowing enough to cover the next phase.

It was a shoestring operation, but in 1977 they opened the center and began serving women in three- to eight-day workshops in writing, theater, carpentry, nutrition, and spirituality. Fifty-eight women attended the first summer. Over the years, more than two thousand women (including nuns, surgeons, flight attendants, poets, artists, factory workers, political activists, and farmers) came to Hardscrabble Hill to write, paint, make music, hike in the forest, and meditate in a peaceful setting.

In 1982, after obtaining an M.F.A. degree from Sarah Lawrence College, Rosa moved to California to help Joanna Macy with the writing, editing, and designing of her book, *Despair and Personal Power in the Nuclear Age*. Rosa has lived in California since, but she returned to Maine each summer to operate Hardscrabble Hill, until it closed in 1986. The three founders of Hardscrabble Hill had become involved in graduate school programs, and they decided, regretfully, to close the center. Today the buildings sit empty, ready and waiting for the next vision.

At thirty-five, Rosa returned to school to study architecture, satisfying a creative side that needed a further outlet. As a poet, Rosa found building interfered with her ability to concentrate on writing. She also discovered that when she did find time to write poetry, she lost interest in building. It occurred to her that architecture might be the perfect vehicle to combine these disparate elements in her life. She envisioned architecture as a form of physical poetry that would draw on both her creativity and her practicality.

"Architecture and poetry are similar not only in the creative process but in their actual structure."

Architecture and poetry are similar not only in the creative process but in their actual structure. The poem is an "open-air" architecture where internal information is partially or fully exposed: walls are peripheries, more like translucent membranes, through which air and light pass. When successful, the reader is able to easily locate a particular entrance, participate in an activity with transformative possibility, and exit at the necessary, appropriate place.

In architecture school, Rosa found her construction experience was both "a blessing and a curse." She knew the nuts and bolts of wood-frame construction, and she knew the implications for the carpenter of all the options she might be considering, but she also found that she tended to design only what she knew she could build. In order to free her imagination from the prejudices of her own experience, Rosa decided to design for a completely different kind of construction technique. She turned to concrete for a time, and the strategy worked—she was able to move into the unknown.

Long before her formal training in architecture, Rosa's design focus had centered on the psychological impact of a design on the inhabitants of a room or a house. She held an underlying conviction that buildings should enhance the well-being of the people who use them. Over the years, Rosa's design beliefs expanded to include the neighborhood and community of the building site. She feels that a designer must consider a building's impact far beyond the structure's boundaries in space and in time in order to be harmonious with and beneficial to human activity.

When approaching a new design, Rosa first thinks about what activities will occur inside the space, then about the effect of design elements. She envisions a person's movements through a house. If there are stairs, she imagines how they will look and what it will feel like to use them to move from one portion of the house to another—in a sense, moving into a different realm. Rosa believes the designer can pleasingly accentuate this transition by creating an atmosphere that feels safe and familiar, yet full of magic and surprise. How the second floor is visually revealed as you near the top of the stairs, how light and shadows change the appearance of a room at different times of the day or year, how the upper level feels compared to the lower one—all of these elements can be manipulated to create a particular mood.

A meeting space they dubbed the "Japanese Teahouse" at Hardscrabble Hill was a good example of Rosa's philosophy. The plastic roof panels made the room feel light and airy; because the plastic was translucent, the light was soft and diffused rather than harsh and distracting. Clear skylights would have created sharp contrasts between spotlighted and shadowed areas of the room. They would also have offered a view of the sky and the trees around the building, providing a distraction. The room was intended to induce peace and contemplation. The undivided and uncluttered space, piles of soft pillows in lieu of furniture, the plain, square shape of the room, and soft light all combined to create a contemplative ambience.

Design is an extremely complex process. The designer must hold several images in mind simultaneously. When working on a floor plan, for example, Rosa must also consider the elevation (how the walls and openings will look when viewed from straight on) and how the building fits into its site.

When she draws in a window, Rosa thinks about how it fits in the floor plan, how it will look to a person standing in the room as well as to someone outside the building, and how it will facilitate or inhibit the flow of light, air, and psychological connectedness or separation in the building. She mentally takes the building apart and puts it back together over and over again as she works.

In order to keep track of these elements, Rosa uses model-making extensively. She builds models with removable roofs, and, if multistoried, floors that can be separated. She uses toothpicks to make models of people, marking eye level. For a child's room or a facility for people in wheelchairs, eye level is lower than for the average standing adult. Then she moves her model person through the model house, imagining what they would see.

Rosa looks, for instance, at how a building might affect someone's reactions. For example, when a stranger enters a building, does the layout communicate what they need to know to find their way around? Are there features that help guide people or reinforce the information they are getting in other ways? Are rooms intended for rest actually restful? Do rooms intended for more activity draw one naturally forward? Rosa tracks through the entire building with her toothpick person, making adjustments wherever problems are revealed. The building changes from being an object to being a series of perspectives that affect the people in various ways.

I relish every aspect of design from initial rendering to electrical diagrams. My favorite, however, is the first phase of design, which addresses the site context. Undoubtedly, there is rich history and a vocabulary that goes with each and every site. The building-to-be can respond to this memory. It can inform future building images and provide seeds for the imagination: farm buildings, barns, fishing shacks, an old stone cellar hole, a rock wall, tree formations, the shape of snow drifts, the house next door, the neighborhood.

One of Rosa's last tasks as a graduate student was to conduct a study of a small coastal community, Bodega Bay, in northern California, in which she evaluated the responsiveness of a waterfront development project to community needs. This tourism-based development was encroaching on the original fishing industry and threatened to swallow not only the remains of the fishing activity by displacing it, but the character of the community itself.

Having grown up in a setting similar to Bodega Bay, Rosa could identify with the dilemma, one that is facing many small communities today. How do you bolster a weak local economy without damaging your resource base or the web of human relations that make up a community? Rosa originally intended to specialize in designing therapeutic environments (such as hospices, nursing homes, and other health-care institutions). But now, inspired and intrigued by her experience with Bodega Bay, she decided to pursue community planning.

What we have are towns and cities which bought a developer's dream of more revenue, and the resulting coastline of schlock which eventually is avoided by tourists. What I want to do is to consult with towns to design for both the short-term users (tourists) and the long-term users (natives) from an understanding of authenticity and basic economics.

Rosa, now forty-five, still lives in California, where she works as an architect. She has developed a model for urban facilities for the homeless and designed several houses, public education facilities, office buildings, historic landmark restoration work, and accessibility modifications to commercial buildings. She still, however, returns to Maine every summer. She now sees her first house with a different perspective. She thinks about how much more she knows now than she did in 1975. Yet the house doesn't look crude or ungainly to her. In fact, she sometimes stands and looks at it almost in awe—impressed with the elegance of its simplicity, and with herself for having done such a good job with so little experience.

In spite of having moved her base to the West Coast, Rosa hopes to reactivate Hardscrabble Hill in 1997 as a place to teach women how to design and build their own houses. She already envisions how the program could work. With a drafting table in each of several private rooms, the women would have an opportunity to design and sculpt their own houses. This would be followed by a hands-on training session in building techniques. Each woman would end up with the support, knowledge, and tools to convert a dream into working plans.

Women have important contributions to make to built environments. To instill confidence in women to begin and continue to design and build is an urgent commitment for me.

Carol Yee

While Carol Yee was growing up in Connecticut, she often vacationed with her parents in Vermont. Carol began building a log cabin in Vermont in 1969. She had no power tools, so she carved and notched the logs by hand, built the fireplace, chimney, and foundation with stones and concrete, and split and shaped the wooden roof shingles by hand. She did most of the work herself, or with the help of one hired woman and the many women who attended her weekend work parties. After living there for ten years, she returned to Connecticut and built a triplex (mostly with hired labor) with two land partners, Michelle Giffin and Christine Acebo. Carol is a cabinetmaker.

Vermont Log Cabin

When Carol was in her early twenties, during the rise of the counterculture in the late sixties, she decided she wanted to live in the country, be self-sufficient, and "do her own thing." She hoped to create a communal land project, but wasn't able to, so she decided to build a log cabin for herself on a beautiful eighty-acre piece of land in Benson, Vermont, where her parents had a summer cottage that, in 1969, was very inexpensive. After she bought the land it took her a couple of years to raise the money and get organized enough to start construction.

When Carol Yee built her cabin, she spent very little time thinking about the design. She figured, "I just want a little log cabin with a porch and a loft. What's to design?" So she determined the cabin's size according to what she thought she needed as a single person and what she could afford to build. She wanted a loft for sleeping that would leave part of the downstairs a cathedral ceiling, as well as stained-glass windows somewhere. And that was about it.

When she began building her cabin, Carol had no knowledge of construction techniques, but that didn't stop her. She just made it up as she went along. Although she did hire a backhoe operator to help get the rafters up, the rest was done with elbow grease, hand saws, and, occasionally, a chain saw. Friends came for work parties. For the initial stages of building the

foundation and lifting the logs into place, she hired another woman, Susan Durrance, to work with her. For income, Carol relied on intermittent painting jobs on Martha's Vineyard. She would work for a while, make a little money, and return to Vermont to work on the cabin until the money ran out. Then it was back to Martha's Vineyard.

Carol had electricity run to her building site, but she couldn't afford to buy power tools, so virtually all of the work was done by hand. To lay the foundation, Carol and Susan made wooden forms, mixed the concrete by hand, poured it, threw in stones, and built up the foundation walls one layer at a time. For the interlocking logs, they bought raw logs and hewed them by hand, notching the joints with a hatchet.

After we finished the first notch we both sat down and got drunk. Because the first notch took us all day. We had no idea what we were doing. Of course, by the second week we were whipping them out in twenty minutes. We coated the ends of the logs with creosote and dipped the ten-inch nails in oil. It was very rough inside. The walls were made of boards from a barn. It was a real rustic log cabin.

We're talking about building a house out of nothing. Everything was gritted out of whatever was laying around. We made a lot of stuff ourselves, so the cash out-

> *"After we finished the first notch we both sat down and got drunk."*

lay was mainly buying the trees. That was the craziest thing. That and the chimney. They were the craziest things I have ever done in my life.

To help out, Carol recruited friends for weekend work parties. In the early 1970s it was so unusual for a young woman—especially one with no construction experience—to build a house, that she invited women she knew from New York, Boston, and Martha's Vineyard to help and be part of the adventure.

We were these freaky, who-knew-what women, you know? We'd have these wild parties on the weekends (my folks' house was right in the middle of the village). There'd be all these women running around, drinking beer. And sometimes we just partied instead of working. A lot of people came to that place and camped and did whatever.

I don't know how I did it. I had a lot of energy. And we drank a lot of beer. It was great in a way. Susie and I would say, "Okay. It's time to move the big beam." We'd go down to the lake—I brought a lot of people down there, they'd come and rent cottages down by Lake Champlain—we'd just go down and scoop everybody up, and nine women would come up and lift the thing into place.

Carol built a fireplace that ran from the foundation to the top of the first floor, with the chimney extending through the roof. She had to carry the rocks up the ladder one or two at a time, as well as haul the cement up. By that stage of the project Carol couldn't afford her helper anymore, and her friends were gone. The worst part was that Carol didn't realize there was no need to do neat masonry work on the inside of the fireplace—such work is done only on the outside,

"We'd just go down [to the lake] and scoop everybody up, and nine women would come up and lift the thing into place."

where it shows. The inside could just be filled with rubble mixed with concrete, like lumpy oatmeal. But Carol diligently set each stone and neatly mortared the cracks. She built it all carefully, putting mortar between every piece of stone. The fireplace, eight feet long and four feet deep, was solid stone and cement all the way up. In spite of that backbreaking ordeal, Carol found the energy to put in two stained-glass windows, one on either side of the chimney.

When it was time to shingle the roof, Carol hired a local logger to cut and haul the white cedar logs from Lake Champlain to her site. She cut the logs into short lengths and split out the shakes by hand with an antique froe she borrowed from a history buff she met in town. Finally, she hand-trimmed each shake as it was placed on the roof.

I feel guilty (now that I know about old-growth timber) that I had these great old cedars cut down. But I couldn't afford to buy ready-made shingles. So I hacked out the rough shakes one at a time. Each shake was about five-eighths inch thick by two feet long. Afterward, I made this crazy thing you sat at. You held it down with your foot. It held each individual shake. And then I took the drawshave, and shaved them as even as I could, because when they came off the log they had ridges on them. Then when I got up on the roof I had my hatchet with me and my rasp. It wasn't just putting down shingles. Every single one had to be shaped to fit. Every one had to be custom-cut and fit to the next one. It took all summer long.

When asked about her background, it was difficult for Carol to say exactly how it affected her personality and skills. On one hand, because her parents were always sensible about things, Carol retaliated for a brief period in her life by being extremely reckless about many things. She was rebellious, wild, and generally in trouble a lot from the time she was a teenager through her early twenties. At the same time, however, she was a very organized person—a trait that's very useful in construction. Since Carol's family didn't have much money, she learned to be resourceful and to make do. And she became obsessive about avoiding waste. She saves everything and is very careful with her money. Carol is especially proud that she was recycling before anyone else around her thought it was necessary.

Certainly, however, Carol attributes some of her individuality and self-confidence to her father, a minister who had immigrated to this country from China when he was an infant, and to her mother, a loving and caring woman.

I always felt that I could do anything that I wanted to. I guess my parents must have given me that self-confidence. My mother was from Vermont, she was born in 1901 and certainly wasn't raised to be independent, but I

"I always felt that I could do anything I wanted to."

think whatever I got from her was because she loved me so much and I got so much emotion. She loved me no matter what I did. My father did, too. Even if he was critical and judgmental, I always knew that he would be there in a crisis.

Carol lived in the cabin for ten years, then sold it and moved to Connecticut. When she built the cabin, she had thought she was going to live there forever. She tried to be friendly, but the neighbors didn't know what to make of her. She made a few friends, but she had a hard time fitting in with the community. As a single, half-Chinese woman, Carol was exposed to the same racial tension her parents (Chinese-American and European-American) had encountered when they tried to buy a vacation home in the area. They had been

turned away from several towns in Vermont—they were told there was nothing for sale.

During her last years in Vermont, Carol felt very isolated. Her cabin was barely accessible part of the year, and the community was facing a severe economic depression—the year she left Benson it won the distinction of being the poorest town in the state of Vermont—which made it difficult for her to maintain the cabinetmaking business she had started there.

It seems funny. With all the struggle and all the good times that we had, the unhappiness only happened in the latter part of my stay up there. But I was really done with it. By the time it was time to physically leave, I was gone already. It wasn't hard to sell at all. I wanted out of there. I was there thirteen years altogether, and probably I should have left after about ten years.

In those days we were all twenty years old. Everybody was mobile. They didn't have careers. Everybody wanted to have a good time. And you know how work parties are. A throng of thirty people can descend on you. And you might find one person you can actually delegate something to. And the rest of the time,

it's more of a pain in the ass than anything. You don't get a whole lot of work done that way. But we were partying, so it was okay; it was fine. It's more a way to keep you going, getting other people involved.

And then all of a sudden people started doing this and that. The traffic to my cabin decreased. I kind of looked around, and here I am sitting on this beautiful porch looking out over a lot of great scenery. But I wasn't making a living, and I was starved for a lot of stuff. In the winter people wouldn't come up because you had to walk up the mountain. I never had enough money to get the driveway plowed. It was really wicked hard, and it was a lot of fun. But it was over.

So I bought this piece of land down here in Connecticut and moved away from my little cabin. When I got down here people were a lot more sophisticated, because the university is so close by. People didn't just stare at me when I walked in the general store.

In 1983, when Carol moved to Connecticut, her first priority was getting a new shop built so she could start work as a cabinetmaker. She was in a hurry because she needed to generate income as soon as possi-

"She liked the idea of owning her own space and was fortunate to find a lovely piece of land."

ble. The shop was a fairly straightforward project, and with some help she started it up fairly quickly. Having done that, she temporarily moved into the loft space above her workshop. It wasn't a very good arrangement, and she realized she would have to either build a house or find another place to live.

Building the shop was not the adventure that her log cabin had been. This was expediency. She liked the idea of owning her own space and was fortunate to find a lovely piece of land. But it was really just a job to do.

Solving the housing problem was another matter. She had passed the stage, financially and emotionally, where she felt the need to do it entirely on her own. Besides that, she was a lot older. If she could have afforded to hire someone to do all of the work, she would have. However, she had spent most of the money from the sale of her cabin on the land and building the workshop. What she needed was partners. When she found them, she began building her second house, the Connecticut triplex, with her partners, Christine Acebo and Michelle Giffin.

Michelle Giffin

Michelle Giffin grew up in Connecticut, took shop and mechanics in high school, went to teachers college, then joined the merchant marine. She built a rough log cabin in the woods near her home when she was twelve years old. She has never married, preferring independence and mobility in her life. After returning from a tour at sea, she went back to school and received a degree in engineering. With her land partners Carol Yee and Christine Acebo, she built a triplex in rural northeastern Connecticut. She currently alternates between stints in the merchant marine and jobs near home in electrical engineering.

Connecticut Triplex

When Michelle Giffin heard that Carol Yee was looking for land partners to share a housebuilding venture, she jumped at the chance. She had always wanted to build her own home, and the small cabin she owned at the time didn't suite her needs. She knew if she sold it, she wouldn't clear enough money to both buy a piece of land and build a house on it. She was impatient and didn't want to wait until she had saved up enough money—that would take years. The idea of a joint venture was irresistible.

Christine Acebo also wanted to own her own home but couldn't afford to either buy or build one by herself. The three women got together and talked about building one house that they could all share. At first the idea seemed a little farfetched. But after much discussion they decided to go ahead. Michelle and Christine bought shares in Carol's property and the three pooled their remaining resources to build, instead of a single-family home for three, a triplex—one building with three separate living spaces.

They started construction in 1988 and finished in the fall of 1989. Michelle had put her cabin on the market in January 1989, thinking it would take months to sell and that the profit would help pay for the tail end of the construction costs. Instead, the cabin sold in two weeks, leaving her without a place to live. She stayed with various friends through most of the winter, then moved onto the land in a small camping trailer during construction.

Building her own home was a dream for Michelle, with roots that go all the way back to her childhood. When she was in elementary school, she had freedom to come and go as she pleased. What she loved best was to roam through the woods and fields near her home in Connecticut. She didn't always tell her parents where she was or what she was up to. She certainly didn't tell them that she and her friends used to hop freight cars for the fun of it. They'd climb on at a place where the cars used to stop just behind a shopping center, ride the trains for a short distance, then jump off and walk home. They knew the spot where the trains usually slowed down and learned to jump off without getting hurt.

When she was twelve, Michelle, with help from a younger brother and a friend, built a small log cabin in the woods. They chopped down trees with an ax, carved notches in the logs, and stacked them up till the walls were about six feet high. They were initially puzzled as to how to put a roof on the cabin, but they finally

> ## "I just had this attitude that I should be able to do anything."

decided to lay logs across the tops of the walls and cover them with tar paper.

They thought of the little structure as their secret hideout. The idea of having a place of her own stayed with Michelle for years. She imagined that when she grew up, she would learn how to build a real house and someday find a piece of land to build on. In high school, she took college prep courses. If she went to college, she could earn money faster to "get to that place on the mountain that I was going to go." She wasn't sure where it was going to be, just that it had to be in the middle of nowhere, safe from intrusion and control by others.

Michelle was the first girl in her school to take woodworking. She also took a mechanics course. She thought it strange that boys could learn things girls couldn't. By the time she was sixteen, she was repairing her own car, an "old clunker" that needed constant attention.

I had this attitude that the only way I'm going to get anything is to go and look and try to achieve it, and just keep moving in that direction. I had a lot of energy, and I just had this attitude that I should be able to do anything. I don't know where it came from.

With four brothers and a sister, Michelle got stuck with a lot of child care duty when she was still a child herself. While this undoubtedly helped her develop a sense of responsibility, it also made her impatient. She wanted to be out roaming and getting into trouble on her own. She was independent, ambitious, and determined. Part of her fantasy of building her own house somewhere far away stemmed from the desire to escape the family nest and the confusion of adult relationships. She felt that she didn't understand people and didn't know how to relate to them. She thought isolation was the answer and read up on wilderness survival and self-sufficiency.

By the time the triplex project presented itself, Michelle had discovered that her home didn't need to be remote from civilization. As long as she had ownership and control over her portion of the house, she'd be satisfied. What remained of the dream was the need for a place no one could take away from her, a place that she could leave and come back to anytime. She no longer needed a hideout, but she did want a base, an anchor, in her life that would leave her free but also connected.

When the triplex project began, the partners' first task was to build a barn to store construction materials and tools. It would eventually be used to house Christine's horse and as a common storage area. Susan Durrance, who had helped Carol build her log cabin years earlier, supervised the barn construction. Susan designed the layout, drew up material lists, scheduled the work, and assigned tasks.

Once the barn was completed, they began to focus on the house. Carol had built her cabin in Vermont almost single-handedly, and by this time she was also an experienced cabinetmaker. Michelle had a degree in electrical engineering, and a practical background from a stint with the merchant marine. She also read up on building technology and energy conservation. Christine collected comparative pricing and quality data on building and decorating materials. By drawing on their collective abilities and pooling their resources, they were able to put together a plan for a large house that would meet all their needs yet be affordable.

Their original vision was to design a triplex that would contain three completely separate living quarters. Each partner would have her own section of the house that would be designed individually but fit with the other two. It was a cooperative planning process that allowed each woman privacy in the finished building and independence in designing and laying out her own section. It was by necessity a complex design process. It turned out that each partner had a very different image of the kind of house they wanted. Carol wanted a gambrel roof. Michelle wanted a cape—a simple, peak-roofed house. Christine wanted an A-frame. So they made cardboard models of each type of house and moved the boxes around, trying different combinations until they came up with a configuration they liked.

This collaborative approach worked surprisingly well. The only major hitch was when they discovered that the town zoning board wouldn't approve plans for a triplex. They were allowed to build a duplex, but not a triplex (by the town's definition, that would be a condominium, not permitted in their zone). They solved the zoning problem by combining Carol and Christine's sections of the house; they would share a kitchen but have separate living areas on either side of it. This satisfied the zoning board, and they were able to proceed.

Once the framework was settled, each woman drew a layout for her section's interior. These plans were combined and sent off to an architect, who supplied them with construction drawings. They had spent nearly a year in the design process, but their care meant only minor changes had to be made once construction started.

"To design a triplex, they made cardboard models of each type of house and moved the boxes around, trying different combinations."

In addition to coming up with a compatible design, the three women wanted to create a partnership agreement and a list of preconstruction duties. This agreement turned out to be the most difficult part of the preliminaries. They knew they should establish in writing how a variety of issues would be handled before any problems arose. They tried to create a document that would deal with equity in the property, decision making about construction procedures and use of the property, and provisions if any one of them left.

They didn't want to start construction until they had a legal agreement, but they were advised that the document they were creating would not stand up in court. Finally, they let it go and started construction without any agreement on paper at all, relying on good will, trust, and honesty. And, in spite of some rocky periods, they never felt the need to resort to a legal contract to resolve differences or to ensure that their rights were respected.

Most of the differences that arose during the planning stages were minor. For instance, Carol and Michelle wanted old-fashioned, divided lites for the windows and doors, but Christine wanted large, single-pane openings.

They all agreed that the effect of different styles of windows and doors would create a cluttered, awkward appearance. What they needed were unifying features. They settled on double-hungs for the smaller windows and divided lites for the larger ones in all three sections. Christine was able to include single-pane sliding-glass doors on her south side, affording her a pleasant view from the living room through a large window.

Perhaps the most complex problem, from a design standpoint, was the overlap of Carol and Christine's sections of the house. The two women have fundamental differences of opinion about designing living space. Christine's priorities were ease of cleaning and maintenance. "My attitude about a house is: How fast can you sweep the filth out? If I had only myself to think of, I would have built it with a cement floor that could be hosed down," she said. Carol could tolerate more clutter and prefers a more complicated arrangement of furniture and cabinets. They worked over how their sections would merge and how the kitchen would look until they had a layout that was acceptable to both.

In designing her portion of the house, Michelle thought a great deal about what she wanted. She drew

"I never knew how much room stairs take up."

plans and sketches, erasing and rearranging walls, stairs, and furniture layout.

I just walked around a million times, trying this and that. I know I moved the chimney around a million times. I moved the stairs around a lot, too. I never knew how much room stairs take up. I put the living room on the south side, because I thought it would be nice to have the sun warm the room.

To open up the space between the kitchen and the living/dining area, Michelle had to figure out how to support the floor above it. The wall that separates those parts of the house was a load-bearing wall. She consulted a mechanical engineer from her workplace who helped her calculate the live-load capacity of the species of wood she intended to use for the beams.

Michelle used wood paneling for several ceilings on the second floor, even though drywall would have been much easier. The narrow tongue-and-groove boards required a great deal of overhead nailing. But the effect is elegant. The walls are light, so the natural wood gives it a warm, natural touch. She also put windows in the sides of some of her dormers to let more light into her sloped-ceiling bedroom and bathroom.

Michelle's first floor ceiling construction is also unusual. The house is basically stud-frame construction, but she laid 8-by-8 beams along the top of her first floor walls. The second floor deck is laid on large 4-by-8s that span the room at three-foot intervals and are supported by the beams she laid on top of the walls. Normally second-floor joists are spaced every sixteen inches. By spacing the deck supports at wide intervals, each carries more weight—too much for a normal stud wall. The beams spread this weight evenly along the top of the wall and prevent sag at the points of support. These beams are tied together at the corners with half-lap joints to strengthen the construction.

Flooring on the second floor is 1¹/₂-inch thick tongue-and-groove pine boards. There is no subfloor or first-floor ceiling material, so the bottom of the floor decking is visible downstairs. The effect is similar to the tongue-and-groove ceiling on the second floor, except these boards are thicker and act as both floor and ceiling. This makes the house look like a post-and-beam structure. The exposed beams are attractive, as is the underside of the floor above, and it was far less expensive than actual post-and-beam construction. Michelle likes the look of all that wood and the sense of solidity the timbers provide.

Wood selection was another area in which Michelle departed from typical building practice. She preferred hardwood, birch especially. So instead of pine or even oak for floors, doors, and trim, Michelle used birch wherever she could. The placement and number of doors was another area she was careful to get right. She thought about where she would want to enter or leave the house, both in terms of inside layout and proximity to outdoors.

The stove and chimney turned out to be the most problematical. Michelle had a wonderful old wood-fired cookstove that she wanted to use in the kitchen. The chimney was placed in the middle of the passageway between the kitchen and the dining room, and an extra flue was installed to accommodate it. But because the cookstove was so old, it didn't have safety features that are now required for stoves of that kind. If she used it, she wouldn't be able to insure the house against a fire. So instead, she bought a modern gas stove, which doesn't require a flue. Although Michelle is satisfied with her chimney's location, it might have been placed differently if she had known it wouldn't be needed for the cookstove.

In general, Michelle feels she did a good job with the design. Taking enough time to get (almost) everything right was well worth the effort.

I like the kitchen the best. I love the color and the counters. It has a lot of counter space. The cabinets are real nice. Carol built all the counters, in her side and mine. I had this friend who came up to visit. I told her I was going to make stained glass for the upper cabinet doors. She said, 'Let me make you some temporary glass.' She took a sample of the wallpaper in the dining room (she didn't tell me she was doing this). She brought it home, and then she blew it up and made this big stencil. Then she sandblasted it. She brought up these pieces of glass for the cabinet doors. I said 'Wow! This isn't temporary.' So that's how I got these beautiful glass doors. They're real nice. It's a real nice kitchen. I don't know. I just like it.

"*I also had the sense to make a map of the wiring system in the house.*"

A few details remain to be completed. Most of these were planned as future projects or options.

There are pipes in the wall for a future solar hot-water system. I can put solar collectors on the roof, and I don't have to tear apart the walls to put in the system. I put in a laundry chute and a bedroom on the ground floor so that as I get older the house will still be easy to live in. Next to the laundry chute, I made a space for a wiring chute. The idea was to make it easier to add to the system or to get at it to make changes later on. I wanted to have the option of adding cable TV or more telephone wires. Now any changes like that will be easy on the electrician. I also had the sense to make a map of the wiring system in the house.

One source of difficulty for the partners was that they had borrowed money from a bank to pay part of the construction costs. Therefore, they had an inflexible deadline to meet. So they hired a contractor, who brought a crew in to do most of the actual work. This naturally was easier and faster than trying to do it all themselves, but it had problems of its own. The carpenters didn't always do things exactly the way the women wanted them to. Also, the contractor wasn't on the site every day. He would go off and supervise other jobs he had going at the same time. Carol tried to keep track of things during the day, since she was around working in her shop. Nevertheless, mistakes would be made or changes wouldn't be communicated. Michelle would come home from work each day and inspect the progress.

That was pretty miserable. I worked all day long, and then I'd come back and see what had happened on the building site that day. And I would either be sad or mad. It was pretty stressful. We weren't very good at dealing with that. We got mad at each other a lot. Toward the end, when we were putting in the driveway, Carol and I weren't even talking to each other. It was crazy.

Construction on the triplex didn't go quite as smoothly as the design phase had gone. When problems arose, the partners didn't always see eye-to-eye on how to solve them. And they discovered things that had been left out of the design process—things they only realized were issues during building. For example, Michelle wanted clapboard siding with painted corner boards, and Carol was determined to have all natural wood shingles. They had each envisioned what the house would look like but had never actually discussed the siding material. By the time they were getting ready to order materials, each found it difficult to alter the image that had become set in their minds. They argued and argued over it. Finally, they negotiated a compromise. They'd go with shingle siding with painted corner boards.

"*That was pretty miserable. I worked all day long, and then I'd come back and see what had happened on the building site that day.*"

The friendship among the triplex partners was bruised, but it survived the building process. It took effort to restore a sense of goodwill among them. Tensions flared periodically long after the building was completed. But the stresses and strains that caused the friction are beginning to fade into memory and their enjoyment of their property and the ease of living they achieved there have done a lot to ease old resentments.

They realize they made a mistake in not setting up a good, formal mechanism for settling disputes from the start. They also didn't have a really detailed budget or a clear-cut division of labor worked out in advance. Since Carol was around during the day working in her cabinet shop, much of the day-to-day problem solving and crisis intervention fell to her. Dealing with house problems interrupted her work in a way that did not affect Michelle's job. Eventually, Carol felt her position was being taken advantage of.

Michelle often worked on weekends to try to even the balance. But she didn't work every weekend, and sometimes she had to bring work home from her job and couldn't focus on the building project. Then her absence would create resentment in the others. At other times, Michelle felt she was the one who worked above and beyond the call of duty. In response to the tension that resulted from the hectic schedules of all the partners, they would either grit their teeth and try to let go of hostility, or hold it in until something triggered a blowup. But in spite of the uneasy atmosphere at times, there was always a sense of mutual responsibility and commitment.

I was committed, and we knew the things that needed to be done and when they had to get done. So we would do them. I would be mad while I was doing them, but always getting the things done. And sometimes not doing the best job because of the anger. One day I stayed home from work and shoveled all the gravel into the cellar because the concrete floor was about to be poured. The gravel had to be down there when the concrete came. And that was wheelbarrowing and shoveling all day long. And spreading the stones around to level it. When Carol and Christine came home, it was all done. Whatever I had to do, I did it.

The partners had friends who helped out occasionally. They knew an electrician, Peg Preble, living in Boston who was willing to help design and install the wiring. Also, Michelle's friend Gina, who was living with her in the trailer while construction was going on, was a professional painter, so the partners hired her to help with painting and other finish work. She advised Michelle on color selection, hung the wallpaper in the

> *"They would either grit their teeth and try to let go of hostility, or hold it in until something triggered a blowup."*

dining room, laid the marble tiles in the living room, and helped lay the kitchen floor tiles.

In spite of the tension among the triplex partners and the magnitude of the project, Michelle wishes they could have done all the building themselves. Even though she didn't have experience in construction, she knew she could have found out whatever she needed to know. She did do a lot of the interior finish work. She made and installed many of the hardwood doors and put in some of the finish flooring and a lot of the trim (which was also hardwood). This contribution is important to her. She can look around her and see the fruits of her own labor, feel the pleasure that comes of not merely designing, but also creating her surroundings.

Overall, Michelle feels that her participation in the triplex project has taught her something not just about building, but about relationships. Building a house as a collaborative effort necessitates a degree of intimacy among the partners that they may not have anticipated or wanted. While there were moments when each of them would have liked to be rid of the others, the process did have its rewards. Michelle feels that she understands people in general a little better now, and she learned something about her own strengths and limitations.

Michelle, who was thirty-five years old when she finished her house, decided it was time for her to break loose again for a while—it seemed that her alternating need for security and mobility had been a continuing theme in her life. She resigned her position as an electrical engineer and rejoined the merchant marine. Her first stint with the merchant marine had been shortly after she graduated from college. Although she had a degree in elementary education, she had decided she wanted some technical training. She didn't feel ready to teach (she thought she still had a lot to learn herself), and she knew teachers aren't well paid. The technical trades offer better pay with less additional education than white-collar occupations. She also wanted more

"I gotta learn as much as I can in my twenties, so I can put it to work in my thirties."

mobility than teaching could offer. She learned that the merchant marine would provide training and pay her a good wage immediately, so she joined up. They sent her to their school, where she learned welding and machinist skills as well as machine operation and maintenance. Being the only female in the class didn't stop her or slow her down.

I don't know how I did it. I just had this attitude that I wanted to learn as much as I could. I said I gotta learn as much as I can in my twenties. I was like a fanat-

ic. I was always reading stuff, and observing stuff, and talking to people. And I had to learn all this stuff so I could put it to work in my thirties.

She worked very hard, and within six months she was first in the class. However, some parts of her studies were easier than others. She was intimidated by the idea of having to learn calculus, for example. But she knew she had to pass the course to continue. She convinced herself that if she just tried hard enough and took enough time with it she would eventually learn it. As a matter of fact, she got straight A's in the class. By the time she was ready to go to sea, she was sure she could do anything the men could do. The work was hard, operating and maintaining all the machinery on board, but she pulled her own weight. It was a tremendous experience.

After a year at sea, Michelle came back for another year and a half of classroom study to earn her license as a marine engineer, thinking she could then get a job as an engineer anywhere. But she discovered that her

license wasn't adequate for a land job. She needed a graduate degree after all. She worked during the day and went to night school for six and a half years, finally earning a degree in electrical engineering.

The idea of a triplex as a way for each partner to own her own home has certain drawbacks they have each had to accept. They knew when they started that it was an investment that would be hard for any of them to back out of later. It would be nearly impossible to sell just one section of the house. Who would want to buy into a situation like that? It would be almost as difficult to sell the whole house. In theory, it could be converted to a two-family house, or Michelle's section could be made into an in-law apartment. Still, there are many outbuildings, and it's a big piece of land. It would be a very expensive and tough property to sell. They are more or less stuck with each other.

But Michelle was looking for permanence. She enjoys having people around. More than the others, she seems to have had a very long range view of it from the beginning. When she was designing her part of the house, she thought about what it would be like when she got old. The room off the living room was designed to be large enough to convert to a bedroom when she is too old to climb the stairs or if she were disabled at some time. That's also why she put a bathroom on the ground floor.

She likes her privacy, but she also likes the convenience of built-in neighbors. In the country, it's a long hike to go next door to borrow a cup of sugar or have a casual chat. She likes the fact that she can go away to sea for months at a time and there will be someone to look after the cat and see that the pipes don't freeze. Although for most intents and purposes she lives alone, company and help in an emergency are always at hand. Ironically, the very fact that it would be so hard to leave has a positive aspect to her. It makes her feel like she really has a home. She has a place where she truly belongs. She lives in a house that she can and must view with a long-term perspective, which gives her a kind of security that she finds reassuring.

When asked what she learned from the experience of building the triplex, Michelle's first response was to say she'd *never* build a house again. But then she became more thoughtful and began to look at how dif-

> *"She likes the fact that she can go away to sea for months at a time and there will be someone to look after the cat and see that the pipes don't freeze."*

ferently she saw things now compared to how they had seemed while they happened.

If I had to do it again, I'm sure there are a lot of things that would be different. Probably everything that happened wouldn't be such a crisis. I think I'd be more flexible now. I may not be flexible on the workmanship. But on handling the situation. I wouldn't get all tensed up, and it wouldn't be such a big deal. It came out nicer than I thought it would. It feels comfortable, and there are just different rooms that seem really nice. I didn't really picture the end. It's all linear in the planning stage. There were parts I couldn't understand at all. The 3-D stuff is kind of hard for me. My head doesn't work with plans very well. Maybe now that I've seen the whole process I could look at plans for another house and relate to them.

She's very comfortable in her house and proud of the accomplishment it represents. She's also impressed by the resourcefulness they all mustered to get the project completed. But most of all, she likes knowing that it is the product of her own imagination, her own design and vision. She can stand in a room and remember having painstakingly drawn it out on paper, calculating every part of it down to the inch. Although that process wasn't fun a lot of the time—"it hurt my head"—now she gets to see the finished product.

That's what's cool. You walk around, and it's pretty much exactly the stuff you struggled and worked and worked and worked on. And there it is.

Debrin Cox & Oceanlight

Debrin Cox and Oceanlight, together with a third partner, purchased a small piece of property along the coast of northern California near Mendocino. Their intention was to build three cabins on the land, one for each of them. After cutting down trees and having them milled into lumber for building, they became discouraged about their ability to continue. Eventually they worked their way through a difficult process, and all three cabins were built. Debrin Cox, who is a masseuse, grew up in Baltimore and the suburbs of Chicago. She had no previous experience in construction before building her cabin but had dreamed for years of having a home in the country. Oceanlight is a psychotherapist who grew up in Lawrence, Kansas. She saw her parents design and have their own home built when she was about five or six years old. The feminist movement of the early seventies impressed Oceanlight in her early teens and profoundly influenced her life.

Redwood Cabins

The idea of a communal building project arose when three friends—Debrin Cox, Oceanlight, and Kim Morello-Moonwater—realized they all dreamed of owning their own home, but not one of them could afford to do so on her own. They first thought of buying a piece of land together and building a house on it that they would all live in. Then a property just outside Mendocino, in the town of Albion, came onto the market that had a small house and a couple of outbuildings already on it. They decided to share the house as a gathering place, communal kitchen, and storage space, then they would each build their own cabin. When first interviewed in 1985, they were all living on the property: Kim in a tiny trailer, Oceanlight in an existing (equally tiny) cabin, and Debrin in an old toolshed next to the main house. These accommodations left much to be desired, but the excitement of their joint adventure at first distracted them from the discomforts of their living conditions. They had several trees cut down to provide a clearing to build, to let in light, and to furnish lumber for the cabins. They cleared brush, planted a garden, and began to plan the cabins. Eventually, the trees were milled into boards and carefully stacked in the middle of the clearing. They were ready, but as it turned out, not yet able to proceed with building.

It was at this stage that I first met Debrin and Oceanlight. I didn't get the chance to interview Kim at that time. Sadly, she was killed in a motorcycle accident in 1988.

None of the three women knew much about building, nor had any of them done much, if any, carpentry before. They embarked on this project out of need and with the belief that they were capable of figuring out the necessary details as they went along. They had a lot in common. They all wanted to live in the country, they liked the area and the active women's community there, they shared an ecological consciousness, and they were interested in gardening to produce their own food. They shared many practical preferences that made them comfortable with the idea of living together. They also had powerful role models in a number of women who had built cabins in the area in the late seventies and early eighties, many of whom had no more knowledge or experience than the three friends had.

Debrin was inspired by the freedom of these women to do things that are traditionally in the male domain. As a child, Debrin was strong-willed herself. The oldest and only sister of four brothers, she had a great deal of responsibility at home. She became well-versed in "boy-type things" by hanging out with her brothers. But she was also responsible for taking care of her brothers much of the time, and for a large share of household chores. By the time she was a young woman and beginning to look to her future, Debrin had already experienced raising kids and being tied down to the house. She didn't look forward to doing more of that. The women's movement helped her articulate what this dilemma meant to her. She ponders how much her own self-image is derived from her mother's example.

Debrin

My mother was a really strong woman, in a lot of senses. And yet she also was totally dependent on her man. She moved from her father's house into her husband's house. What was strong about her was her personality, her wit, and her intelligence. And yet she didn't have any skills or a trade. There was the boys' work and the girls' work. And I kind of grew up that way, also. I was responsible for the girls' work. My mother did give me more choices than she ever had. But I was very held back from learning nontraditional skills.

"Everyone felt as though they were a part of the process, that it was a family project."

Oceanlight could identify with the homesteading women of the Mendocino area more readily than Debrin could. She appreciated their initiative and courage, because she had a role model in her own family of a woman who decided, after years of dutiful conformity, to take control of her own life. Her mother was intelligent and well educated, with a master's degree in social work. But she stayed home and took care of her family, until Oceanlight was in seventh grade. Then she went back to work, working nearly as many hours as her husband, while still doing all the cooking, cleaning, and child care. Oceanlight's sister had severe asthma, so Oceanlight, being robust and naturally active, was called upon to help out with the housework. Though she feels a little cheated of a carefree childhood by being pulled into an adult role so early, Oceanlight is also grateful to her parents for the message they imparted: they clearly had confidence in her abilities.

When Oceanlight was a teenager, her sisters introduced her to feminism, and together they challenged their mother to question the roles she and the entire family were playing. Reluctantly at first, Oceanlight's mother gradually agreed that she was sacrificing too much and denying too much for herself. She stood up to her husband for the first time and began to drastically change the way she lived. This hidden capacity for power and decisiveness made a big impression on Oceanlight.

Another early experience that stayed with Oceanlight was her exposure to housebuilding. When she was only five or six, her parents designed a house and hired a contractor to build it for them. That was a happy time in her life. They visited the site at different stages of construction, and when they moved in they had fun arranging things. The children were allowed to participate in some decisions, mainly about the furnishings in their bedrooms. Everyone felt as though they were a part of the process, that it was a family project. From this Oceanlight gained not only the image of taking charge of a house's construction, but also the satisfaction of a successful group venture.

Debrin, Oceanlight, and Kim took their commitment very seriously. They developed a detailed agreement covering the issues that might affect their lives in important ways. They agreed that decision-making would be by consensus. Each one also committed a specific number of hours per week to work on the property. Each woman would design her own cabin, subject to approval by the others. Regular group meetings were planned to ensure that differences would be ironed out, and shared goals would be reevaluated periodically.

The project started out with a surge of energy, enthusiasm, and self-confidence. Once they purchased the property, the very first task for Debrin was to fix up the shed she was going to live in until her cabin was built. This was her first carpentry experience, and she dove right in.

Debrin

When we moved here, this was a toolshed. It didn't have any of the porch structure out in front. It was very much a boarded-up, not-used toolshed. It had this huge, solid big door on it. The windows were all painted shut and had torn screens. The guy who owned it had nails all over the place. They were the hugest nails—and then everywhere else, all over the walls, there were little finishing nails where he hung his plane and his hammer and so forth. Every tool was outlined with these little finish nails. I had so much nail pulling, sanding, plastering, and sanding again, it was enough for a lifetime. I figured out how to build a porch. Now it's quite a gorgeous space. I feel such a sense of accomplishment.

The property was densely wooded, mostly with fir and pine, but also with several grand old redwood trees. It had a lovely, almost enchanted-forest atmosphere. But in order to build, they had to remove some of the trees. Getting them cut and milled was the high point of this early phase. It let sunlight onto the property and made it easier to look at the available building area. It also helped them feel they were making progress.

Debrin

Well, the first thing we had to do was to get some of these trees taken down. We wanted to get more sun on the land. I don't even know if you can imagine what a huge process that was. These trees were huge, huge grandmother trees. They filled up the whole sky, and they would block all the sun that's shining on us right now. But they were gorgeous. And we really needed them to come down. It was painful to have them cut down. And then, in the process of big trees coming down, other areas are wiped out. But we decided we had to do that.

Oceanlight

We did a ritual with the trees the night before the guy came to cut them down. And we said, "Oh, trees, we're sorry," and, "Thank you for giving your lives that we may have shelter and light," and that sort of thing. The guy was great. He'd do some trees, and then he'd come and say, "Well, I'm going to do these now; is there anything around them that you don't want to have hurt?" And we'd point out the trees to him that were important for us. He was really careful. And he was really good. I mean, when he felled a tree, he could place it precisely. We selected which trees to cut by which were blocking the light to a really great extent. And there were some that were rotten in the base. So we picked trees that were unhealthy.

Debrin

And we had another guy who we hired who came in with a portable saw to mill the wood. Rather than him hiring an assistant, we were his assistants. We grabbed the lumber as it came off and stacked it. So that was all new

for us. And muscle-building. It was wonderful, because we were really able to be with the process all the way along, from the emotional choice to take down the trees, to helping the person clear the brush as the trees came down, to helping mill the lumber, to designing the cabins. That was a lot of concentrated work and money during that period, which was going toward the cabin building, but they were still preliminary steps.

Because her toolshed was so small, Debrin had to build a platform for her bed, leaving the area underneath it for clothes and general storage. There was no place to stand up. As time went by, these cramped quarters began to lose their charm. The climate in California is mild, but they do get a lot of rain in the winter, and Debrin found herself using the main house more and more. Although her first stab at carpentry had been successful, she began to doubt her ability to build a whole cabin by herself. She considered expanding the toolshed so she could be more comfortable and better able to muster the energy and confidence she'd need to build a cabin. Then she considered giving up the idea of building a new structure and simply putting an addition on the toolshed. But she finally decided that if she could do either of these, she could build a cabin.

Tensions arose over her use of the main house.

They had agreed that Debrin's cabin would be the first to be built since she had the most miserable accommodations. But her initial design was rejected by her partners as too large. Personal conflicts arose. The decision-making agreements proved difficult to maintain. Discouragement set in as the momentum was lost and the magnitude of what they had taken on began to seem overwhelming. First one building season and then another passed with little to show for it. Resentments alternately simmered and boiled over

Debrin

It's really hard, the collective process. To be working with two strong-willed, independent, creative women who have different opinions, and to really feel strongly about your opinion, but to try to be compassionate about the other opinions.

By the spring of 1985, Oceanlight was getting very impatient. Good building weather was once more upon them, and she didn't want to go through another winter without some real progress on the cabins. She believed their uncomfortable living conditions were contributing to their sense of helplessness. Oceanlight knew they needed to restore a sense of cooperation

*"I was just laughing
all day."*

before they could proceed. But another part of her kept saying, "Let's get to work. Let's just do it. Let's get out the bow saws. Let's have work days. Let's have friends over here. Let's get the work done. Let's start doing it." She felt sure that a lot of energy and a renewed sense of shared enterprise would be generated by getting to work. She remembered the thrill of getting the trees milled, and how inspiring that had been.

Oceanlight

The day we got the logs all milled and the lumber stacked up here, I had a blast. I was just laughing all day because I had looked out my cabin door at this pile of logs for so many mornings. I was just thrilled.

But by this time regular meetings had become irregular. Mistrust and hard feelings interfered with cooperation. The tension between the need to be independent and the need to be responsible to the group was classic in its paralyzing impact. Debrin, Oceanlight, and Kim made a valiant effort to keep their venture

from falling apart. They tried a variety of techniques to get things moving, including affirmation rituals, meditation, marathon negotiation sessions, outside mediation, and periods of "time out" in which one or another of them spent time off the land.

Once, when she found herself increasingly frustrated by the lack of progress on the cabin building, Oceanlight decided to escape from it for awhile and visit her family. While there, she became ill and found herself with time to reflect on the process. She realized how stressed and discouraged she had become. She felt the goals the three partners had set for themselves were hanging over their heads. She was convinced they needed to either get moving again or let go of those goals.

Oceanlight

Just coming home, I feel how I really love this place. I love living here. That it really is home. I walk the path, and I feel the familiarity and the depth of having walked that path countless times. I have roots here and they really stabilize me. I love it. It holds me. It's a cradling sort of thing. I saw that I was really scattered. I was trying to do a lot of different things. Each of them takes a lot of centered focus. I wasn't doing anything well. And I was feeling like a failure all the time. I was miserable. And embarrassed, and ashamed. It was awful. So I prioritized. I stopped doing a lot of things. I said that my priorities were to do healing work on myself and to get my money togeth-

*"I walk the path,
and I feel the
familiarity and
the depth of
having walked
that path
countless times."*

"I really say, 'Okay cabin, where are you supposed to be?'"

er. And the way that's played out has shown me that those choices I made were excellent. It's really worked.

Oceanlight, an active meditator, began to try visualization. She tried to conjure up an image of what her life would look like if she were at the end rather than the in the middle of the building venture. She allowed this process to inspire her as she began to focus on the design of her cabin.

Oceanlight

I think I can build something really simple and really basic, and I'm going to be so happy with it. I don't want it to be complicated. I don't want the money and the time expense of little frills and things like that. I know it will be a process inside of myself of birthing a newness, as well as something outside of me. I need to just leave it open for that to happen.

Debrin found it difficult to stay focused on the building project. She was deeply involved in both political organizing and dancing, and she wanted to keep active in these areas, even though the building project dragged on and was constantly hanging over her head. A part of her wanted to be involved in working on her home, but she found herself spending all her free time on outside interests. Looking back, Debrin realized, "I needed to grab the bull by the horns, but I didn't know where to reach for the horns."

Debrin's style was to worry for a while, then to calm herself by sitting quietly and gathering her thoughts. She sought a solution from the land itself. She walked around the property for hours, scrambling through the bushes and looking at the land and the issue from all sides. Since she had been living on the land where the cabins would be built for two years, Debrin could call up the vision she was searching for. Living intimately with the sounds of the forest, the smells in the air, and the feel of the place gave her a sense of connectedness with her home and the building project. She felt grounded there. When she needed to know that the next step would be, she had a basis in her

experience of the land. That familiarity, that deep knowing about the land and her relationship to it, gave her the guidance she sought. Her technique was simply to calm the chaos in her mind enough to grasp it.

Debrin

I really say, "Okay cabin, where are you supposed to be? Energies come through to help me figure this one out, because I really don't know." And it works.

Around that time, she also made what felt to her like a revolutionary discovery. Committed to feminist principles, Debrin had been assuming she'd have to take charge of every bit of the building of her cabin. She could get some help with the labor, but she would have to be the responsible party. It finally dawned on her that this requirement came out of an idea she had about what it means to be a liberated woman. In fact, doing everything herself, learning about construction, directing the work, and supervising every step of the process wasn't really an essential part of her goal. She just wanted to get her cabin built. She didn't have to do everything herself in order to retain her self-respect. She was very willing to do work trades, to rely on someone more

experienced to take charge, or to hire someone to do the work if necessary. This realization helped her enormously in getting unblocked and back on track, ready to tackle the next step.

Kim, meanwhile, concentrated on the gardens and planting fruit trees. A priority for her was self-sufficiency in food production. They had agreed that Debrin's cabin would be built first, so Kim felt less pressure to have her cabin design ready or to begin the process of building.

Finally, they agreed that raising money was going to be the key to getting their cabins built. They got the idea that they might hire someone who could supervise construction. They all felt competent to be the "brawn" of the project. But none of them wanted to take on the responsibility of directing the work, and none felt able to muster the energy or acquire the knowledge necessary to do so on their own. So they started looking around for someone experienced in building to help them and made a concerted effort to save the money they'd need for materials and labor.

In October 1985, Debrin began building her cabin. She hired an experienced carpenter, Diana Wiedemann, to supervise construction. Oceanlight and another woman Debrin hired on to help made up an all-woman framing crew. On weekends, Debrin and a friend would get as much done as they could before the hired crew showed up again on Monday. The basic structure went up in about two weeks. During the rest of October and November, they finished the outside work: sheathing and partly siding the walls, installing some of the windows, and shingling the roof.

Debrin moved in the spring. Even though none of the inside work had begun, it was a vast improvement over the toolshed, and she was happy to be in her new home.

Debrin's cabin is a shed-roofed rectangle, 16-by-24 feet and 14 feet high on the tall side. There is a small bay at the front entrance and large windows on the front (south) side of the building. A sleeping loft runs along one side. The large windows on the front wall let in a good deal of sunlight, which reaches all the way to the back of the cabin. A large mirror mounted on the back wall for dance practice reflects the view of the trees and garden and brightens the north side of the house.

There is no bathroom and no real kitchen; the

main house still serves its original function as dining area and social center and for facilities not available in the cabins.

Debrin used a post-and-pier foundation. The wood for her cabin's joists, girders, rafters, and studs all came from the trees they milled on the property. That didn't mean the wood was free—they had paid to have the wood milled and there was a lot of work involved—but it was cheaper than purchasing lumber.

During the summer and fall, Debrin sided the front of her cabin in redwood shingles (the sides and back had been done in fir during the initial building phase) and installed the last of the windows. The following year, she worked on insulation, drywall, and trim. Debrin was once again burned out by the time the finish work needed to be done. She made herself be patient and do a careful job, but it was not a joyful part of the project. In 1988, she met her current roommate, Brenda Johnson (who is a journey-level carpenter), and together they completed the last details. Brenda built cabinets, a desk, and some built-in shelves.

> *"Breaking the logjam and getting work started on the cabins, one right after the other, raised eveyone's spirits tremendously."*

The building of Debrin's and Oceanlight's cabins actually overlapped in time. As soon as the crew had gotten Debrin's cabin framed, they moved over to start on Oceanlight's cabin. After that, Debrin and Ocean-light each worked mostly on her own cabin, supplemented by work parties and work trading among the land partners as the various stages of construction were staggered over the next couple of years. Kim wasn't ready to start her cabin until the spring, so the question

of whose cabin to build after Debrin's was settled.

Breaking the logjam and getting work started on the cabins, one right after the other, raised everyone's spirits tremendously and helped them resolve most of their personal conflicts. It also produced, as expected, a surge of energy and self-confidence.

Oceanlight's cabin is a polygon, twenty feet in diameter (the design is based on a yurt). It is one big room with sixteen sides, each composed of 4-by-8 foot panels. The roof is made of sixteen pie-shaped pieces with a three-foot diameter, round skylight in the middle. The prefabricated roof panels were lifted into place with a crane by a local company that specialized in wooden yurts. The siding is redwood clapboard. Most of the wood used for framing is fir and pine from trees cut and milled on the land. Her front door is made of wood with a single glass panel and faces due south. A small window on the opposite wall provides an opening to the north. She placed three large five-foot-high windows on the east side, the middle one facing due east. Three smaller windows open to the west, looking out to untouched forest and a giant old redwood tree. There is some clearing in the south, north, and east, and indigenous huckleberry bushes and wild rhododendrons surround the cabin.

Once the basic structure was framed and closed in, Oceanlight moved in and finished the rest a little at a time. All of the cabin's interior trim is redwood. The walls are drywall painted a light peach color, and the ceiling is pine with fir trim. A maroon carpet covers the plywood subfloor. A woodstove sits in front of a brick hearth inlaid with personal ritual objects.

Oceanlight

The first part of the building was a very high, exhilarating time for me. As it dragged on, I longed for it to be all done. Passing the series of building inspections was tense and then happy. I liked it better when I was working with people, though I also liked experiencing myself fully when I was working alone. Sometimes I didn't think I could do it, but then another piece of it would move forward, and I'd be encouraged and just keep going, push on, day by day.

Two and a half years after she began working on it, Oceanlight completed her cabin. She lived in it most of that time, but a week after she finally got the last piece in place (the living room carpet), she moved to New Mexico. She had fallen in love and decided the relationship was worth the relocation.

However, she wasn't willing to give up her partnership in the property, so she rented her cabin as a hedge against changing her mind. Although she was happy in Albuquerque, she missed her cabin and the redwood forest home she worked so hard to establish. In February 1993, she moved back to Albion and into her cabin. Debrin is glad to have her back. She said that

> "*The first part of the building was a very high, exhilarating time for me. As it dragged on, I longed for it to be all done.*"

sharing the property with tenants is not at all like sharing with land partners. There's something very special about that experience that goes beyond economy and touches the deeper values that led to the idea of a commune in the first place.

There were a number of points along the way when they thought they'd never get through it. But they did get the trees cut and milled, they did get all three cabins built, and their conflicts were put to rest. Kim's death was traumatic for Debrin and Oceanlight. But overall, their success at a collaborative effort, their per-

severance in realizing the dream of having their own home, and their gratitude for the support they got from other women at different stages seem to them to outweigh the painful aspects of their experience.

Debrin

You know how things can roll through in your life, and there you are at the next step. You don't quite know what it's all about, but there you are. If I could, I would start with more money. Of course, if I had the money to hire more skilled carpenters from the beginning, I suppose I wouldn't be the person I am, and my home possibly wouldn't emanate the warmth that it does.

Gail Atkins & Gwen Demeter

Gail Atkins and Gwen Demeter have lived in the Memphis, Tennessee, area for many years. On land they bought to create a women's commune in nearby Holly Springs, Mississippi, they built a central core of public spaces, such as a kitchen and a bathhouse, and later added cabins for private housing. Gail learned her building skills by reading as much as she could on construction techniques. Gwen, whose father had studied architecture, shared in the designing and building process. The buildings were made of inexpensive materials and cooperative labor, leaving Gail and Gwen free of a mortgage. They try to live simply and gently on the land. Gail taught school for many years and is now an educational administrator. Gwen, who enjoys photography and writing, spends most of her time at home, tending the garden and the household.

Silver Circle

Gail Atkins and Gwen Demeter wanted to create a place for women to live communally, sharing resources yet retaining privacy and individuality. Together with five other women who shared their dream they bought some property in Holly Springs, Mississippi, and established a commune called Silver Circle. The main house was to be the central gathering place, a social space, and the location of shared facilities, as was the laundry and bath house, while cabins and other buildings would provide personal space. The entire property was intended to be separate from the rest of society, offering women a place where they would be respected, could build their own kind of relationships and physical structures, and would be free to express themselves.

Gail

I just do real well, personally, in a collective situation. I really learned that when we started a collective house in Memphis. But I think collective houses in the city are just . . . You've got so many people in just a little amount of space. Out here you've got room to spread out, and if you've got the grumpies, you can walk up to the

"We wanted to have a place where women could find out what they could be."

pond and just sit there and get over it. More space is just psychologically more healthy.

Gwen

We wanted to have a place where women could find out what they could be. If they wanted to have time to do artwork or writing or whatever, to be able to do that along with maintaining survival, without having to go to an eight-hour-a-day job. That was our hope. Kind of a place to grow old, maybe.

Gail and Gwen, along with the other women who were in on the project at the beginning, started to build their first communal structure, a tool shed, in September 1982. No one was living on the land full-time yet, so they needed a secure, dry place for tools. Next they built a temporary kitchen. Until then, they were cooking over an open pit next to a table they used for food preparation and storage. It worked well, except they needed a place safe from bugs, raccoons, and possums. The food storage area had a plastic cover to protect it from rain, but the arrangement was less than satisfactory.

Gail

At the time, we had some women who were staying here. You know when something new gets going, you've got hangers-on who just want to be in on the high. We did a lean-to out of plastic that we could move out of the way in the daytime so we could have access to everything. And we agreed that whoever was down there at night would put the plastic back over it. Well, you know, all it took was one time. One woman *forgot to put the plastic up, and it rained and everything was wiped out in the whole kitchen.*

Building a kitchen became a top priority. One of the women saw a kit on sale for a small geodesic dome. She bought it, thinking it would be the easiest way to get a kitchen up fast. Actually, they would have been much better off building a simple shed from scratch;

"When Gail and Gwen began to design the main house, the most important consideration for them was that it be a passive solar design built in an ecologically responsible way."

putting the dome together turned out be a lot more complicated than it looked. But once they had bought the kit, they were committed to finishing it.

Gail

We started on it in June, but we couldn't work on it regularly because it just rained and rained. This was the year we had just unbelievable amounts of rain down here. By July we had the refrigerator in. But the roof was plastic. By November it was pretty much like it is now, except for the door. We went through that winter with a quilt over the door. But it was an exceptionally mild winter. It only got below freezing two times that whole winter.

They grew to love the little dome kitchen, with its whimsical, unconventional shape.

Gail

Something about the triangles, the whole thing is really appealing to me. I almost laugh every time I look at it. It reminds me of a little fairy house or gnome house or something. Like something out of a children's book. It looks real weird at night. The way the windows look and all. One window's high, and one window's low. I like the irregularity of it. It's different. I like that.

When Gail and Gwen began to design the main house, the most important consideration for them was that it be a passive solar design built in an ecologically responsible way. They selected post-and-beam construction, for three reasons. First, their intuitive sense told them it would be the most stable and earthquake-proof. Second, they liked the flexibility of post-and-

beam construction. They knew they might be adding on to or changing the house at a later date. With a post-and-beam frame, they could knock out wall sections between the posts without compromising the integrity of the structure.

Third, the post-and-beam frame allowed them to put in as much glass as they wanted without having to worry about sizing headers correctly or getting enough diagonal bracing. When the wall itself is bearing the weight of the building, you can't just cut holes in it for windows anywhere you please. But in a post-and-beam structure, you can do what you want in the spaces between the posts.

The precise size and shape of the house were determined in part by how much room they needed and what kind of a space they wanted to live in. Another consideration was fitting the house into the land. They wanted to impact the environment as little as possible. Conventional foundations involve digging a large trench around a building. The trench and the piles of dirt that come out of it cut a path of destruction fifteen to twenty feet wide around the entire perimeter of a house. To avoid digging a trench, they eliminated the foundation wall. They placed concrete blocks directly on the ground to support the post and sill beams.

Also, Gail and Gwen didn't want to cut down any more trees than they had to, so they picked their site carefully, keeping in mind sun and wind exposure, and with an eye to doing as little damage to the trees and plants around the house as possible. Oddly enough, long-term durability was not an issue, at least for Gail.

Gail

I want this building to last my lifetime, but beyond that I'm not concerned about resale value. I'm only concerned about it meeting my needs. And if somebody comes along who can use this after I'm dead and gone, that'll be fine.

The building site was at the edge of an open meadow, but the house nestled into a wooded portion of the property, so it is shady in the summer and open to the winter sun. The house is 16-by-24 feet with a shed roof fourteen feet high on the south side. It has a loft over half of the main floor on the east side, which gives the kitchen below it a seven-foot ceiling. The rest of the living room has a thirteen-foot ceiling at the south end.

They ran the loft at right angles to the pitch of the roof, resulting in a very low ceiling at one end of the

> *"I wanted a loft. I wanted that sense of upward, in spiritual terms, of everything that is symbolized in that movement upward."*

loft, but they retained some open, dramatic space over the living room.

Gail

I wanted a loft. I wanted that sense of upward, in spiritual terms, of everything that is symbolized in that movement upward. That's why we put the loft at the low end of the space, to leave the high end open.

The house is small but creates the illusion of spaciousness rather than making absolutely most efficient use of space.

Stud walls were installed between the posts to hold the insulation. A 14-by-24-foot screened porch provides a nice area on the north side. They have one-inch-thick, rough-sawn oak, board-on-board siding and a metal roof. The inside wall covering is mostly rough-sawn boards. All windows and glass were bought secondhand. The only plumbing is a sink drain to the yard. The house, which took two years to build, required a total cash outlay of just over $3,000.

The heating/ventilation system is somewhat primitive but effective. The tall side of the house faces south and has generous window space. In winter, it warms up quickly during the day. The sleeping loft at the top is warm at night. Gail and Gwen also installed removable panels along the bottom of the first floor wall in the living room and the kitchen that were covered by screens to keep out insects and mice. In hot weather they remove the panels and open a window in

the loft to draw air through the house. As an added measure, they put an opening in the floor on the north side of the house and another opening under the porch that allows cool air to be drawn in.

Gail

It's tropical in the summer—it gets to be 100 degrees down here, and the humidity is 80 percent. But with the amount of insulation we have, and the ventilation, it'll stay cool. We sleep in the loft all summer long. It's fine.

The layout of the interior was a collaborative effort. By the time Gail and Gwen built their home, they had lived in a number of different places and had a pretty good idea of what they liked in a house. Fortunately, they didn't seem to have any disagreements about the design. Gail didn't want the space broken up into small rooms, so the house is one big, open space. The loft is open to the downstairs, and only the back wall of the kitchen and some closets break up the space.

One of Gwen's primary concerns was keeping the house clean, so she used smooth surfaces wherever possible. Otherwise, building materials were selected mainly on the basis of price. They picked up secondhand or salvage materials, and they bought things on sale. In general, they shied away from high-tech products. They were uneasy about the potential dangers of toxic substances in building materials. Wherever possible, they kept to "plain old wood."

Gail checked out books from the library on carpentry and housebuilding, and Gwen read everything she could on solar design. Gail described their system as an organic process. She would come up with ideas, Gwen would come up with ideas, then they would get together and work on the design. They had fun with it.

Gwen drew up the plans based on the sketches. She drew all the plans to scale, and even drew all the furniture in, but, unfortunately, she forgot to allow for things like hats and coats and boots and all the miscellaneous items you accumulate and have to find a place for.

Gwen

It always seemed to turn out smaller than it looked on paper. No matter how much you draw to scale and all that, it still seemed to turn out smaller.

During construction they did a good job of squaring the building themselves (using the 3-4-5 triangle proportion method). When they finally put the roof on, it all fit together—a vindication of their faith in themselves. They also put in big, 2-by-6-foot panes of 1/4-inch-thick glass in the south wall. They have had no problems with the windows for ten years. In the living room, they installed one large section of beveled glass in the south wall. It's a beautiful window, one that is a continuing source of delight to them.

They began construction on the cabin in September 1983. During the winter while they worked on the house, Gail and Gwen lived in the back of a pickup truck with a cap on it.

Gail

Living out of the back of a pickup truck, we didn't have the normal creature comforts, like a hot bath every night. We were taking showers out of milk jugs, being each other's faucet. So we were not working under the best conditions. That got, physically, very demanding.

By March they were able to move in. It was a magical moment for both of them. They felt relieved after the discomfort of a difficult winter and satisfied at finally having a place of their own with absolutely no strings attached—no mortgage, no obligations, no limitations on what they could do. Even with minimal financial resources, they were able to achieve the often elusive dream of home ownership.

Gwen

The whole reason I did this was to have an affordable home. I wanted to be involved in the building process so I would know that the electrical wiring and plumbing were safe, and so that I would be able to do my own repairs and maintenance. It was so much cheaper to do the labor ourselves than it would have been to hire someone.

"It always seemed to turn out smaller than it looked on paper."

Gail's motivation for wanting to build a house was also economic. She had been a schoolteacher all her adult life, and the purchasing power of her salary was decreasing every year. She wanted to continue teaching because she loved it. She also wanted to provide a safe place for other women.

Gail

I wanted to build a place where women could come and have a home if they were willing to work. That has happened. Although we don't have women living here all the time, women come through here who are seeking certain things in life. They come here and they live awhile and they do work exchange. They learn a lot while they're here. Many of them go on, and some of them come back on a regular basis.

Gail had never been involved in building before Silver Circle. When she was four years old, though, her family had moved into a little three-room house in Memphis which her father eventually expanded into an eight-room house with a big workshop and a carport. Gail had helped out by holding things for her father and fetching tools. She knew what was involved, and knew it was possible to build without hiring professional help. Even though she had no building experience, she decided it was something she could learn how to do.

Gail

I was an inquisitive child, and my father would answer my questions. So I had that back there in my apperceptive mass. I had not learned to use tools, but I knew what their names were, and I knew what their functions were. I knew what a chalk line was for. I knew what you do with a plane. I knew what a chisel was. That information, I realized, was something rare for women. And so, when I got the idea to build my own house, I just got out all the books. You know, I can read. I'm a relatively intelligent woman. I just got out all those books and read and read and read.

"Being female, I did get a lot of that negative kind of training to helplessness. But it didn't take with me."

Gail hadn't been exposed to many role models for women in nontraditional work, but she did have a close friend who was studying to be a union carpenter. And Gail's grandmother ran a farm single-handedly for many years. Even though Gail describes her mother as a helpless kind of woman in some ways, she was able to instill in Gail the idea of independence. Gail also took care of her younger brother and sister, and so was familiar with responsibility as a child both by example and through her own experience.

Gail

All of these things in my background influenced me in my own work. I was raised to work, for one thing. I was raised out in the country in a blue-collar working-class family. Work was real important. The Puritan work ethic was definitely a part of my upbringing. About the worst insult that could be made about you was that you were lazy. Being female, I did get a lot of that negative kind of training to helplessness. But it didn't take with me. I was always a tomboy. People teased me about that. But at the same time, my family continued to rely on me and give me responsibility, which made me more and more confident that I was all right the way I was.

Design and construction were also new experiences for Gwen. In the early seventies she visited hippie communes where she saw buildings being built, and once she helped assemble a dome for storage space at a friend's father's business. But building at Silver Circle was her first real construction experience. She credits her childhood experiences with giving her the self-confidence to see the project through.

At eight or nine years old, Gwen developed an interest in design when her stepfather went to architecture school. Around that time, she began drawing house plans and received a Girl Scout's badge in architecture. She also did some carpentry projects, such as cages for her various pets.

Gwen

I think my parents inadvertently instilled self-confidence in me. I guess they encouraged me to try things, though they didn't give me much positive feedback about the results. The confidence must have come from the doing, or outside feedback from teachers, Scout leaders, church, aunts and uncles, and grandparents.

Gwen was also influenced by watching her mother, an accomplished seamstress, work. Gwen was enthralled by seeing her mother turn flat pieces of cloth into coats, suits, and evening dresses. Thirty years later those memories of her mother working would inspire Gwen to tackle carpentry. She found, as have many other women, that manual and cognitive skills are surprisingly transferable; strong analogies exist between carpentry and cooking, sewing, and even writing. Such tasks require assembling and shaping the components, then connecting them in a structurally sound finished product. All the basic elements of a good carpenter or a good designer can be learned by absorbing the example

of any competent worker engaged in a constructive activity.

The overall building plan at Silver Circle was somewhat open-ended, completed in stages. When the main house was finished, two other cabins and a bath house were added. The seven women whose names are on the deed originally intended to develop a commune using the main house as a group living space. But Gail and Gwen were the only ones to settle there permanently, so the main house became their home.

By 1992, several new women had joined them and moved into the other cabins, and Gail and Gwen were building an addition to the main house. The dome kitchen has been reactivated as communal space, although Gail and Gwen sometimes cook for the entire group in the main house.

As the community has evolved, Gail and Gwen and the other women at Silver Circle have continued to explore group decision-making strategies and the personal politics of shared responsibility among women with different degrees of investment in the property, of

> *"The structures that they've built have allowed them the flexibility to keep altering the living arrangements, and Gail and Gwen are pleased with how it has all worked out."*

different ages and skill levels, and with different financial resources. The structures that they've built have allowed them the flexibility to keep altering the living arrangements, and Gail and Gwen are pleased with how it has all worked out.

Gail

We're just thrilled to death with this place. I think it's wonderful. I built myself a home for $3,000. No mortgage, you know? None of that crap. I mean, I've owned homes all over Memphis and West Memphis. And I've done the suburban number, and done the midtown number, and the old house that you redo. You know, I've been all that route. And I've hated it. I mean, I have really been through the whole rat race. Been mortgaged up to the hilt. For me, the peace of mind of not having to go that route— there's no comparison.

*"I think it's wonderful.
I built myself a home for
$3,000. No mortgage,
you know?
There's no comparison."*

Leona Walden

Leona Walden came to the Mendocino, California, area in 1972, during the peak of the back-to-the-land movement. She and her partner, Max, built a cabin there completely by hand. In 1974, Leona moved out. Since she was the one who was handy with tools, Leona sold Max her share of their cabin and designed and built a second cabin for herself and her daughter. Before moving into the cabin, she fell in love with another man and moved into his house in town. After they married, she designed and built a huge California barn-style house for them, this time using hired labor. After her husband died, she designed a fourth house for herself. She works as a commercial artist.

Salmon Creek Farm

Leona Walden grew up in a suburban Los Angeles neighborhood, where she had her first job at the age of nine, working at a children's pony-ride stable. Unfortunately, two years later her father had a stroke, sending the family into a financially difficult period. Her mother went to work as a secretary, but Leona says the change didn't disrupt the emotional structure of the family.

Both before and after her father's stroke, Leona's family was warm and loving. Leona appreciates and draws on the love and the sense of well-being that her mother instilled in her. Leona's father set a positive example, as well. He never discouraged her from using his tools, and he never gave her the message that it was inappropriate for a girl to be handy at repairs.

I've never felt that I couldn't find out what I needed to know in order to accomplish something. I guess I've just had a lot of positive feedback in my life about my abilities, or who I am. I've met a lot of people who are smarter than I am, but I'm very quick to pick up on things. The type of intelligence I have is very down-to-earth and very functional. If I don't know what I need to know, I can find out. And I can put it into the format that I need to make it work for me.

Evidence of her self-confidence and intelligence can be found just outside Mendocino, California, where

Leona built four houses on or near Salmon Creek Farm, a commune founded in the early seventies by Robert Greenway and River (Sally Barnes Shook). Leona's first house was a tiny cabin in the woods overlooking a small canyon.

We arrived in July of 1972. I had a three-year-old daughter at the time. I heard they had terrible winters (and it's true—we get sixty to seventy inches of rain in the wintertime). I had moved onto the Salmon Creek Farm property, but at that time there weren't any buildings on it yet. We were all camping out in tents. So I just got it in my head that I'd better get a shelter built. So I started in. I had never built anything before but a bookshelf with boards and bricks. I didn't know how to start. So I just asked every carpenter I came across. And I looked at books. Basically, if I found three people who agreed on something, that's how I did it.

Although most of her knowledge of construction practice came out of books she found in the library and what she could find out by asking friends and neighbors, Leona had another source of information—a book called *Dwelling*, by River, which Leona had illustrated. River's philosophy advocated building without damage to the environment, leaving no permanent scars on the land. The cabins built at Salmon Creek

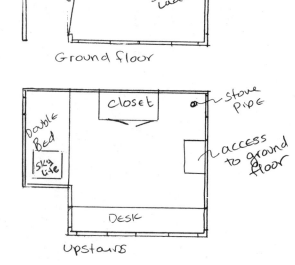

Ground floor

Upstairs

> *"I had never built anything before but a bookshelf with boards and bricks."*

Farm had foundations made of stones or were built with posts and piers that could be taken apart later. Even if the buildings were abandoned and left to deteriorate, all the materials would decay and eventually disappear. The forest could reclaim its own.

In the course of looking at the houses described in the book and talking to builders, Leona picked up many ideas, including what works and where the pitfalls lie. She asked lots of questions and stored away the information.

Her first cabin was only 12 by 16 feet and was two stories high. Leona pretty much built it on her own. Max, her partner, was very good at helping her carry boards, but his design instinct and carpentry skills were minimal. So the cabin was basically Leona's design, and was built mostly from carpentry skills she acquired as she went along. She and Max tore down chicken coops in Petaluma for some of the lumber; some was given to them by a man who owned a mill. When the cabin was finished, Leona had spent exactly $300 for materials.

Although Leona admits she didn't really know what she was getting into when she started building, it didn't seem insurmountable to her. In fact, the cabin only took about three months to build. There was no electricity to the site, so all the work was done with hand tools. The path to the building site was once a logging road that was no longer drivable, and the canyon was so steep that the only level spot to build on was right on the old roadway. All the materials, including the lumber, had to be carried the quarter mile from the main road.

It actually was very exciting, one of the most exciting things I think I've ever done. Up to that time, I had been doing a lot of artwork, on paper. I found that one sixteen-hour day raised an entire wall (on a house that's still standing twenty years later). Sixteen hours on paper produced one small drawing that would probably end up in the trash basket, or in the rain or something.

The cabin had a small sleeping alcove on one side of the building facing the view over the canyon, and there was a bank of windows that ran the length of the front and partway along the east side. In the early morning, sunlight came in the window at the crack of dawn. Wide eaves kept it from shining directly on the bed, but it lit up the room. Leona remembers waking up and dozing off, then waking up again as the sun slowly came up over the horizon. And at night she would look up through the skylight and watch the stars as she settled into bed.

The commune members shared their meals in a central kitchen/dining hall. Leona liked that arrangement, because it meant she cooked one night a week and came to dinner six nights. Additionally, the inclusion of a communal kitchen meant the members' individual cabins could be very small, since they were basically just places to sleep and have privacy. A large gar-

"I found that one sixteen-hour day raised an entire wall. Sixteen hours on paper produced one small drawing that would probably end up in the trash."

den served the entire community, and there were always many hands to help with work parties or emergencies.

Leona lived in the cabin for two years, then broke up with Max and moved out. He wanted the house, and she knew she was more capable of building another one than he was, so she agreed to sell her half of the house for $300. After traveling and living in San Francisco for a couple of years, she and her daughter returned to Salmon Creek Farm, and Leona built a second cabin, virtually next door to the first one. There was still no electricity, so she again built a house without power tools. This time, the walk to the road was nearly a half mile. Although she had a twelve-inch chain saw to cut the heaviest timbers, beams, and girders, the rest was done by hand.

My second house was small like the first one. It was for myself and my daughter. But I never actually ended up living in that house. I only stayed there a couple of nights. I built it, and then I was dating a fellow and I fell in love with him. He had a house in town, so I moved in with him.

Leona's new companion, Jack, had been married for twenty-six years. He had accumulated a lot of belongings he stored at his rented house. When he and Leona decided to buy a sailboat and sail around the world together, he began looking into the cost of renting storage space for all his things. Leona, however, suggested he build a barn on some property he owned nearby. Jack thought that was a great idea, and Leona offered to design it. She liked the idea of doing a California barn-style structure (with a tall center section and two side sheds). The barn was planned to be two stories high, with a small loft and a set of windows under the eave of the center section that would imitate the style of a cathedral clerestory. Leona drew up detailed plans, and construction began in 1977.

When deciding the overall shape and size of the barn, Leona looked at houses in her neighborhood and tried to analyze why some appealed to her and others didn't. One roof pitch would look too steep. Another appeared too shallow. She calculated the actual pitch in each case and used that to determine what would be right for her barn. Then she considered how easy each roof would be to shingle and repair. She ended up putting a fairly steep pitch on the central roof, but she made the side shed roofs slightly flatter. The combination was visually pleasing and practical—if the central roof ever needed repair, the flatter shed roofs would make it more accessible.

"I still found I was very economy oriented. And actually, the building ended up costing us $25 a square foot."

Well, so we started. His half of it, besides financing it (which was a big part of it) was to keep saying, "Bigger, bigger." I came from having built everything by hand and having carried everything on my back to the house site. I kept thinking, "Smaller, smaller." And he kept saying, "No. Bigger, bigger." And so we ended up building a 4,600-square-foot structure that's forty feet long and sixty feet wide.

Having lived on $150 a month for a good number of years of my life, and suddenly being in a position of sort of unlimited resources, I still found I was very economy-oriented. And actually, the building ended up costing us $25 a square foot. I just did a very good job of shopping around. I knew most of the major resources in this area because of having built before. A lot of the materials I got really good deals on.

Among the good deals Leona found were the rafters and the beams for the house, which were either made from wood milled by local sawyers or obtained from "wood butchers" who provided her with salvaged leftover wood, such as old beams from a bridge in Oregon. She even used timbers that were too far gone for structural members as edges along the lawn. She paid less than 20¢ per board foot for the wood. The 1-by-12 redwood siding was milled by a local sawyer and cost $410 (the most expensive lumber outlay for the whole building). She bought 4-by-8-foot thermopane replacement glass panel seconds that cost only $23 apiece.

This time around, the actual construction work was done by hired carpenters and contractors. Leona and Jack hired two men to be in charge of the work. One of the men had quite a bit of experience as a contractor, and the other one had been a carpenter's helper. Leona quit her job teaching at the College of the Redwoods to concentrate on the building project, and she and Jack moved into a trailer on the land.

The line separating the functions of client and contractor became fuzzy, which is often a problem when the client wants to be involved in the construction of a building. Conflicts developed between Leona and the contractor. He had been hired to supervise the work, but Leona was buying the materials and making many of the arrangements and decisions that are normally the responsibility of a general contractor. Leona suspected that some of the problems stemmed from the contractor's discomfort with a woman telling him what to do; she didn't have credibility with him in terms of construction expertise. On the other hand, Leona didn't want to leave all the decisions to him merely because he was a professional contractor. Eventually, Leona and Jack fired the contractor and turned the job over to the carpenter to finish the building.

Because the building was to be a storage barn, Leona obtained an agricultural exemption from residential building code requirements. That meant they had more latitude in using nonstandard building materials. About halfway through construction, the carpenter expressed amazement that they were building the huge barn just to store their belongings. He said, "You mean to say you're going to store all your stuff in this great big beautiful building, and you're going to live in that funky little trailer?"

They scratched their heads and thought about it. It did seem a little silly. So they decided to convert the

"You mean to say you're going to store all your stuff in this great big beautiful building, and you're going to live in that funky little trailer?"

barn into a house. To prevent problems, Leona hired an engineer to go over her revised plans. He made only one suggestion: lower the rafter ties to the very base of the rafters. They liked that idea, especially since it made the loft a much more usable space. They waited to inform the building department of their revised plan until they were at the point of closing in the walls—figuring the further along in the process they were, the more likely they would be to get away with it. The building inspector came out to look at the building while the structural framework was still visible and, in spite of the nonconforming materials, allowed them to continue.

The first floor of the center section of the barn house was nine feet high. In the middle was a six-car garage for Jack's antique-car collection. There were two side sheds, one of which was divided in half. Originally, one half of the divided shed was Leona's studio. Later, it was converted to the master bedroom. The other half of the shed was a workshop. The shed on the other side was a hay storage area with two stalls for horses. While there were some disadvantages to having animals housed in the same building as people, it was convenient to feed the horses during bad weather.

The second floor included an open dining room/kitchen area at one end with an adjacent deck that has an ocean view. The middle area was less defined. At the other end was a very large living room. The second-floor level rose above the side sheds and was lit along the sides by the clerestory windows. Large windows at the two ends and an open floor plan prevented the space from having the gloomy atmosphere associated with barn interiors.

The loft covered about two-thirds of the second

> ## "We have very little glass for the amount of open space. And yet you have this total feeling of openness and light and airiness."

floor. It was under the sloping roof rafters at the top of the house, and as a result it had no vertical wall space. To alleviate the cramped feeling, Leona put in two skylights and two large dormers. The dormers were each eight feet wide, large enough so one of them could become Leona's studio. She had storage space for her drawing materials built into the north dormer. With its lighting, it was an ideal studio. The south dormer became Jack's office and personal space. The rest of the loft was a bedroom.

While Leona had always favored simple shapes and traditional styles, her ideas about how to design comfortable living quarters changed during the conversion of the half-finished storage barn into a building that combined the functions of garage, attic, stable, and house.

What I would have done, before I lived in the barn, is I would have built a house with a lot of different rooms. And what I would do now is very much like the barn—basically open space. What we have inside is posts, as opposed to walls. It allows this flow that I talk about, and yet still divides the rooms. Instead of having walls, we have furniture that breaks up the space. Also, we have very little glass for the amount of open space. And yet you have this total feeling of openness and light and airiness. I would try to do that again. Rather than do a huge bank of view windows all along one side, I'd try to devise a plan that didn't do that, because you lose so much heat and you have so much sunlight to deal with if you do.

Leona and Jack were married in 1981. They lived in the barn house for several years and were extremely pleased with it. As it happened, they never got around to taking the sailboat trip that originally spurred this major building project. Jack died in 1989, and his estate was divided between Leona and his children by his previous marriage. Leona ended up with a large portion of the land, but not the house. So once again, she needed a place to live.

"I work from the inside and design the house around flow and inside space."

In July 1990, Leona began construction on her fourth house, a 2,200-square-foot basic rectangle with a shed on one side and an entranceway on the other. The lumber for the beams and other structural members and the redwood siding came from trees on the property that she had cut and milled. Leona acted as her own general contractor. She didn't do any of the hands-on work, but she designed and planned the building, ordered materials, and supervised the subcontractors' work. Although she had to be accessible to answer questions as problems arose, she worked a part-time job throughout the construction process.

In this new house, Leona placed windows for maximum advantage. Although her kitchen is eighteen feet long and has only one small window in it, it is flanked on two sides with rooms that have a great deal of glass. On one side is a dining room with a double set of glass doors. On the other side is a solarium, which is glass on two sides. The kitchen is separated from the solarium by a glass door so the outdoors can be seen from the kitchen. Both in this house and in the barn house, Leona managed to create an illusion of many windows without actually having them.

Leona always enjoyed the conceptual work of design: thinking out what kinds of rooms are needed, the flow of activities from room to room, and how a house will look. She concentrates first on how the different functions of interior space will interact.

I like to work from the inside out. I like to figure out what is needed, what kind of space is needed. Things like, how do you live? Where would you want your kitchen to be in relation to your living room? Where would you want the deck to be in relation to your bedroom? How do you like to live? Do you need office space? What's important to you? So I work from the inside and design the house around flow and inside space.

In spite of Leona's very practical approach to building, there is always a romantic element or two in her designs. Her barn-house had clerestory windows like a cathedral, and the sleeping loft had a secret passage to the living room—a panel concealed in the living room wainscoting led directly to the loft.

Some of Leona's favorite features came about by chance in one house and were then designed into the next house. In the first cabin, the roof had an overhang on the south side of the house. It projected just far enough to block the high summer sun but did not block the warming rays in winter, when the sun is low in the sky. She hadn't thought of calculating the angle of the sun when she built the roof, considering the eave's function to keep rain off the side of the house. Because the spectacular view was to the south, there was no question that most of the windows would be oriented in that direction. But as she discovered by happy accident, heat and light were moderated perfectly.

The back wall of her first cabin faced north toward the steep bank of a hillside with no windows. On the ground floor, a bank of windows ran across the front of the cabin, and an east window went almost to the floor. The east window gave a lower-level perspective on the room that, besides being good for children, was a psychological invitation for adults to use the floor, too. This was especially appealing to Leona, who spent a fair amount of time doing yoga or playing with her daughter.

By the time she built her fourth house, Leona was much older, and her desire for convenience was stronger than it was when she built her first cabin. This time she gave more thought to how easy a house is to clean, where you can set down your groceries when you come in the door, and how you get firewood to the stove from outside. Having become accustomed to ample space, plumbing, electricity, and other conveniences, Leona didn't want to go back to roughing it as she had in the cabin. Some things she knew she could live without—electricity, for example. But she didn't have to. She wasn't so sure, however, that she could still live without hot and cold running water, even though she had done it for years.

Her kitchen counters are mounted high, because she is tall and doesn't want to bend over to work in the kitchen. She has a dishwasher, which she can load and unload standing in one spot. There is a shallow drawer over the dishwasher for silverware. Directly over that is a cabinet that holds glasses and plates. Leona describes this setup as somewhat symbolic of most of her structures. There is an easy flow from room to room, and she has analyzed the tasks that are performed in each room, always thinking ahead of ways to make life easier. Another example is the indoor/outdoor wood box. She fills it from the outside and unloads it from the inside, so she doesn't have to carry firewood through the house.

Leona also thinks about long-term maintenance needs. She put forty-year composition shingles on her

> *"It was a treat to build with no one to please but herself and to have the experience of three other building projects behind her."*

scheme, there is a connection between inside and outside. However, she hasn't designed the living room to feel as though it's a part of the outdoors; rather, the outdoor view is a picture to look at from inside the living room.

There's also a simplicity about Leona's designs. Even in her last house, she resisted the temptation to add ornate features. Basically, her most recent house is as simple and straightforward as the first three.

It was a treat to build with no one to please but herself and to have the experience of three other building projects behind her. She feels more settled now than she ever has before. She views her succession of houses as progressive steps. Each has been more comfortable and sophisticated than the one before, but each, in its turn, was appropriate for that time in her life.

I have little fantasies. And without any effort whatsoever, they come true. So my fantasy is, I'm going to set myself up in such a way that in my older years (you know, from sixty on), I'm just going to be a painter. And I'm not going to have to sell to make money. I'm not going to have

new roof. She used treated redwood exterior siding and windows with aluminum frames. And her exterior doors are made of steel though they appear to be wood.

A further distinguishing characteristic of Leona's designs is her lack of concern for melding the inside with the outside. Instead, she makes the outside visible only as a discreet image. At her current home there is a three-acre pond within thirty feet of her window. She chose her carpeting to match the color of the pond. Since she used the view as an integral part of her color

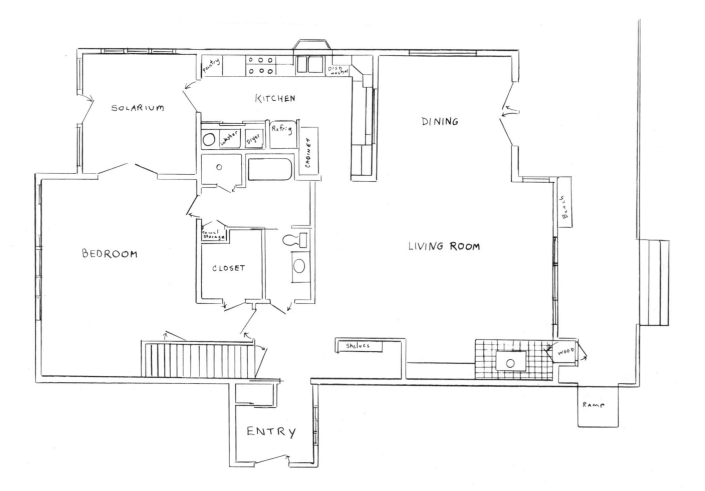

*"I have little fantasies.
And without any effort
whatsoever, they come
true."*

*to work outside. I'm just going to paint for the shear joy of
painting. So that's my fantasy . . . I'll just paint.*

*I've learned a lot. I've got a lot of skills as a result of
doing what I'm doing. We'll see what happens. I'm not
going to work on it. I'm just going to see what happens.*

Dawn Hofberg

Dawn Hofberg came to Mendocino in the early seventies. After Leona Walden moved out of the cabin she had shared with Max, Dawn moved in with him. With Max's help, Dawn expanded the cabin with several additions. But that relationship also came to an end. This time Max moved out. Dawn stayed and continued to make improvements over the years. By 1988, she had married and, with her husband, Robert Schlosser, built a new house on nearby property. Dawn had done most of the work on the cabin by herself, without power tools, but local contractors built the new house under her direction. She has worked as a landscape gardener, forester, waitress, midwife, and family practice doctor's assistant.

Canyon Overlook

Dawn Hofberg's life at Salmon Creek Farm was very different from her life as a child in a suburban middle-class family in Los Angeles. However, she credits her mother's tales of summers on her childhood farm, her own experiences at summer camp, and her family travels with giving her the idea of living in the country.

My mother has always thought that some of the things I've decided to do were kind of crazy, but she liked that I would try to do them. So I got a lot of support from her. She just really liked that I would do what I wanted. Anyway, I was happy doing it, so that was really what she cared about. I can't say my parents directly encouraged carpentry (probably neither of them could hang a door), but they always did—and still do—support me in any harebrained or sane scheme I can think up.

Dawn moved into her cabin in 1975 and had her first child there. Even though she had little prior build-

ding experience, she was inspired to work on her cabin by the examples of strong, resourceful women who were around at the time, such as River, cofounder of Salmon Creek Farm, who firmly believed that anyone could build a house. Dawn, in particular, was encouraged to build and add onto Leona's cabin, even though it stretched her skills and entailed structural alterations she didn't know how to perform.

Dawn and Max made a number of improvements, including a small addition on the west side and another on the east side that is larger than Leona's original cabin. The original section of the cabin was never insulated, so it warmed up quickly on summer days and cooled down just as quickly when the sun went down. However, the additions Dawn built, which are insulated with fiberglass, hold the heat better. Other than that, the additions were built in much the same style as the original cabin. Dawn introduced walls that cut corners off at interesting angles, and she altered the roof line in

"*When you have a site like this, what else could you do?*"

several places. The result was a building with complicated segments that would look almost Victorian if there were more peak-roofed sections instead of mostly shed roofs.

Dawn also added a bathroom and extended the back of the cabin to provide extra storage space, and she built a pantry off the back of the kitchen. Because she had no power tools, she had a problem when she ran into a large tree stump she couldn't remove by hand. As a result the pantry doesn't run the full length of the back wall and is raised at the back. Despite these inconveniences, the pantry worked very well. It was cool and dark. Dawn cans lots of vegetables from her garden, and the pantry provided perfect storage conditions. The only flaw was that the pantry wasn't mouseproof. Canned goods did all right, but winter squash and carrots didn't last long.

Dawn especially liked the cabin's simplicity and the dramatic setting. The view determined the design of the original cabin and most of the additions. It was obvious that all the rooms would be oriented toward the south, overlooking the canyon, because, as she explained, "When you have a site like this, what else could you do?" When Dawn began expanding the little cabin, she wanted as many windows as possible, so the rooms she added at either end of the original cabin have large windows.

Eventually Max moved away, and Dawn stayed on with her daughter. In 1983, she married Robert Schlosser. Dawn and Robert put in solar panels for hot water and electricity. Two of the panels were water panels that siphon into a tank by the side of the cabin, and the others were small photovoltaic panels, which charge storage batteries that supply electricity to run the few appliances in the cabin. The house didn't need much electricity; there were only five light bulbs and a radio/tape recorder. The refrigerator ran on gas.

The cabin had a wood stove with a coil in it that heated water when it was cold—a fire was made in the morning to heat the water. In warm weather, the solar panels heated the water. In early spring, when mornings are cold but the days are sunny, the water was boiling hot. The water came from a small feeder creek in the hill behind the house. Since the photovoltaic panels couldn't supply the load an electric water pump would require, the water was pumped by a hydraulic ram pump.

Dawn enjoyed living off-grid and felt proud their needs were so modest. She felt a special comfort in keeping life simple, knowing she was consuming minimal resources and causing minimal waste and pollution.

"*I feel proud of living without electricity—without the power company.*"

We used kerosene lamps for a long time. I always liked the light. But the smell and the fumes from the kerosene are not good. And it's not good light to read by. The fire hazard doesn't bother me that much, because we're real careful about kerosene. We've lived with it so many years it doesn't seem like a big danger. It's like a wood stove. You get used to it. You get so used to being careful, it just becomes a habit.

I feel proud of living without electricity—without the power company. The fact that I have electricity now, and it's still not the power company, makes me even happier. And we don't have ugly wires overhead. But I don't wash my clothes by hand. There is a point at which your time is worth more. So I go to the laundromat. Diapers, you know.

In spite of all her additions and the improvements Dawn and Robert made to the cabin, when Dawn's second child was born they began to think about building a larger house.

Robert, who is an architect, was eager to work with Dawn to develop a new design. And on all but two details, they agreed on what they wanted in the new house. The primary bone of contention was the finish floor in the living room. Dawn wanted it to be hardwood, her husband argued for concrete. His rationale had to do with creating a heat sink for the sunlight that would be coming into the house from the southern exposure. Her priority was to have a floor that would be comfortable to sit on and that children could play on without breaking absolutely everything they dropped. The agreed-upon compromise consideration was to put in a wood floor, but to build a stone wall behind the wood stove. It wouldn't get direct sunlight, but it would store heat from the stove.

A secondary area of disagreement was on the site of the house. Although the land is nearly as steeply sloped as the cabin site, there were more options on the new location, and Dawn wanted the house to be situated on the most level part of the site.

He wanted to have a really dramatic view. I said, "I want a lawn in front of the house. I want to walk out and be able to be on the earth." We're kind of perched here on the edge of the canyon. I have to walk a long way to get to my garden here. I don't like that very much.

Dawn's vision of the new house seemed to center as much on the outside as the inside. She was concerned about where to plant fruit trees, where an herb garden would go, how the irrigation system would work, where she would keep her tools, and where the kids could play. Because she lives in a mild climate, her children spend a good part of their lives outdoors.

Having gone through a few winters in a tiny house with small children, Dawn also placed a high priority on indoor space. She imagined her new house as big enough to hold meetings, maybe even dances, without feeling cramped. As far as she was concerned, bedrooms were only for sleeping, so they would be very small.

Because she planned to live in the new house for a long time, it was important to Dawn that it have all the features she really cared about. By far the most important room for Dawn was the kitchen. She wanted the house to be large enough for visitors to sit at the kitchen table together. The kitchen also had to be big enough to accommodate group activities like canning and joint meal preparation. She also wanted a house that was easy to clean. Most of the interior wood surfaces in the cabin were rough-sawn lumber (a real dust catcher).

The new house would have all smooth surfaces. She also wanted to be sure any stairs in the new house were enclosed and designed so children couldn't climb over or through the railings.

Dawn planned on some very traditional rooms in her house, like a mudroom for hats, coats, and boots, and an old-fashioned pantry off the kitchen. She also wanted two bathrooms, one downstairs and one upstairs. The only really modern touch would be a loft over the living room for her own work space. She would use part of the loft as an office and part of it as a place for her loom.

In 1986, Dawn and her husband started construction on land next door to Salmon Creek Farm, on the same slope as the cabin and with much the same view. Although they thought about the design off and on for months, the actual plans were drawn up during a vacation in Mexico (it rained for ten days, so they took the

opportunity to have uninterrupted design time for working out the final plans). Having lived next door to the building site for ten years, it was relatively easy to plan the new house. By then, Dawn knew almost exactly what she wanted.

In many ways, the new house is a larger and more comfortable version of the cabin. Like the cabin, the new house has a bank of south-facing windows as its main focus. But an original feature in the new house is a two-story living room that "makes up for in drama what it lacks in efficiency."

The new house is both on- and off-grid. The lights and electrical outlets are supplied by photovoltaic cells, the water is solar-heated, and they have a wood stove. They did end up compromising as they had anticipated. The living room floor is wood, with a large brick-and-tile hearth that is an effective heat sink.

There is a system for heating water with a wood stove. They now use about half as much wood to heat their 2,500-square-foot house as they used in the cabin, which had only one thousand square feet of living

"Robert had seen many marriages break up under the stress of building and decision-making, so he and Dawn braced themselves, took each step as it came, and kept their lines of communication open."

space. Double-glazed windows and generous insulation in the walls and ceiling created most of the heat savings.

The refrigerator, washing machine, a few lights, and a backup water heating system are all powered by electricity from the power company. Only rarely do they need to heat water this way. The power kicks in after a few days if it is foggy but not cold enough for a fire. Her only regret is that they never put a drain in their roof-mounted solar panels, because they circulate the panels to push the water through the system continuously. However, if they leave town for several days in the winter, when the water might freeze, they have to climb up on the roof and put blankets over the panels.

For the new house, Dawn had help with the construction: four local carpenters and a plumber, an electrician, and concrete and masonry subcontractors. Dawn and Robert stayed in the cabin until the house was completed. Being next door was handy for overseeing construction. Robert had seen many marriages break up under the stress of building and decision-making, so he and Dawn braced themselves, took each step as it came, and kept their lines of communication open. Perhaps most importantly, they did not make decisions without consulting each other unless they had previously agreed that one or the other would be in charge of a given task.

Dawn describes their new house as an architect's modest dream: energy-efficient, simple, comfortable, and attractive. In planning the house, Dawn drew primarily on her knowledge of family and community living. Her husband provided the architect's eye for lines and detail. The result is a satisfying blend of the practical and the aesthetic.

"When we walk home at night, she says, "Aaaaaah, it's so nice to come home. It's so quiet here."

In some ways, Dawn doesn't feel she has really moved. Her attachment and sense of "home" are more tied to the place (a ridge, a view, a social community) than to the building itself. She felt some sadness at leaving the cabin where her first two children were born, but her third child was born in the new house, and that gives her enough of an emotional connection to make it feel like her permanent home.

I feel all the time lucky. It's really nice, because I hear my daughter say it now, too. When we walk home at night, she says, "Aaaaaah, it's so nice to come home. It's so quiet here." It really makes me feel good.

Ronnie Sandler

Ronnie Sandler, who grew up in the New York City area, moved to Detroit in the early 1970s and became the first woman to enter any of the building trade unions in Michigan. She became a carpenter, then started her own business as a general contractor doing remodeling and additions. She bought a tiny house on a mountainside in New Hampshire, which she totally renovated. Then she took off the roof and added a second story. She still lives in New Hampshire and served for nine years as the executive director of a training program for women in the trades. Ronnie now works as a consultant helping federal agencies enforce compliance with affirmative action programs.

Another Story

Ronnie Sandler bought her house in 1973, when she was twenty-five years old. Before that, she had been living with a group of people in Whitefield, New Hampshire, and was getting tired of the communal scene. She happened to be in town one day and spotted an ad on the town bulletin board that read, "House for sale, Dalton, New Hampshire, maple trees, views, $3,000."

It turned out that the people offering the house were hippies from Tennessee. They didn't actually own the house; they had only bought the right to the deed. But they had already gutted the house, planning on fixing it up. Now they didn't want it. They were so eager to sell, in fact, that when Ronnie met them to look at the place, the first words out of their mouths were, "You can have it for $2,500 dollars."

The only other people who had been by to look at the house were hunters, and they didn't want to sell to hunters. Ronnie looked around the little 16-by-30-foot house. The basement and the good, solid foundation were the only reasons the house hadn't fallen down the hill. When the sellers brought the price down to $2,250, Ronnie gave them a $50 down payment and was on her way to owning her own home for the first time.

The house didn't have running water. It wasn't insulated. It had fifteen-amp electrical service. The siding was made of green roofing shingles on the front and black roofing shingles on the back. It had an outhouse and a porch that was falling down. But it was still a bargain, and Ronnie was thrilled.

Fortunately, Ronnie was already a skilled carpenter. She had learned carpentry on her own by taking classes and working with other people, and she had found she loved working with tools.

I was a real tomboy. Why? Boys got to do all the fun things, that's why. I have an older brother, and I always wanted to do what he got to do. I always wanted to take shop in school, because my brother had taken shop. And so in junior high school I went to my guidance counselor and said, "I want to take shop." He said, "Girls don't take shop. Girls take home ec." And I said, "But I don't want to take home ec. I want to take shop." And he said, "Girls don't take shop. Girls take home ec." And I said, "But I don't want to take home ec. I want to make a salad bowl."

Finally the guidance counselor said, "Go see the assistant principal." So I went to the assistant principal, and I said, "I want to take shop." And he said, "Girls don't take shop. They take home ec." I said, "I don't want to take home

> *"Boys got to do all the fun things. I have an older brother, and I always wanted to do what he got to do."*

"I knew I always wanted to build my own house. It's so important that I have a place that's mine. That no one can take away from me, and no one can kick me out of."

ec." He said, *"You will take home ec. That's the end of it."*

So I took home ec. We had to sew a skirt and wear it to school for a day. It was an ugly A-line skirt. It was awful. To this day, I do not sew.

My mother always says that I'm just rebelling. Everything I do is because I'm rebelling, and I've always been doing it. I sometimes wonder if they had let me take shop, if I would be a nurse now.

Ronnie was able to develop a strong and independent nature, and to see herself as a competent and intelligent person. Though she attributes it largely to her father's tremendous confidence in her, part of Ronnie's sense of independence comes from being raised in a subculture with strong female role models. As a member of a Jewish family in Brooklyn, New York, she was exposed to a familial system in which her grandmother was the matriarch. Even when she was very young, Ronnie was aware of a tradition of strong women in her family.

Another factor that might have increased Ronnie's level of self-confidence was that, like some of the other women interviewed, she saw her family's home being built. When she was in the second grade, Ronnie's parents bought an unfinished house on Long Island. The house was already framed when they bought it. The family would drive out to the house on weekends to watch the progress. As a family they chose the flooring, planned the den, and decided on window design and placement. They would sit down together and discuss the new house. And even though she was only seven years old, Ronnie was invited to contribute to these discussions.

It was really exciting. We'd stand in this room. We'd stand in the garage. We'd say, "Well, that's where the bedroom's going to be," "This is what we're going to look out on," "What color shall we paint the house and the trim?" It was a great house. It was wonderful. I suppose it had something to do with my thinking about building my own house later on.

Two years later, Ronnie's father died. When her mother remarried, Ronnie had a difficult time accepting her stepfather. Later, when she was in college in Vermont, she just didn't feel comfortable returning to her mother and stepfather's house. In her mind, it wasn't "home." As a result, she feels, the concept of home became extremely important.

I knew I always wanted to build my own house. It's so important that I have a place that's mine. That no one can take away from me, and no one can kick me out of. It's mine. It can always be mine if I choose it to be.

Before moving into her new house, Ronnie installed a loft and insulated part of the house. When she moved in, she hooked up an electric coffee pot, an electric frying pan, and an ancient refrigerator. For heat, she had an Ashley wood stove (eventually she added an oil furnace), and she ran well tiles from a spring. (A couple of dry years without water, however, forced her to have a well drilled, which cost more than the house.)

The first winter I lived there, there was a blizzard. I was upstairs in the loft I had built, and I could feel the snow coming in on me. There was frost around the edges and the corners of the room. I had a wood stove at the time. I remember getting the stove cherry red trying to keep the house warm.

In 1976, Ronnie closed up her Dalton house and moved to Michigan, where after joining the carpenter's union, she started a training program for women in the trades called Step Up. Two years later, she returned to Dalton, started her own construction company, and continued working on her home. In 1985, Ronnie recreated her Step Up program in Vermont, becoming executive director of Northern New England Tradeswomen, Inc.

Finally, in 1987, fourteen years after she had bought it, Ronnie had just about finished renovating her house. The work she had done had consisted mostly of necessary and basic improvements. Now that the house was functioning well, she began to think about what would make it better. More space would be the biggest improvement—the house was too small for more than one person, and she might not always be living alone. The problem was figuring out how to make the house bigger.

Generally it is easier to expand a house horizontally, adding rooms on one side or another. However, Ronnie's house was located on a steep hillside, very close to the road. It seemed like the only way to expand was up.

My fantasy was always to take a chain saw and go around and cut the roof off, and get a helicopter to come pick the roof up. Then I'd build the walls for the second floor and drop the roof back on. That had always been my fantasy. Then I read an article about someplace where they did that. I laughed. But my roof was not in good enough shape to do that.

Ronnie decided to take the old roof off, build a second story, and quickly build a new roof. She reasoned that if she planned it carefully and got enough help, she would have the house open to the weather for only a short time. Her strategy was based on prefabricating the walls on the ground first, then taking down the old roof. The new walls would be lifted into place by a crane as soon as a new platform was built over the first floor.

The first order of business was to come up with a design. The outside dimensions were already set by the size of the house itself, but how to lay out the rooms on the second floor and where to put the staircase took more thought. She knew she wanted a master bedroom, a bathroom, and a guest room. And she had a good idea about the dimensions she preferred. Her grandparents had given her a large, beautiful Chinese rug that she had never been able to use, and this predetermined the size of the master bedroom; and the bathroom had to be big enough to contain a large Jacuzzi bathtub. The guest room would take up the remaining space.

Ronnie also had to consider the house's orientation. She had a spectacular view of the mountains to the east, so there was no doubt the bedroom would be on that side of the house. She put it on the south end so she could build a deck out from the bedroom that could catch the afternoon sun. She already had a deck on the first floor on the east side, but by early afternoon it was shaded by the house.

The next step was planning window placement. Ronnie wanted large windows facing east for the view. But if she tried to line them up directly over the windows on the first floor, the window placement on the second floor would be awkward. The windows also

> ## "In some ways this was twelve years in the design stage. But in the immediate sense, it took a couple of evenings of intensive work."

turned out to be smaller than she had intended, because she forgot to account for the height of the floor joists in her calculations.

Positioning the stairs was even more problematic. Fortunately, one of Ronnie's friends had studied architecture in school and helped her determine the best layout. Another friend who was taking a drafting class drew up some plans for her.

It was fascinating. In some ways this was twelve years in the design stage. But in the immediate sense, it took a couple of evenings of intensive work.

To minimize the time the roof was off, Ronnie chose a simple peaked roof. To make the process easier, she used prefabricated roof trusses, which go up very quickly, instead of building her own rafters. She just couldn't afford to leave the house exposed to the weather for the length of time it would take her to build rafters.

She organized a four-day work party, scheduled the crane, and began measuring the house. The first measurement was the length of the house, which came up 30 feet, 4 1/4 inches, a very odd size. Usually houses are built in increments of 16 inches, 2 feet, or 4 feet; her measurements didn't make sense at all. She measured six times to be sure. Finally, she had to accept it. She proceeded to build the walls to those exact measurements, worrying the whole time that something would be wrong somewhere.

Ronnie sent out a flyer to all her friends describing what she planned to do and inviting everyone to come. She recruited a woman she knew who was an experienced carpenter to help out. The rest of the crew was made up of women friends, some who knew how to hammer and saw, some who did not. She scheduled her volunteers so that there would be people there on each day. Of course, everyone wanted to come on the day the crane was going to raise the walls. People who didn't want to build were to cook or bring food or help in some other way.

The walls were prefabricated in late July, about two weeks before they were to take the roof off. It seemed like a good choice—August is usually the driest month in New Hampshire. She and her crew constructed the walls in the reverse order they were going to go up. Since the crane would have to reach over the house to drop the back wall in place, that one had to go up first, otherwise the front wall would be in the way of the crane. So the front wall was built first and sheathed. That formed a platform on which the other walls could be built and stacked one on top of the other.

They built all four walls in one day—one *long* day. The first wall was the hardest because it was laid out on the uneven ground. The next three went quicker. The whole time Ronnie was working, she kept worrying about that 30-foot, 4 ¼-inch measurement.

The plan was that we were going to start early on a Saturday morning. We were going to rip off the old roof totally. On Sunday, we were going to put down joists for the second floor and cover that with decking. And on Monday, the crane was going to come in at eight o'clock in the morning. We were going to lift the walls into place. On Tuesday, we were going to do the roof trusses. So it would be all closed in by Tuesday night. This was the plan.

While all this was going on, Ronnie was working three days a week running Step Up and four days a week on the house. It was a grueling schedule. She borrowed a VW van to live in while the roof was off, and she moved everything out of the ground floor of the house. Some of it went into the porch, some of it was under plastic in the yard, and a good deal of it was put in the basement to keep dry. The rest was taken to a neighbor's house and stored for the duration.

On Saturday morning at about eleven o'clock, the all-woman crew arrived. The day went well—the only hitch discovering that once the roof was off, the walls of the house were neither level nor square. The top of the walls was about six inches lower at the back of the house than it was at the front, and the middle wall was out of plumb by several inches. There was also a bulge

along the front of the house. The whole thing was like a large parallelogram.

I was in a total daze. I mean, here was my house, which was the most meaningful thing in my life. I used to joke that when I bought the house, it was only four walls. But now it was really only four walls. . . . You could stand in the kitchen and look up at the sky and the trees. I felt too weird. I think I was in denial. I was just so disoriented. I felt violated. I felt like, "What have I done? Oh, my God. Whose idea was this? I liked my house. Whose idea was this?"

On Sunday Ronnie and her crew began leveling and squaring the tops of the walls. Using a come-along, they straightened the wall and resheathed it with plywood to stiffen it. Using line levels, a carpenter's level, and wedges cut from 2-by-4s, Ronnie built up the low walls to match the highest point on the high walls. It took almost all day Sunday to get everything on one plane and level.

The crane was scheduled for eight o'clock on

"You could stand in the kitchen and look up at the sky and the trees."

Monday morning. Sunday afternoon at four o'clock they were just getting ready to put the second floor joists down. Ronnie realized there was no way they were going to be ready in time, so she rescheduled the crane for Monday at noon. At the end of the workday Sunday, the house was totally open. To make matters worse, there were clouds in the sky. To be on the safe side, they covered the whole place with huge sheets of plastic.

So I'm sleeping in the van. Two friends of mine are sleeping in a pup tent. About two o'clock in the morning, the sky literally opened up. It just poured. Tat, tat, tat, tat, tat. After about half an hour, one of the women who was sleeping in the pup tent came over and knocked on the door

"It looked like a house had fallen on my house. It's an image I'll never forget."

of the van. She said, "I think it's leaking into your house."

We went out and tried to push up the plastic to get the water to run off. It was just draped across the top of the house with some boards across the walls to hold it up, but of course it sags in between the supports. So we're trying to push up on these bulging puddles. We realized there was nothing we could do. It was hopeless. Then these big swimming pools worth of water would break through and drench the house. There was an inch of water on the floor. An hour later, there was an inch of water in the basement, which was where I had put everything to stay dry. We had an inch and a half of rain in an hour.

They started in again at seven o'clock Monday morning. With the help of her crew, Ronnie laid the joists down as quickly as possible, and started in on the floor decking. They got half of the floor decked by eleven o'clock. They could see they wouldn't be ready on time for the crane, so they ran decking around the rest of the edges in order to have a base to put the walls on. Then they laid plywood down over the rest of it so they would have places to stand. The crane arrived at noon, and amazingly they were ready.

They began the second story by lifting the back wall first. Ronnie was still nervous about that 30-foot, 4¼-inch measurement, convinced that something must be wrong somewhere. But the back wall dropped into place perfectly. They had just gotten the back wall braced when a big dark cloud rolled in. For the next five minutes, it poured down rain. They just kept working, finishing up the bracing, working in the rain. Then it stopped and didn't rain again for a month.

They tied all the walls together and braced them thoroughly. By this time, it was half past four or so. The original plan had been to use the crane to pick up the roof trusses and hold them in place, one at a time, while Ronnie and her crew nailed them down. But it was too late in the day for that, so they just had the crane pick up the trusses and lay them upside down across the walls. On Tuesday morning, they started putting the trusses up, flipping them up one by one. Then they sheathed the roof and put tar paper over it. By Tuesday night, the roof was waterproof again.

We had sheathed the walls before we put them up. But we hadn't sheathed the space at the ends of the joists. So there was this space between the top of the ground floor walls and the bottom of the new walls. I slept in the van that night and looked out the window. All I could think of was The Wizard of Oz. It looked like a house had fallen on my house. With that gap at the top of the old walls—that's just what it looked like. The second floor was a total house by itself. And it had fallen on my house. It's an image I'll never forget.

On Wednesday morning, Ronnie went back to work—she had never been so relieved to go to a job. She continued to sleep in the van. She could take showers, and she could cook, since the downstairs bathroom and the kitchen were still functioning. But the house was a total mess. She basically lived in the van for the next three weeks.

I would never recommend to anybody to build up. Because when you build up, you totally expose and open up your living space. At least when you build out, you can separate the new construction from the rest of the house

with a temporary wall or at least a plastic sheet. Your living space is on one side, and the construction zone is on the other side. When you build up, it's like, "Here I am. Turn my house into a construction zone. Forever." I can't tell you how many times I swept and vacuumed up sawdust. I'm still doing it, because I'm just finishing trimming out the downstairs.

Finally Ronnie put the strip of sheathing around the joists. She got most of the windows installed, and put shingles on the roof. Inside, she covered the stairwell with plywood so no one would fall down the hole before she got her finish stairs installed. And she put a ladder on the woodshed roof to the bedroom door that would eventually open onto a deck. She used this as her access to the construction zone on the second floor. The idea was that the sawdust and clutter would be contained

and she could stay sane until work was completed.

Once all this was done, Ronnie breathed a sigh of relief. She moved into the downstairs portion of the house the next weekend. Of course, everything was still a mess. She started to think it had all been a ghastly mistake. Her house, which had been perfect and all together and almost finished, was total chaos. She would come home from work at night and walk right into a second job. But gradually things started to come together. As more progress was made and the house started looking better, Ronnie began to enjoy herself again.

Over the years, Ronnie had been collecting materials she thought she might use someday. She had some windows from Maine and two-hundred board feet of cherry wood she had been drying for six years. Ronnie decided to use the cherry for door and window trim on

"There's nothing else in the world going on. Except for me and this piece of wood that I'm working on."

the second floor. However, Ronnie had never used hardwood for trim before, and she didn't realize how much work it would be. With hardwood, you have to predrill every nail hole before you nail it, and sanding is very tedious. She found that the work dragged at a time when she was already tired of it. But once she adjusted her pace and accepted the fact that it was going to take

a while, she became absorbed in it and actually enjoyed the challenge.

There's also something almost Zen about doing trim work. When I'm doing carpentry, and especially trim work, there's nothing else in the world going on. Except for me and this piece of wood that I'm working on. Taking the time to get the cuts right. Getting it to fit just right. When I was doing trim work in the union, you didn't have time to do that. I just love working on my own stuff. I would literally lose myself trimming the upstairs. It was amazing.

The next project had to be the stairs. Once again, Ronnie chose native woods: the treads are all cherry; the risers are all beech; and the stringers are made from two 13-foot by 13-inch-wide pieces of cedar. The stringers are impressive, especially since cedar boards

that size are extremely rare in Vermont.

There were also two stained-glass windows in her house that were in the gable slated for demolition. The windows, which had originally been set on the diagonal, served as the house's landmark. When she built her second floor, Ronnie wanted to retain something distinctive about the appearance of the house on the side facing the road. Ronnie saved the stained-glass windows and put them next to the stairwell. She set them at different heights, following the ascent of the stairs. The effect is interesting and also breaks up the boxy appearance of the house.

In spite of the hard work and the sometimes harrowing moments, Ronnie is pleased with her decision to add on to her house. Admittedly, there are some aspects of the old house she misses.

There were things about my old house that I loved. In my old house in the loft, there was a window that looked out the back. My bed was right next to the window. I would sleep with my head looking out that window. I miss that. I remember times of waking up and coming back from being in the stars, into my body.

When the renovation work was completed, Ronnie turned her attention to the way the house related to its setting. She terraced her hillside and planted gardens; she thinks of it as expanding her remodeling activity to the outdoors.

Ronnie has only about an acre of land—not a big piece of property. But it's plenty for her. She is surrounded by forest, much of it protected from development, giving her a sense of continuity between her property and a vast spread of wilderness. She finds tending her small lawn and her gardens plenty of responsibility.

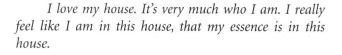

"There's something about the long-termness of that. The gardens and the house. This is mine."

In 1994, Ronnie quit her job as director of Northern New England Tradeswomen and started a for-profit consulting company called Compliance USA, Inc. She and a business partner do on-site inspections for civil rights contract compliance. Right now they are working for the Main Department of Transportation overseeing a major bridge construction project, making sure that women and minorities are adequately represented in the project's workforce. Ronnie has to travel a lot for this job. Though she loves the work, she is also always glad to return home.

Ronnie especially loves her perennial gardens. She has been single for several years and jokes that perennials are her long-term relationships.

I sort of have this fantasy of what it's going to be like when I'm eighty years old. I'm going to have these wonderful perennial gardens all around, and I'm going to be this little old lady in this house with these incredible gardens. That has become an important piece for me, planning the perennial gardens. There's something about the long-termness of that. The gardens and the house. This is mine.

Ronnie's house is a symbolic center and anchor in her life. It is also a physical repository for her own identity, a place where she has left her mark. Remodeling, for her, was a form of self-expression.

I love my house. It's very much who I am. I really feel like I am in this house, that my essence is in this house.

Patricia Liddle

Patricia Liddle grew up in Halfmoon, New York, a suburb of Albany. After years of living in rented apartments, she wanted a place of her own in the country. She found some land in nearby Canaan, New York, and moved into a trailer that came with the property. Her first building project was a barn for her three horses. Building a house for herself came only after five years of living in the trailer. With the help of a friend, Pat constructed a small, traditional-looking New England saltbox house. Solar panels preheat her water, while windows and doors on the south side and a wood stove in the center of the house keep her heating costs to a minimum. Encouraged by the mostly positive experience of building and tired of teaching elementary school after fourteen years, Pat decided to use her carpentry skills professionally. First she helped found a small construction company, later she worked for a general contractor, and she is now cashing in on her knowledge of construction by working as a property adjuster for an insurance company.

New England Saltbox

Pat Liddle's is another sweat-equity story. She bought property in Canaan, New York, and moved into a trailer on the land. But after living in the trailer for five years, she wanted a real house to live in. Although relatively unskilled in construction, she had undertaken some small projects before: a chicken coop, a porch addition to her trailer, and part of the work on the barn for her horses. As a schoolteacher, she had free time in the summer, so she decided to build the house herself.

Pat had picked up the basics of carpentry and tool use as a young girl by watching her father work around the house. He allowed her to use his tools to do simple projects of her own. She built a bird feeder and organized several forts with the neighborhood kids. But thinking back to her childhood, Pat couldn't really pinpoint any significant experiences that influenced her future as a builder of her own home. She was just always a tomboy, and her parents didn't try to discourage her activities or tell her they were unladylike.

Since her parents didn't make a big fuss about gender-appropriate behavior, there was no "girls'" or "boys'" work at home. Like most children, Pat wasn't aware of how other families operated. So it was somewhat of an unpleasant surprise in junior high school to discover the elaborate rituals of femininity that began to play an increasingly important role in the social life of her friends. To her, these represented rather pointless restrictions on her freedom. She learned to conform where necessary, but never really internalized that sense of helplessness and restraint women often adopt.

Pat believes she learned good work habits from her mother. While her mother wasn't particularly handy with tools, she did know how to use a hammer and a screwdriver and was very good with wall papering and decorating projects. Her work was always neat and efficient, and she took pride in a job well done.

Pat's father, on the other hand, was a master of the temporary fix that invariably became a permanent fixture. He was always saying, "That's good enough, for now." But he never did the job over. Whatever block of wood was propping up the end of the bookcase would probably be there for the next ten years. He did have a fair amount of repair knowledge, which he shared with Pat. And he had a lot of tools.

As a young woman, Pat hadn't dreamed of building or even owning her own house. When she left her parents' home, she rented happily for years. She felt that land ownership had more to do with stewardship than with possession.

Pat did, however, grow tired of having to board her horses at a stable, and she had developed a strong interest in gardening. She couldn't afford to buy property large enough to provide the pasture and garden space she wanted with a house already on it. When she found several acres in Canaan with a trailer, she figured it was the best she could do.

Later, when she became fed up with trailer living and began to seriously consider building a house, Pat sought advice from Clint Gove, a friend who had a fair amount of building experience. He had helped his family convert a farm building into a house. Since he was between jobs at the time, he offered to help her with the framing. The catch was that she would have to start right away. She had wanted more time to think it over and plan the project, but she recognized this was a great opportunity, so she accepted the offer.

Pat's preference for uncomplicated design can be seen in her old-fashioned New England saltbox. One of the reasons she chose the steep, peaked roof of the saltbox was that her property is flanked by two long, fairly steep ridges. She felt the shape of the roof would mimic the hillsides in a harmonious way. The saltbox shape was also a good choice for a solar house. The back of Pat's house faces the road, which is the north side, and the ridge line of the house is parallel to the road. Pat put the long side of the roof toward the road. She wouldn't have wanted to put many windows on that side anyway,

because not only is there traffic noise, but it is also the cold, dark side of the house.

To prepare for the project, Pat read books on house building and talked to friends who had building experience. She felt capable of making the major decisions on her own. There were some drawbacks to that choice, however. She knew enough to draw her plans to scale, but since she had never designed a house before, she didn't think to draw in furniture, calculate how much space a person takes up, or consider how much space is really needed for different activities.

I went through a number of versions, erasing and changing. I gave the walls thickness. It might not have been real precise, but it was close. I think I used one-quarter inch equals one foot or one-half inch equals one foot, I can't remember now. But I must have envisioned myself as this minuscule little object inside this house. I must have figured I was the size of a toothpick on the paper, when, in reality, I should have made me more the size of a Tootsie Roll or something.

Once Pat had her design worked out, she made only a few changes. She extended the dormer on the second floor to accommodate a larger stairwell, and although she had originally designed the house with only one bathroom, shortly before construction began she realized she wanted another one on the second floor. Fortunately she changed her mind before the concrete slab was poured for the floor and the plumbing lines were literally cast in concrete.

The house is basically a 1 1/2-story rectangle with a peaked roof, so framing it was pretty straightforward. Pat bought green lumber from a local sawmill. Her walls were made of rough-sawn, 2-by-6 pine with two-inch, foil-faced rigid insulation on the outside of the walls. The walls were therefore much thicker than is standard, which meant she had to make her own extension jambs for the windows and doors. She also had to make her own doorsills.

Pat had started out thinking she would follow the instructions in basic carpentry books and buy whatever materials she needed—it would simply be a matter of assembling and installing parts. But by deviating from standard practice, she ran up against the most basic challenge of construction.

"It seems overwhelming until you break it down into parts."

You end up having to do things yourself. There's a lot of different things like that, that you think, "Well, where do I buy this?" But you don't buy it. You make it. You just make these things. So I thought, "All right, I get it. I'll just figure out what I need to do, and I'll do it. This is no big deal." So I did. I made extension jambs for all the windows. I made the sills.

It worked out okay. I was very grateful to have someone there who had some little tricks of the trade to show me, some knowledge I could fall back on. But it wasn't that hard. It's pretty basic, most of it. It just seems overwhelming until you break it down into parts. You look at what you have to do first. Then you look at the next step. And so on.

Working intensely for two months during the summer of 1979, Pat framed, roofed, and sheathed the house with Clint's help and direction. After that, she was on her own. Progress slowed during the winter, but she continued to work evenings, weekends, and during her vacations. Although she hired an electrician and plumber to put in her mechanical systems, Pat did the insulation and drywall herself.

Pat's house depends partly on solar energy for heat. She has solar hot-water panels on the roof, and her windows are oriented for passive solar gain. The only backup heat source is a wood stove. However, Pat burns only about a cord of wood each season. Her house is very energy-efficient. The outside temperature in her area can drop to five or ten degrees below zero, and is often zero to ten degrees above in midwinter, yet when she goes out of town for a weekend in the winter, her house temperature never drops below about fifty degrees.

Although the chimney is large (about 2 by 4 feet), with a double flue, and takes up a great deal of room in such a tiny house, Pat placed her chimney in the center of the house. This resulted in an awkward layout but avoided several potential problems. For one, the smoke rising from the firebox doesn't cool down as quickly as it would if the chimney were on an exterior wall, which means less creosote deposited in the chimney flue by smoke condensing as it cools. It also means that whatever heat is lost from the chimney is gained by the house.

Pat hadn't done any masonry before, but she decided that she could teach herself how to build the chimney. She bought books on housebuilding, went to the library and looked up what kind of mortar mix was right for her application, and started in.

"I learned how by trial and error."

I learned how by trial and error. You can tell at the bottom I was just learning. It gets a little better. The further up you go, the straighter it is. I really enjoyed doing the chimney. I never thought I would, but I did, because it was all mine. Nobody had any suggestions—nobody from start to finish—it was me. And it was not your normal chimney design. It was not elaborate—I didn't have a fireplace, so I didn't have to worry about a firebox or anything. But it was big—double-wide. I had an extra flue in there to blow warm air from upstairs back down to the first floor. It was actually a lot of fun.

Inside the veneer of brick are two standard ceramic flue tiles. Pat filled the space between the flues and

the brick with sand and gravel to create a heat sink. The brick wall behind the wood stove and the sand and gravel around the flue radiate heat back to the house for hours after the stove has gone out. The second flue was put in to blow warm air from the top of the house back down to the first-floor level to even out the temperature gradient, so that the top wouldn't have to be too hot in order for the bottom to be warm enough. But Pat gets such good convective air flow in her house (probably due in large part to the open floor plan) that she hasn't needed to use this technique.

Pat incorporated both practical and aesthetically appealing features into her design. By placing her kitchen on the same side of the house as the driveway, she is able to set her groceries down as soon as she comes in the front door. This arrangement also allows her to carry in firewood, carry out trash, and get at the tools in the utility room without traipsing through the living room. Large sliding-glass doors off the end of the living room help make the house seem larger than it is.

Pat enjoyed building her own house, though it involved a tremendous amount of hard work and totally absorbed her time and energy for over a year, leaving her perpetually exhausted. While Clint was helping her, he expected her to keep up a strenuous pace, and she was never able to get everything done by the time he thought she should. If she had questions or needed help lifting things, he was there, but much of the time his role was to prod Pat to work harder and faster.

Left to her own devices, she would have worked at a slower pace. Living alone, Pat had no one else to do the grocery shopping or laundry, cook meals, or make phone calls. She had to determine each night what supplies she would need on the job the next day. She had to watch her lumber piles and buy more wood before she ran out.

It was very intense. Very hard. Absolutely exhausting. Long days. It was probably the hardest I've ever worked in my entire life. But I enjoyed it. Framing a house is fun. It's just so immediate. From the foundation, within a week you have the outline of the house. It's amazing. You put up the green lumber, nailing the nails, and the juice is spurting out at you because it's green. But it doesn't matter.

Pat especially enjoyed doing the window trim. She used a hand plane at a little bench she set up. She liked to see the shavings curl off the plane as she worked. She went at her own pace then—fussing around with the trim to get it to fit and having a good time with the challenge of it.

I enjoy learning how things get put together, whether it's a watch or a house or whatever. I have always enjoyed the mechanics of a thing.

One thing Pat learned is to recycle materials constantly on a construction site. Pat assumed she would have to buy scaffolding, but Clint showed her how to construct safe scaffolding by nailing 2-by-4s to the house and cross-bracing them for sturdiness. She didn't have to invest in expensive commercial scaffolding she would only need once, and since she made her scaffolding out of leftover lumber, she didn't have to buy anything. She found that the boards that hold the concrete for the foundation footings can be reused for bracing the stud walls before they are pinned by the rafters and sheathing. Those braces can be used again—along with cutoffs from studs, plates, and rafters—to make scaffolding. You use scrap wood to make sawhorses, blocking for drywall nailers, and bracing for the joists. The list is endless. One way and another, materials keep cycling through the job.

"I enjoy learning how things get put together, whether it's a watch or a house or whatever."

Pat moved in to her new home as soon as she possibly could. The trailer was taken away and its porch converted to a storage shed. She has since added an attached garage. Her current plans call for a patio and some landscaping to soften the transition between inside and outside, which will also help to make the house seem roomier. The only real regret Pat expressed was that she did not make her house bigger.

When she is alone, there is plenty of room to move around and get things done. But when she has guests over, it starts to get crowded. Pat might have alle-

viated this problem by dividing up her interior space more than she did. And if the house were just slightly larger, she could have divided the second floor into two bedrooms, which would have provided the privacy the house now lacks. A door closing off at least part of the upstairs would also conserve heat downstairs. Yet, even given the inconvenience of inadequate space, Pat is happy with her home, and she knows she can always add on.

Another thing Pat would do differently is to include a formal entryway. In fact, now that she has added a garage off the kitchen, the main entrance isn't even an exterior door.

I never really realized how important that is to a house. It does make a big difference. It helps finish it, helps kind of complete it. Now I'm realizing that it's really critical. It can make a small house look much larger or feel much larger. It lets you feel connected to the outside when you're in and to the inside when you're out.

Once she began landscaping, Pat found that her attitude toward the house and yard changed slightly. For a long time, she didn't bother to plant flowers. She had a horse, which she occasionally allowed to chew on the lawn. But when her horse died a few years ago, Pat was surprised to discover how much difference a few flowers around her house made.

It's kind of interesting. Up until now I wouldn't have been happy about moving, but I could have done it. But just landscaping the outside is making me more interested in staying here than before. Before, I always tried to keep my distance. Even though I built this house. I would say to myself, "Now Pat, it's just a bunch of wood. You could do it again if you wanted to. You can leave this, right?" It's just all coming together in a way it didn't before. It's more connected now. It looks like it belongs here. It would be hard to leave.

Sandy Seth

Kristina Wilson

& Valerie Graves

Sandy Seth, Kristina Wilson, and Valerie Graves live in Taos, New Mexico. Sandy is a writer who coauthored with her sister, Laurel Seth, Adobe! Homes and Interiors of Taos, Santa Fe and the Southwest. Kristina weaves rugs and blankets, many of which are made of wool from her own sheep and llamas. She is also a skilled carver and finish carpenter. Valerie is a painter. Her landscapes of the desert countryside around Taos are expressive of her love of the land and its natural beauty. Sandy and Kristina collaborated for many years, building and remodeling adobe houses. They learned their basic skills by making traditional adobe fireplaces, an art which they turned into a business. Later, they renovated an old house. Their next project was to buy land and build three houses on speculation. Finally, they remodeled and added to their own houses and joined Valerie in building a home for herself.

Adobe Tradition

Kristina Wilson lives outside of Taos, where she raises sheep and llamas and runs a weaving school during the summer. As a young woman, she had very little money and was raising a baby on her own. Determined to spend as much time as possible with her son, she invented ways to earn money at home. The most successful of these activities was weaving, which also brought her an enormous amount of satisfaction.

Kristina built her own house, a small adobe, that started out as a one-room cabin. It was very primitive at first—no electricity or running water—but little by little, for the last thirty-five years she has added on and made improvements to create a comfortable home. She also built a studio for her weaving and other projects.

"It also satisfied a deep pioneer instinct, and still does. Over the years, the house has grown by adding on a bit each summer."

Kristina and Sandy Seth first started working together on an old house Sandy bought to remodel.

Kristina

It also satisfied a deep pioneer instinct, and still does. Over the years, the house has grown by adding on a bit each summer and by adding amenities as I could afford them. I get a tremendous sense of security, belongingness, and . . . at-homeness. I feel this place is an extension of myself and a clear reflection of me.

Sandy

That was my first experience of building. The house was built on a shallow foundation of rocks. To make it more heat efficient and cleanable, the previous owners had covered the beam-and-pole ceilings with drywall. The individual sheets of drywall were painted pink, yellow,

"I learned how to build fireplaces from an old Taos Indian woman."

and blue in alternating pieces. Can you imagine? The house was broken up into tiny square rooms, with a light bulb in the middle of the ceiling of each one. I broke out two or three rooms, ending up with a sort of dance hall feeling—a long, skinny dance hall.

I wanted to fix it up to live in. It was in terrible shape. It didn't have a well, didn't have a bathroom. And it had linoleum floors everywhere. There were fourteen layers of linoleum. And they went back in time as you went down through the layers. The newest were little, delicate, pretty patterns. Colorful, light prints. Going down

you came to darker, gloomier layers, ending up with these heavy, morose, giant maroon-colored flowers.

About that time, Kristina offered to build Sandy a fireplace as a housewarming present.

Kristina

I learned how to build fireplaces from an old Taos Indian woman so that I could add fireplaces to the house that I was living in. Then Sandy wanted to renovate an old house for herself, and I said I'd help her build a fireplace. We decided to make it outrageous. It became like a flower unfolding. Sandy would be working on one side and I would be working on the other. And we'd say, "How about doing this?" Or we'd say, "Let's try that." I'd start doing something, and then she'd just almost imitate me, and vice versa, back and forth. And somehow we made it seem balanced. It was a lot of fun.

They enjoyed working together so much that they decided to start a fireplace-building business. It was very successful and kept them busy off and on for several years.

Sandy

It was a great partnership. It consisted of Kristina, myself, and an Austrian woman, Inga Davis. She was our fancy plasterer. She did absolutely elegant plastering. Almost too elegant, in a very European way. It had to be done and redone, I think, a minimum of seven times. The plaster would be applied—first coat, then a second coat, and then a third coat. And then it would be rubbed down with milk and a piece of sheepskin. Rub, rub, rub, rub, rub. In order to make it really shine and in order to have it incredibly smooth. And just very beautiful.

Then one day we heard about a house that was supposed to be for sale really cheap. It was in the middle of a funny part of a real small town that was real junky. We thought how wonderful it would be to take that and make it absolutely gorgeous. Just make it this little gem in the midst of this mess.

Well, fortunately, we did not do that. Instead, we got a piece of property, went into partnership, and built our very first spec house.

Kristina and Sandy designed the house together. They didn't really have any cash beyond the price of the materials. Kristina did most of the carpentry, including all the handmade, carved doors. Sandy worked mostly on adobe.

They worked well together throughout the project; they seemed to think along the same lines. Each time there was a question about what to do, they found they were both considering the same solutions. Sandy attributes this easy relationship and decision-making process partly to the fact that the project was their own—there was no customer to please. They were free to do whatever they wanted to with the house. Building for a client to a certain set of dimensions, utilizing materials that they might not like as well, would have spoiled a lot of the fun.

For Sandy and Kristina to consider building a house on their own isn't as unusual in this area as it would be in most parts of the country. Women in the tricultural area in and around Taos and Santa Fe grow up in an environment with a strong women's cultural component that seems to foster building activities by women.

Sandy

Many women in the Southwest have built at least portions of their own homes for hundreds of years. Pueblo Indian women and Hispanic women both have long traditions of working with adobe. In the case of the Pueblo, women often own the houses as well. It is common for Indian women and Hispanic women to build fireplaces and plaster their homes inside and out.

Having mastered the basics of adobe construction in their fireplace business, much of the mystique of building that inhibits many women had been dispelled for them. That didn't mean it was easy, though. The overall effect of the adobe design is relaxing and soothing, but building adobe houses isn't relaxing—it is extremely hard, backbreaking labor. There is no relief from the long and tedious task of lifting, carrying, and stacking adobe bricks, and it puts a lot of wear and tear on the body. It's also very hard on the hands, especially if you work in the winter. Many of the older people around Taos who plaster or build fireplaces have arthritis.

Nevertheless, Kristina and Sandy built two more spec houses, each one larger and more ambitious than the previous one. Each time they were able to find a buyer and make a profit on their efforts.

Their design procedure was at the opposite end of the spectrum from that of most professional architects. They just sat down with a piece of paper and a pencil and sketched out what they thought would be a good plan. Then they started to build, making changes along the way—sometimes on a whim.

Because of their open-ended approach and the forgiving nature of adobe, a high degree of spontaneity was possible. Batting ideas back and forth, relishing the freedom and creativity of adobe, they made the building process itself their central focus. From their first project together, the ideology behind their work was a constant: to make buildings comfortable for people, to make each space reflect and support spiritual and psychological needs as well as physical needs.

Sandy

It was a thoughtful kind of process. We wanted the house to have a great view. And we wanted it to be done in a traditional framework, be made of all those neat old materials, native materials that not only look nice, but feel good for the person who lives in it and those who perceive it as neighbors or passersby. We were looking for a harmonious structure, not an aggressive structure that is disagreeable to the eye or to the heart.

Their first spec house had only two bedrooms. They had wisely decided to do something modest for their first project and had developed a budget that designated fixed amounts for materials and acted as a constraint. But within that limitation, their primary consideration was to make the house absolutely beautiful. As new ideas occurred to them, they would confer, then try them out. They would build a room, stand back and

"We were looking for a harmonious structure, not an aggressive structure that is disagreeable to the eye or to the heart."

look at it, then decide whether to continue according to plan or make a modification on the spot.

Sandy

We kept continually jogging the walls in designing that first house—partly to make an interesting shape, but also to have this feeling of an old hacienda, where you did

ramble a bit. And ramble within a small structure. I mean, it was only about 1,300 square feet, and that includes the outside portales. *The other reason for jogging the walls was to let more south light into the house. On the second house, we did that even more. We used handmade tiles from Mexico and some wrought-iron things. We carved out little niches in the adobe walls. We could do whatever we wanted, in a creative way, within this sort of wonderful boundary of what's already been established out here.*

> *"That's the wonderful thing about adobe, that you can have these curves and soft lines."*

For the second spec house, they had a spectacular view, with the Taos Mountains in the east. The large windows facing the view also let in the morning light. Taos is surrounded by high desert, and the site of the second house is almost seven thousand feet above sea level. It gets cold there in the winter, so it helps to have sunlight warming up the house early in the day. Their use of south-facing windows for light and heat was an

intuitive decision. At the time they were building, there wasn't the widespread consciousness of solar heating there is now. Looking back, they regret that they weren't more attentive to the development of solar technology; otherwise they would have done even more passive solar design in their spec houses.

Kristina

The second house we did was also very successful. It was like a river to me. It just meandered. We tried to catch sunlight in every room. It was quite a large house. There were a lot of organic shapes to it. That's the wonderful thing about adobe, that you can have these curves and soft lines. If you look carefully around here, a lot of what looks like adobe houses are fake. They're built with wood or cement blocks and plastered over. But you can see the edges are too straight. Look at the corners and the edges. But with authentic adobe there's a subtle irregularity to it that's very pleasing, very soothing. I love that. The shapes are caressing, almost sensual. It gives a wonderful warm and natural feeling to a room. It takes a lot of work. But it's beautiful. It makes a big difference when you get all done with it. I don't want to build any other way.

Their third spec house was even more ambitious. Success built confidence and enthusiasm for further projects. Although it got to be more work, they never lost the sense of fun and collaborative creativity that made the first house so rewarding. And though they did have an employee helping them on the bigger houses, they resisted the temptation to expand the business and

hire a whole crew. They loved working together and didn't want the pressure of having to attend to the needs and schedules of other people.

Sandy

Kristina and I had a real good relationship in which we didn't have to talk very much. We'd just start out with a little something on a piece of paper. We never had any real official blueprints or anything like that. They usually were on a very small piece of graph paper, or a paper napkin. It was not a logical process. Anything that was made that wasn't precisely right according to the plan that we had—well, the plan was flexible. If we thought another opening was necessary, or we wanted to change a wall or something, we would just do it. Do whatever we wanted to do. And each time that came up, each time the question arose, we seemed to agree on it.

> *"We'd just start out with a little something on a piece of paper. They usually were on a very small piece of graph paper, or a paper napkin."*

Kristina

It was great being able to plan these houses as we went along. It's like weaving. If you try to transfer an idea onto a piece of paper, paper is a different material. So if

you plan it on paper, it's not going to be the way you are visualizing it. And if you follow your plan, you can't respond to the material as you encounter it. I'm really glad we had the flexibility to make changes as we went along. For example, there were some carved posts that were going to be inside the house. We needed some posts there, and I made these elaborate carvings. But then they didn't look good in that spot after all. But here we had the posts already made (and it was an awful lot of work, believe me). So we found a place outside by the garden gate and put them there. It worked out just fine.

"And if you follow your plan, you can't respond to the material as you encounter it."

Kristina

We had some clear ideas to start with about what we wanted it to be. We both feel very strongly about the traditions around here. In the Southwest, you know, you build a house, it's seen for miles around. It's not like building in the trees back East. The old houses around here are very soft—they look as if they grew up out of the land.

Sandy and Kristina got ideas for many design elements from old crosses in the cemeteries around Taos. In keeping with tradition, they used iron fixtures, brick floors, and Mexican tiles. Even Kristina's window treatments were inspired by Southwest jewelry she had seen. Although Kristina wanted to keep the houses very traditional in feel, she also wanted to introduce some subtle departures from that tradition. For example, she wanted a great deal of light, which the old Spanish and Indian houses didn't have. The constant attention to traditional as well as practical detail is what set these houses apart from others. Kristina and Sandy had a financial budget, but they clearly had a psychological balance sheet, as well—if a design wouldn't be aesthet-

The third house had a sunken garden on the south side based on a garden Kristina's mother had made from an old cellar hole back in New Hampshire. Though it appears to be a one-story house from the road, it actually has two stories in back; the lower level opens out onto a walled patio with flower beds around it. It is very private, yet the beautiful surrounding landscape is visible. By creating a sunken garden, they could nestle a two-story house into the landscape and make it look smaller, "and the house doesn't stick up like a sore thumb."

ically rewarding they didn't consider it worthwhile.

Building a house places the builder in a very intimate relationship with her materials. It is like a contact sport. Every single piece is handled repeatedly as it is collected, stored, sorted, measured, marked, cut, and fitted into place. The weather, your moods, the good days and the bad days, the mistakes, the "perfect" fits are all associated with the materials being handled at the time. In stud-frame construction, this intimacy is usually not visible in the final product, especially to a stranger. In a post-and-beam structure, you can sometimes see evidence of the craftsperson at work in the chiseled joints of the framing members. But adobe building is more like pottery. The imprint of the work of the body is literally on the walls of the house.

For an adobe-like effect without using the traditional process, cinder block can be plastered over to look like adobe. But then wire lath must be put on the surface before mud is applied. If you want any kind of shape or curve in the wall, you have to plan it in advance. With adobe, the shape is a reflection of the movement of your hands. You can feel the difference—not just through the curves and irregular shapes, but also through the material itself. Even the acoustics are different in an adobe house; the mud walls absorb sounds and muffle sharp noises.

Following completion of the third spec house, Sandy went on to build two houses on her own property. The design of Sandy's second house featured spectacular views of the Taos Mountains to the north and a wide vista of sagebrush and the distant, pale blue Jemez Mountains to the west. South-facing solar windows and eastern morning sunlight were incorporated in each room. The long, rambling hacienda-style building is open and cozy at the same time. Traditional round vigas and aspen *latilla*s in a herringbone pattern form one of the ceilings. Another ceiling has split cedar between the vigas.

The walls are soft-plastered with a light tan earth called *tierra bayita*. Little flecks of straw used in the

mud mix show on the surface and shine a soft wheat color when the light catches them. The floors are brick, laid in a herringbone pattern in one room and a basket-weave pattern in another room. A large, south-facing sunroom has a Mexican tile floor. The kitchen and baths have hand-painted talavera tile on the walls surrounding the tub and sinks. All doors are handmade, traditional *peñasco*-style doors (as are the kitchen cabinets) detailed with Southwest-style flat spindles.

Sandy built all the doors and cabinets and constructed all the other aspects of the house, from digging the trench and pouring cement for the foundation to laying the adobe walls, plastering, and building the ceilings, roofing, and flooring. Each room contains a traditional adobe fireplace.

Neither Sandy nor Kristina is inclined to make a career out of building houses. They've enjoyed what they've accomplished but have had enough. Spontaneity and creativity were the driving force in their work. To turn this into a career, to become full-time contractors or developers, would not be the same experience.

Sandy sees herself primarily as a writer and has turned to documenting the aesthetic values she sees in the traditional architecture of the Southwest. Kristina will probably never be truly finished with her own house; there is always one more thing to add or change. Her primary focus, however, is her weaving, and other activities unrelated to building.

While Sandy and Kristina were working together, their friend Valerie Graves was looking for a new place to live. Valerie's marriage had recently ended, and she was considering buying a mobile home. Sandy and Kristina convinced Valerie that she would be happier in a house she built for herself. They promised to show her what to do and to plan work parties to help her get it done.

This was not Valerie's first experience with building. She and her husband built a log cabin together, a project that turned out to be extremely difficult. They had gone up the mountain and brought down every log themselves. By the time the cabin was done, Valerie was physically and emotionally exhausted.

"They said, 'You can do it. We'll tell you how to do it.' So they did. It was great. I had these big work parties. And lots of women would come to help."

Valerie

I'd never built anything except that log cabin. But they were encouraging me not to get a mobile home. They said, "You can do it. We'll tell you how to do it." So they did. It was great. I had these big work parties. And lots of women would come to help. And everybody sort of picked out a spot to work. Each one would be working on a different corner. And it was funny. I'd go around to each corner and tell everybody it was the best corner. That's what they all wanted to hear, because they were all competing. In their corners. These gals are real competitive, I think. And they all wanted to hear that theirs was the best corner and they were doing a fabulous job. But they were all super supportive. They came even when it was snowing. It was amazing. It went up really fast. And it's turned out to be very comfortable. I like it. I still like it. I've always liked it.

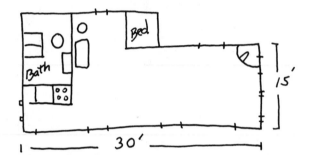

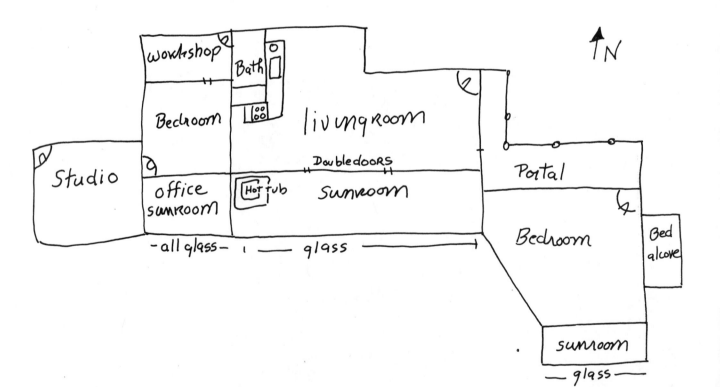

Valerie started small, with just three rooms in a total of 750 square feet of living space. Over the years, however, she has added on one room at a time until it had ten rooms, including two sunrooms, a painting studio, a workshop, and an office. There are seven skylights, including one in the middle of the studio, affording it a great deal of usable wall space and plenty of light.

In contrast to the solid, earthy adobe walls of the central rooms, glass-fronted sunrooms adorn the south side in three places. These sunrooms are made of large panes of glass framed in wood. Vigas in the ceiling are made of branches cut from the mountains near the house that had been in a forest fire, so the wood is hardened and cured. The outside is a combination of cement, plaster, and stucco.

Valerie

It's been really comfortable. I like the feeling of it. I have a great studio now for my painting. I had a really bad place to work before, so I really appreciate this one. Most of all, I like the fact that it's an adobe house. Just the feel of the rooms. It's got to do with the material itself. The mud and the straw. The look of a hand-shaped surface. It's just wonderful. I love it.

> *"It's got to do with the material itself. The mud and the straw. The look of a hand-shaped surface."*

In the house are five small fireplaces which provide decoration and heat. Two small propane heaters are used for backup. There is a hot tub in one of the sunrooms and there are solar collectors on the roof. Sandy made her traditional Spanish-style wooden cupboards to adorn several of the rooms.

Samantha Morse

Samantha Morse grew up in a small town in central Pennsylvania. She was something of a tomboy as a kid, but she didn't plan a career in construction. She majored in art in college and wanted to be a painter, but found it isn't easy to make a living as an artist. She started house painting, began to do minor repairs as well, and eventually entered the trades. She has been a carpenter, painter, mason, and general contractor and ran her own business for ten years. She then worked for a neighborhood redevelopment agency, overseeing the rehabilitation of deteriorated houses in Philadelphia. Decisions about the design and selection of houses slated for renovation were her responsibility. She is dedicated to making home ownership available to the working poor and to revitalizing urban communities. "Sam" now works for Philadelphia Neighborhood Housing Services, where she administers programs to provide housing rehabilitation assistance to low- and moderate-income people.

Philadelphia Row Houses

When she was initially interviewed, Samantha Morse was the project manager for New Kensington Community Development Corporation, a private, non-profit agency that promotes renovations of low-income neighborhood houses in Philadelphia. With substantial funding by the city, the agency buys, rehabilitates, and resells single-family houses in the Kensington neighborhood. It also provides assistance to families who are trying to purchase a house or who need to weatherize or improve an existing house. Sam often was a liaison with homeowners who encounter problems. She also participated in the acquisition of houses targeted for rehab, supervised the renovation work, and provided technical assistance to other community development organizations.

Sam's parents taught her to be independent—to think for herself and to ask questions. She relished this independence to an extreme, however, and resisted her parents' efforts to teach her proper girl behavior. She enjoyed spending time with her aunt, who wrote books

for her in which girls were active. When she was nine or ten years old, she was fascinated watching a construction project in a field near her house.

When Sam entered junior high, she wanted to take shop, but girls weren't allowed in shop class. Later, when she was a senior in high school, she wanted to take drafting, but she met the same obstacle. She persisted and was finally allowed to take drafting, where she learned how to read blueprints. It was the only formal training in construction she would receive.

Sam didn't plan a career in the trades. As far as she knew, carpentry wasn't an occupation open to women. But after she got out of art school she found she wasn't making much money. She began working as a house-painter and immediately found that her customers often asked her to do small repairs for them as well. Gradually the jobs got bigger and bigger, until Sam finally gained the confidence to take a job as a laborer on a construction crew.

Whatever jobs the crew asked her to do, she did. She didn't resent the menial and housekeeping tasks like sweeping up and getting coffee. She realized that the person at the bottom of the totem pole does the grunt tasks. Even if they were asking her to do things because of her gender, she took it in stride. She worked hard and tried to learn as much as she could about carpentry and construction. She also found that she was very naive; she really didn't know the most basic tools and practices.

I remember seeing this guy's combination square. I had been cutting and measuring for him, but how I did it was I took the tape measure and went to the end of the board twice. I'd take a measurement from each edge to make sure my cutting line was parallel with the end of the board (and therefore square). Anyway, one day I was cutting and measuring for this guy, and he had this combination square. I went, "Wow—look at that. What is that?" And he said it was a combination square. I said, "Where do you get them? That's cool!" He was real low-key, a really nice guy. He said, "They got them in the hardware store." I was impressed.

I didn't know how to read a ruler, either. They'd say, "How long is it?" I'd say, "Uh, three lines past the half." The guys used to give me a hard time about it. This one guy was particularly scornful. He would say, "Get her out of here!" And when the guy said that, I thought, "It ain't going to be 'Get her out of here.' If anybody leaves, it's going to be him."

"If I didn't tie it off right, the scaffold would give and I would fall off the scaffold, forty feet onto a brick courtyard. To have your own life in your hands like that. It was incredible."

Sam knew she had a lot to learn and was determined to teach herself what she needed to keep her job. And she was right—she stuck it out, but her detractor quit in frustration.

Sam's next construction job was for a bricklayer. Her on-the-job training included learning how to work on a scaffold. Sometimes, to get to the stationary scaffolding she would have to walk across planks that hung out of windows fifty feet in the air. And Sam would say to herself, "Jesus Christ. Why didn't I listen to my mother and marry a heart surgeon?"

Sometimes Sam would say to the guys on the crew, "I'm afraid. I'm afraid to walk out on this plank." They were very understanding and would say to her, "Don't do it if you're going to panic. Just sit until you're cool with it. Take your time. But do it." Once she braved the planks, she still had to deal with the perils of the scaffold itself. Having mastered stationery scaffolding, Sam then had to learn how to work off swing scaffolding, which is suspended by ropes.

I'm up there on the swing scaffold for the first time in my life. The boss comes out, and he says, "Look. This is how you tie the rope to secure it. If the knot's not right, the scaffold's going to give." And that's all he said. He sets me to work and says, "Call me when you're ready to move to a new position." He gets off the scaffold, and I think, "When I call him, he's going to stop what he's doing, and he's going to come back up onto the scaffold, and he's going to watch me do it, and he's going to hold my hand, and everything's going to be fine." So, when I'm ready to move, I go, "Charlie. I'm ready." He goes, "All right." And I'm waiting. And he's standing on the ground. He says, "Hurry up!"

So what I did was I pulled the rope up, which loosened the knot so I could raise the scaffold. I had my life in my right hand, literally. If I didn't tie it off right, the scaffold would give and I would fall off the scaffold, forty feet onto a brick courtyard, and probably be pretty hurt, if I wasn't dead. And he says, "Hurry up. What are you standing there for? Let's go." So I tied it off. And I let go of the rope. And it held. It was the most fabulous feeling! To save your own life. To have your own life in your hands like that. It was incredible. I felt like a trillion dollars when I went home that day.

Although Sam eventually started her own business as a general contractor, after twelve years of being the boss she welcomed the opportunity to work for someone else.

In her role as project manager at New Kensington Community Development Corporation, Sam worked on creating decent, low-income housing in urban neighborhoods. Her projects were primarily single-family houses or duplexes, most of them classic Philadelphia row houses. As the client's contact and the person who scouted out potential houses for rehabilitation, Sam thought about how people use their houses, how they relate to their neighbors, and how a sense of community is created and maintained.

She drew on her background as a self-employed carpenter and general contractor when supervising construction work or evaluating the development of plans for each new project. Although she did not grow up in the Kensington neighborhood, Sam understood that residents must have some control over their lives to create a successful community. Poverty, crime, and other effects of urban blight devastate even those communities in which the residents have lived for generations. New Kensington Community Development Corporation is not an outside do-good organization

that tries to impose its solutions on its clients. While there are bankers and businessmen on the board, there is local representation as well.

It's people from the neighborhood who make up the board of directors. And they're the people who decide what happens in the neighborhood, what's appropriate. They've grown up there. It's a ghetto. They live there.

They die there. If they want something I think is totally inappropriate—if that's what they want, then I know they're right, and I'm not. I just know that.

The houses Sam worked on were generally property that had been confiscated for unpaid taxes, abandoned homes, or occasionally, houses that have been donated to New Kensington directly. Sam's first action

"If that's what they want, then I know they're right, and I'm not."

after acquiring a house was to assess how much work must be done to bring it up to code. Inspecting buildings on the verge of collapse was not fun.

Sometimes they're really falling apart. It's scary to go inside sometimes. I've had floors collapse right out from under me. I've had some close calls, I really have. It's part of the business, I guess.

Sam always inspected these sites herself, because the architects who draw up the plans for renovation don't always know how to look at a building to see how much has to be rebuilt and how much can be saved. Sam's years as a contractor gave her an edge here. She knows that however sound a building may appear at first look, months later, when it is time to begin construction, much more deterioration may have taken place. Underestimating the cost of a job is a danger Sam is well aware of.

Most of the houses in New Kensington are brick row houses, with exterior walls only in the front and back. When houses are condemned and torn down, there is a side wall facing an empty lot which becomes an exterior wall. Generally, these houses aren't abandoned until they have deteriorated to the point of becoming unlivable. Sometimes all that is left to work with is the four walls; sometimes not even that. Often the party wall (the common wall shared by neighboring houses) has to be repaired—which must be done without disturbing the occupants of the house next door.

Making repairs to shared property, such as party walls, can turn into trouble quickly. More than once neighbors have claimed they were having problems that began only when the excavation started next door, allegations that are difficult to prove or disprove. Situations like this pose a dilemma for New Kensington. Sam had to determine when repairs to shared property warranted the risk, and when to leave things the way they were.

Financial considerations often dominate the design process. Whatever Sam wanted to do with a house had to meet a very tight budget. If she could improve the layout and make the house more pleasant at the same time, that was okay, but the more structural damage she ran into, the less money she had left over to put into the amenities she would have liked to provide.

Sam has developed what she considers to be a good prototype for urban renewal projects. She has done enough of these rehabs to have a good feel for what is possible within the constraints of the budget and the type of structures typical of the neighborhood. Unfortunately, most of the buildings New Kensington acquires are in such bad repair that she didn't even have to look to know she couldn't save any of the major mechanical systems.

Of course, the copper's all gone. You just assume everything else is bad. You rip it all out. Lots of times the

wood is rotted, too. We have to put in new joists and beams. We sometimes rearrange the interior partition walls. Sometimes there's a one-story addition off the back that is too far gone to save. We rip the whole thing down. But we try to stay within the basic style that was original to the house. Usually there's a bay at the back, if it's a two-story row house. Or you stack it. If there's a one-story addition, you might go up another floor level to get more space.

Sam was also involved in the layout of the interior rooms in these homes. Sometimes the architect drafted a plan for Sam's approval; sometimes she got into the act early and came up with the design herself. Either way, she fought to get more square feet of living space into these very narrow row houses. The basic pattern is one room wide and three rooms deep. Sometimes she could get a little extra space by putting a bay window on the second floor, cantilevered out over the street or over the backyard. Bay windows are Sam's specialty. They are traditional, so they provide a sense of continuity, and they allowed her to increase the bedroom size without enlarging the house. Sometimes she had to remove the old bays if they were rotted out, but she tried to replace them with new ones, even though it was expensive. Many of those old houses had tiny bedrooms, which make them difficult to sell, so every inch she could add to a bedroom helped.

Sam often has to rebuild bearing walls. Sometimes, in fact, she had to tear down so much of what was there, she ended up with little but the party walls. The advantage, however, of a house that is being totally gutted is that it gave Sam a chance to move stairways, change rooms around, and extend or eliminate additions. By the time she left that job, Sam had her architects pretty well trained. They know where to put the kitchens and how to lay out the bathrooms in a sensible way.

This one guy, George, used to put the laundry sink in between the washer and the dryer. I said, "George, please. I can tell you don't do laundry. I mean, what do you do? You take the clothes out of the washer. Then you put them on top of the dryer, and shove them in the dryer, right? And then you want to use the top of the dryer to fold. You don't put the sink in the middle. Trust me, George."

Sam was always constrained by the amount of cabinet space she could have in the kitchen. The city would pay for eight linear feet of base cabinet and seven linear feet of wall units. No islands or forty-five degree turns. Sometimes she could talk them into paying for a U-shaped kitchen, but not without a fight.

"They said, 'We're building these houses for working people. Keep those uptown ideas to yourself, Sam.'"

I wanted to put in a skylight in this house, but they said, "We're building these houses for working people. Keep those uptown ideas to yourself, Sam." I wanted to put sliding doors in the dining room. But that's too fancy. The city won't pay for it. We can only put two windows there. It's stupid. I thought sliding-glass doors would be great. It's a difference of about $300, installed. I can't do it. The city's not going to pay for that. So, okay. Our budgets are that close that I can't always find $300 someplace else and make a trade for it.

Sam also realized that even though the backyards of the houses are tiny, these little bits of private open space in the city are vital. Most of the owners have small children, and the backyards are the only relatively safe places for the children to play. Therefore Sam insisted on placing the kitchen sink under a window facing the backyard. Although it would have been more economical to put the sink on an interior wall, back-to-back with bathroom plumbing, Sam believes a parent working in the kitchen must be able to keep an eye on the yard and the alley in back of the house.

Unfortunately, not much landscaping goes into these projects, but when Sam could influence the setting, she did that, too. When there was an empty lot next door, she decided which trees would be cut down and which would stay. Sometimes she could wedge a little extra from tree cutting that she would put to use somewhere else. When the job was being bid initially, the contractor saw twenty trees on the property and gave a bid based on the assumption they would all come down. Later, when money was getting tight, Sam might have said, "Well, the trees that are growing out of the foundation, get rid of them. But leave the ones in the middle of the yard." Not only did that free up some money, it saved some trees to soften the bleakness of an otherwise empty lot.

Sam is deeply committed to her work. She believes every person is entitled to a decent place to live. She also believes that the currently existing housing stock should be rehabilitated (and a lot of it is in need of repair) before we use up precious resources to build new structures. Although much of her work was piecemeal and depended on houses being made available to the city or to New Kensington directly, Sam was thoughtful about selecting the houses her agency acquired. Rehabilitating a house in the middle of a block undergoing change could have a big impact on the houses around it. When she can acquire several houses on the same block, it can make the difference between further abandonment and revitalization.

There is one block in particular that Sam called her "dream block." Most of the residents have been there for a long time, so there is a sense of community, fragile as it is. New Kensington has already rehabilitated a couple of houses on the block, and several other houses are in good enough shape to be viable candidates for rehab. Sam was convinced that an investment in this block would really pay off. She wanted to fill in the empty, rubble-strewn lots where houses had been torn down. She wanted to rehab the buildings that had been abandoned.

Sam thought she and her agency might be able to build a two- or three-bedroom house that would sell for $40,000 dollars. The land is free (donated by the city), and the houses would probably have to be wood-frame construction. The neighborhood is mostly brick or brownstone, materials that are currently too expensive. But the fronts could have a brick veneer, or the whole house could be stucco-sided.

Philadelphia is a brick and stucco town. The Italian and Irish immigrants that came over—that was their trade. It built the city. It's real common around here. I want it to look like the other houses on the block. I don't want to put a bunch of ranch houses in the middle of that neighborhood. So a brick veneer on the front will make the houses compatible with the rest of the block without costing too much.

Sam has been inspired by the work of Avi Friedman of Montreal, who has developed a prototype for affordable urban housing called the "grow home." It derives from the Levittown model, in which the second floor is left unfinished for the owners to complete themselves as they can afford to. Major systems are all complete, including subfloor, wiring, insulation, drywall, windows, exterior doors, and primed walls. But leaving out second-floor partitions, closets, floor cover-

ings, interior doors, trim, and the final coat of paint saves a big chunk of the construction cost.

Lack of closets is a serious sacrifice, but owners can purchase cheap wall units or freestanding cupboards at a discount store as a temporary solution. Eventually, at their own pace, they can finish the house to suit their specific needs.

Housing stock used to be built for the nuclear family—Mom, Dad, and the kids. Well, that doesn't apply anymore. You got single people, you got gay people, you got single-parent families, you got elderly people, you have roommates. God knows what you have. But it's not just Mom, Dad, and the kids. And that's the way builders build houses, which are no longer appropriate for the needs that you have. So this concept, aside from making it affordable, is also: leave it so the person who buys it can decide how to use that space.

Sam also hoped to develop a large property on the corner, which is actually several empty lots. She was working with other organizations to try and promote the construction of a youth center or community building on part of the corner lot, leaving the rest for a park.

A park is something New Kensington has never done before. To develop the park, Sam wanted to initiate a joint venture with another community development corporation. She believes there is strength in unity. She targeted a horticultural society that receives

"So this concept, aside from making it affordable, is also: leave it so the person who buys it can decide how to use that space."

federal money for their projects. She thought if someone could come up with a plan, they might be persuaded to invest in the project. Although Sam left New Kensington Development Corporation before her "dream block" was developed, she holds out hope that this idea will survive and someday come to fruition.

Sam feels the park is likely to be developed before anything else gets off the drawing board. Nobody else wants that property; it is extremely expensive to build in the city. The owners aren't going to reclaim it. In fact, the difficulty is tracking down all the owners and getting them to agree to sell or donate the land. Some of the owners may be dead or have moved away and left no forwarding addresses.

A large commercial building on the corner opposite the park would make a good multifamily residence. The police or the YMCA might become interested in helping create a youth center on the park property. The

Police Athletic Association has been very helpful in promoting recreational opportunities for teenagers in the past.

Sam knows there is support for this idea from the people from the neighborhood who are on the New Kensington board of directors. The neighborhood badly needs a place for kids to play—kids who are currently hanging out on the street, constantly being exposed to drugs, crime, and violence. The neighborhood people want to see something for the kids.

Sam's job wasn't easy. Dealing with city and agency bureaucracy was very difficult. She had to convince each new contractor of her competence, and convince each new architect that her ideas would work for the people who were going to live there. Getting around the neighborhood safely, inspecting buildings without getting hurt, and maintaining patience for all the red tape involved with publicly-funded projects was stressful. Labor politics, city politics, and office politics represented a burden for a woman whose first love is being out in the field improving buildings and neighborhoods.

Sam visited the neighborhood frequently, inspecting buildings and dealing with problems on the construction sites. She also surveyed potential acquisitions and tracked down the owners of houses that looked like good prospects. And she dealt personally with the residents of the neighborhood. These parts of the job were all rewarding to her.

One of these properties had a squatter in it. The lady who lived next door called me up to complain about it. When I get a call like that I have to go out and deal with it. When I get there, they say, "What are you going to do with these houses? Who are you going to put in these houses?" This is a predominantly white neighborhood.

They're very paranoid about blacks. They don't want the neighborhood to change. There's a lot of racism. I've had to control myself. I say, "We do have a priority for people from the neighborhood in these houses. But we will sell to the person who fits our criteria, and you are welcome to apply. Period."

Problems with racism are a large part of the neighborhood's overall problem. When New Kensington sold a house to a Puerto Rican man who was married to a Vietnamese woman, neighbors made a very real threat to firebomb the house. New Kensington called out the city's human relations department and arranged for a community meeting. The people moved into the house without any further incident. Amazingly, less than a year later, one of the neighbors who had been very vocal about living next door to "those kind of people" came into Sam's office. "I'm just here about my neighbor. He had a problem with his plumbing. He doesn't speak English too well, and he's hard to understand. I'm just here to see if you

can do anything about it." Although that was an unusual incident, Sam would like to think that she and her firm were able, on occasions such as these, to intervene to help lessen the problems of racial tension at least a little bit.

Sam's biggest frustration is that there are so few women working in the field.

I've seen plenty of men take younger men under their wing and help them out. But nobody helped me out. When I had my own business, I had women and men working for me. It was nice. But I hardly ever see women on these jobs. I miss seeing women. And so, when I give men a hard time for something, I don't lose a lot of sleep over it. I go, "Why should I give him a break? He hasn't even given her a break to let her in the damn door." I see men in the field as standing in the way of the women in the field. It gives me a certain righteous anger, if you will, and it allows me to never back down when I think I'm right.

Unfortunately, there was disturbing inequality in the treatment of the staff at the agency where Sam worked. The person who had been there the longest was a black woman, and she was paid the lowest salary. Their receptionist got a 25¢-per-hour raise after three years when the white males were receiving $3,000 to $5,000 raises.

The staff eventually went on strike, joined the Teamster's Union, and demanded seniority and a grievance procedure. The strike lasted eighteen weeks. When Sam went back to work after the strike, the atmosphere

"I see men in the field as standing in the way of the women in the field."

was less than friendly. She was laid off about nine months later.

For a while, she returned to contracting, doing repairs and remodeling. It felt good to again do the physical work of construction. Still, Sam missed the planning and the sense that she was in a position to make changes in her community. So in May 1994, Sam joined Philadelphia Neighborhood Housing Services Network. The agency administers a loan program to help low- and moderate-income people secure mortgages. They also buy and rehab housing stock, which they resell to eligible families, and provide rehab services to homeowners.

As manager of the rehabilitation, Sam now oversees a staff of four, running four programs in eight neighborhoods scattered around Philadelphia. She does site inspections, develops bid packages, does some design work, and provides technical assistance to neighborhood community development corporations.

Sam's "dream block" never did get developed. New Kensington has cut back its development activity and has less funding to work with. However, Sam continues to promote her progressive ideas in other neighborhoods, and she loves her new job.

Lynda Simmons

Lynda Simmons grew up with total confidence in herself and in women's capabilities. She lived in New York City as a child and returned there as an adult immediately after graduating from college. Always attracted to the arts, Lynda studied architecture at night while working for a publishing company, receiving her degree in 1963. Lynda then worked for several different architectural firms before joining Phipps Houses, Inc., a large nonprofit housing agency where she later served as president from 1982 until she retired in 1993. Phipps Houses builds, maintains, and provides human services for subsidized housing in Manhattan, the Bronx, and Queens. Early in her career, Lynda recognized the importance of community in housing designed for large numbers of people. Lynda has been an innovator of program strategies designed to humanize the huge, high-rise apartment complexes being built for middle- and low-income people in the city.

Urban Renewal in the Big Apple

Although she was born in Miami, Florida, Lynda Simmons spent her early years in New York City. The family moved to Georgia when she was a teenager, and she attended college in North Carolina. Her earliest ambition was to be an artist, but in her freshman year she decided to become a history professor. By the time she graduated, however, she had changed her mind again and despite being awarded a graduate school scholarship, took a year off.

I wanted to go to New York and see what the big, wide world was about and learn something about the arts. So I came to New York in 1955. I was twenty years old. Of course I found that my Phi Beta Kappa key and summa cum laude, plus a subway token, would only get me on the subway. Nobody was interested in hiring young women at that time.

In the '50s, however, New York was an exciting place to live—it was much safer then for women to walk around alone—and Lynda delighted in exploring it. She got her first job as a clerk-typist at Intercultural Publications, which had been set up after World War II by the Ford Foundation to publish the art and literature from various foreign countries. The company published a supplement to *Atlantic Monthly* four times a year, edited by James Laughlin, who then founded New Directions Publishing House and became influential in the publishing industry.

I was typing letters every day to Ezra Pound, and T.S. Eliot, and William Carlos Williams, and Kenneth Rexroth, and all the great figures of American literature. So when the grant ran out for Intercultural, I moved over and worked for Laughlin at New Directions. I spent four years working for Laughlin. I got very much into writing poetry then, and I thought of myself as a poet. But it was clear to me that I was not the starving artist sort, that I really needed to have something to rely on to make a living. And I thought of architecture. It was a good combination of art and practicality.

Lynda enrolled in the demanding night school program at Cooper Union in 1958 and completed it in five years. Although her aunt offered to loan her money to attend daytime classes, Lynda was very independent and didn't want to be indebted to anyone. Now she regrets having passed up the opportunity. The night course, although it was long and challenging, was not a

degree course, so Lynda had to take the exam for her architect's license based on only her experience.

Lynda attributes some of her independence and self-confidence to her mother's example. Lynda's mother had obtained a scholarship to acting school, only to have the school go out of business before she started, so she had attended teachers college instead. However, she continued to pursue her interest in acting, by giving readings and by putting on one-woman shows at women's clubs, churches, and schools.

So all through my childhood I saw my mother doing this, taking the initiative, being the strong one. She really ran the family. She kept the family together and did all these outside activities. When I got out into the world and found out that people considered women inferior, it was a terrific shock to me. I never had allowed it to enter my mind. I think that when I was a child I didn't really differentiate between men and women. I don't know how that happened. That has a lot of ramifications. I was fearless where I should have had a lot of fear. A lot of women

"*A lot of women have to overcome a lack of self-confidence, but I never did.*"

have to overcome a lack of self-confidence, but I never did. I think that is genetic. I think it's the personality I was born with.

For the first four years after she received her architect's license Lynda worked in a small architectural office, which mostly did residential work, where she did everything from answering the telephone to bookkeeping. She had deliberately sought a small firm, with the idea of getting a better overview of the field. She also learned a lot about the reality of being a female in a male-dominated field.

I remember one particular job I went to supervise. It was a brownstone down in Chelsea. I think I was twenty-four, and I looked about fourteen. And I went, and here was this contractor who was old enough to be my grandfather, practically, who was running the job. And I delivered what I was supposed to deliver, and the instructions, and talked to him. And then I turned around to leave and was walking away, and he'd forgotten something. So he yelled out, "Hey, girlie!" [Sigh.] That's the way it was.

I did the City Building Department work for the firm, because there's an advantage in having a young woman doing that. And I was smart, you know, I knew how to answer the questions and all that. And at the end of this job, getting the permit, the inspector patted my knee and he said, "You know, sweetie, your boss, he never gives me nothing. But I'm gonna give you this approval, 'cause you remind me of my daughter."

Lynda's strategy paid off. After four years she had a well-rounded education in architecture, then was hired by a much larger firm to run the production of a twenty-six-story building, Columbus Park Towers, a middle-income housing project built under the Mitchell-Lama program, which made subsidies available to bring down housing interest rates. The basic design had already been set. Lynda was responsible for coordinating the project. She worked under an older, very experienced architect, but she had a great deal of

autonomy and was actually able to influence the design in several ways she wouldn't have expected.

Her ideas about design didn't only help to create comfortable and pleasant surroundings but also had an impact on the tenants' very survival.

This was a much bigger job than anything I had done before. I took a vacation and went up to Maine. While I was in Maine, I thought about what it would be like. One day I was lying in a blueberry field, looking at the sky and the green trees . . . the blue sky and the white clouds. And thinking that this building that I was going to be designing contained over two hundred apartments. That was bigger than a lot of small towns in America. I decided that I needed to think about that. That this was a whole community, and that it should be looked at as a community. And that really was the genesis of the rest of my career.

I thought a lot about what it means to create homes for 250 families. That's a lot of people. I started thinking about people using the building. We're creating homes. Here are all these people living together, conjoined physically. So it wasn't just a matter of making the apartments good. It was also a matter of trying to create a sense of community within this huge structure. And I was convinced that every part of the building could be made to be supportive of the people who lived in it. Every part of the design could be looked at in terms of how it could enhance people's lives.

Lynda tried to imagine what design elements would make it easier for those families to function as families and as members of a community. How could people be provided with privacy and security, yet have opportunities to interact constructively?

The basic plan had already been determined, so she was only able to alter bits and pieces of the existing design. For example, she changed half of the units from having a separate kitchen and living room to a combination kitchen/living room/dining room to make the space seem much bigger. She knew some people would prefer the open plan. But Lynda also knew that some people, especially people with small children, would want to have a kitchen separate from the rest of the house so it could be closed off at times. Her changes offered the tenants a choice.

Lynda didn't go out of her way to promote her ideology to her employers as an explicit political agenda or a topic of debate. She just looked at the job and suggested changes that supported her philosophy. And over the next few years she was able to introduce, with her employers' support and participation, a variety of design concepts that began to have an impact on how public housing is viewed.

In 1965, Lynda went to work for Davis, Brody & Associates, where she was immediately given responsibility for the Riverbend Apartments in Harlem, another Mitchell-Lama project. The Mitchell-Lama program was very successful; thousands of housing units were built under it. But the general attitude on the part of city and state officials was pretty unimaginative in terms of design. The image of public housing was that it should be unadorned and boxy. It had to look cheap whether it was or not; as if people were supposed to feel bad about being poor. (The original public housing of the thirties didn't include toilet seats on the toilets or doors on the closets.)

But Davis, Brody & Associates took a different attitude. Their goal was to design a fine building. They began to design public housing that was much more interesting and comfortable than any previous attempts had been. They were successful, because they were

smart enough to figure out how to work with the city.

After completing the Riverbend project, Lynda worked on East Midtown Plaza between Twenty-third and Twenty-fifth Street along Second Avenue in Manhattan, where she was fully able to apply her philosophies on community development.

East Midtown Plaza is my pride and joy as an architect. One of the things we did was cut off the corners of the buildings. We put the living rooms in the corners, so that when you looked out you didn't look sixty feet across the street into somebody else's window. You looked into an intersection, and you had much longer, diagonal views.

Cutting the corners off and varying the heights improved the appearance of the buildings by breaking up their monotonous, boxy shape. Lynda also gave the balconies solid brick fronts instead of railings—a very small detail, but important because many people are afraid to be out on a high balcony with just a railing. At street level Lynda created a connection between the indoor and outdoor activities by placing a wonderful plaza next to one of the low-rise buildings which contained all the community space.

Lynda's innovations did not go unnoticed in the architectural world. She actually became famous for her laundry rooms. Most laundry rooms in city apartment buildings are in the basement because that is the only place that doesn't contain rentable apartment space. Every square foot of rentable space is crucial to support maintenance costs and pay off the mortgage.

But Lynda had experience raising small children and knew how much trouble it is to do laundry when you are tending children. The rate at which kids dirty clothes condemns their parents to many hours a week in the gloomy basements of their apartment buildings. Lynda designed laundry rooms with windows overlooking garden-playgrounds located on the roofs of ground-floor extensions. Parents could keep an eye on their kids and enjoy a visual connection to the outdoors while they did their laundry. Having the playgrounds above street level also meant the kids couldn't wander

"East Midtown Plaza is my pride and joy as an architect."

off. A place was created for people to relax a bit and chat with one another in a pleasant atmosphere—a far cry from the dingy basement laundry rooms that represented nothing but a chore to tenants.

One of the wire services picked up the story somehow, so those laundry rooms became famous nationally. Unbelievable. But we broke the mold. And so after that, the Mitchell-Lama housing program became known as a place where, if you could get the cost within certain limits, you could do a good design.

"I was able to add $2 million to the construction cost without raising the rents."

For these conceptual design innovations to work, the client has to decide that such amenities are worth the loss of valuable rental space. Since clients who fund public housing projects are interested in their tenants' welfare, it is sometimes possible to incorporate such amenities. But the bottom line is still money. Lynda had to find ways to keep her changes within budgets that, although enormous compared to single-family houses, are still restricted. In many instances she had to make a trade-off somewhere else in the project. She is extremely creative in coming up with ways to pay for her "extravagances" and in overcoming resistance to altering conventional design formulas.

Every time she suggested an innovation for East Midtown Plaza that cost a little more, the contractor would yell and say, "You can't do that. You're going to raise the rent if you do." At that time the Mitchell-Lama program had a limitation based not on the cost per square foot to build, but on rents.

Rent is determined by what it takes to cover the mortgage payments, along with the management and maintenance costs. The mortgage is determined by how much the building costs to build. An increase in the mortgage could, however, be offset by income from commercial and garage space as well as apartment rents.

In order to assess the meaning of various changes she might want to make in the design, Lynda had to learn how the financial statements worked. She had to understand both the capital statement and the operating statement—what it cost to build and then what it cost to operate—because the rent was a function of both costs. Once she learned that, she could take the cost of X and translate it into the cost of Y. She quickly figured out that if she had additional income other than the apartments (for example, from laundry machines or the garage or from commercial space), she could raise the capital cost without raising the rents.

So East Midtown Plaza started out with about 18,000 square feet of commercial space, and by the time we finished I had put in 40,000 square feet of commercial space. I was able to add $2 million to the construction cost without raising the rents. When the job was built they had a hard time renting at first, but now they are making money hand over fist. Twenty-third Street is a bonanza. There is a whole block front on Twenty-third Street, and they have kept their carrying charges very low because of the tremendous bonanza of having all that commercial space. And they have a beautiful building that we were able to build because of that additional $2 million.

Another coup for Lynda was getting the street closed. There was an entire block of apartments from Twenty-third to Twenty-fourth Street, and a midblock portion from Twenty-fourth to Twenty-fifth Street. Lynda realized it would greatly enhance the project if they could close the part of Twenty-fourth Street that separated the two blocks and develop a plaza. It took six months to get approval, but now there is a plaza that connects all of the buildings in the complex. Lynda and her group also included a large fountain and an outdoor amphitheater in the plaza. Kids can play outside their buildings without having to cross a street, and there's no traffic separating the members of the community.

I learned then where the big decisions are. They are not with the architect. They are with the developer. Of course, now that I've been a developer for twenty-one years, I see that there are other places, too. Everybody had a little piece of it. But that's where I got a vision of what a developer could do. Because, had I not worked on those financial statements, I would never have been able to afford all those good things that (as an architect) I wanted to do.

In November 1969, Lynda joined Phipps Houses, which had just been set up as an independent organization and was still very small, with only six people in the central office and about thirty in the field. (When Lynda left, they had more than sixty in the central office and over 420 out in the field.) When Lynda came aboard, Phipps Houses had just been designated as the sponsor for several major urban renewal areas in the city.

Lynda moved ahead quickly and became director of development in 1970. In 1975, Phipps Houses creat-ed Phipps Plaza West, located across the street from Bellevue Hospital. It has nine hundred apartments in eight salmon-colored buildings on Second Avenue just a block uptown from East Midtown Plaza. It is basically moderate-income housing, with about a 15 percent low-income component, and it is the project Lynda is proudest of as a developer. Because it was proposed at a time when there was more money available for housing, Lynda was able to put into practice many of her design philosophies.

At Phipps Plaza West, the design problem was how to make a huge building a place where people would love to live. She wanted to do something that would enhance the tenants' lives. She reasoned that since Phipps was also going to manage the building, it would be a beneficial consequence of her design if the tenants were happy and, therefore, had a vested interest in its maintenance. But how do you take a building with nine hundred apartments and make it something that gives people a sense of individuality, that makes them love the place and call it home?

First, Lynda broke down the scale of the building. Instead of the single, enormous human warehouse that had originally been planned, she broke it into eight towers of different heights with about five thousand square feet per floor each. The buildings are all ferroconcrete, constructed by pouring concrete one floor-level at a time. Ten thousand square feet represents an economical concrete pour; anything smaller wastes time (and therefore money) in the setup and staging in proportion to the amount you can pour at one sitting. But apartment buildings with ten thousand square feet per floor are intimidating and impersonal for the people who live in them. When stepping out from the elevator, the tenants only see a long narrow hallway, which doesn't encourage them to feel at home or to get to know their neighbors. At Phipps Plaza West, Lynda wanted to make the towers half that size, but the concrete pour would be uneconomical and it would require twice as many elevators.

To confront this problem, Lynda called in the contractors and made them part of the design team. The solution: rearrange the eight building modules so the crane could stand in the middle and pour three buildings at one time in each of two locations, and pour two at once in the third location, which was extremely economical. Once again, her idea saved about $2 million on the structure—which more than paid for the extra elevators.

An additional benefit of having only six apartments on each floor was that four of them could be corner apartments, with cross ventilation and views in two directions. She repeated the pattern from East Midtown Plaza of cutting the corners off the buildings. At street level, Lynda improved the appearance of the buildings by moving the underground garage wall five feet back from the street side. Because of zoning restrictions the above-ground part of the building is back from the sidewalk, anyway. By pulling the underground portion back as well, Lynda was able to have a double row of trees planted along the front of the building. The sidewalk runs between the trees, creating a small promenade. Of course, there was a cost. Smaller garages mean less income—a big sacrifice for five feet of dirt.

We're still making a lot of money off the garage lease. So it's turned out not to be too much of a problem. But I doubt if a commercial developer would have done it. I'm sure that if New York survives for another fifty years, they'll be doing a lot of things like that. They're going to have to; otherwise it isn't going to be a livable city.

Lynda was also able to work her magic in the public park behind the buildings; Phipps Houses played a role with the city in developing the park. Before the park was created, there was no play space whatsoever in that area. The park—filled with flowers, shrubs, and trees—is like an oasis in the city. The lushness (and the shade during the hot city summers) are physically and psychologically refreshing. The park and gardens provide a refuge from the noise and traffic and from the general intensity surrounding every living space.

A private backyard was also added for each of the three clusters of buildings, accessible only from the buildings they correlate to, with an attractive six-foot wrought iron fence around each one, creating a private, secure space for residents.

Another, more subtle touch that Lynda added was the treatment of the buildings' main entrance areas. The front doorways are surrounded by a paved area

"If New York survives for another fifty years, they'll be doing a lot of things like that. They're going to have to; otherwise it isn't going to be a livable city."

about three feet higher than the public sidewalk just beyond them, so the transition from outside to inside is gradual, and the general public is not hanging around literally right outside the doorstep. The barrier to street traffic and loitering at the doorways is psychological, rather than physical, but has been very effective.

A large complex of indoor public spaces at Phipps West includes a five thousand-square-foot-community center with a stage, a kitchen, and a lounge for the elderly; a five thousand-square-foot day-care center on

the second floor; and a privately run theater at the end of the commercial space on the ground floor.

Lynda employed a number of visual devices to make the interiors of the apartments seem larger and more pleasant. The window sills are two feet above the floor, substantially lower than standard practice. This increases the apparent height of the ceiling and allows a sitting view from the living room. The windows are taller and wider than usual for public housing, so the apartments have a great deal of light. (These buildings were built before the fuel crisis, so heat loss wasn't considered as important as it would be now.) Most of the apartments also have a balcony next to the dining room. The kitchens are open to the dining areas, allowing a view through the opposite sliding-glass doors.

That's something I became conscious of as a feminist—not building kitchens like black holes of Calcutta, which is the standard in New York City apartment buildings. The kitchen is often made into a kitchenette, which means that you can make it a totally interior room, with no windows and with mechanical ventilation. Now, my kitchens are in the center of the apartment, too. But they're closer to the outside, and there's always an opening from the kitchen and a big window opposite it.

In apartments where the kitchen is separated from the rest of the house—it's a terrible thing for social isolation—whoever is preparing the meal is cut off from the rest of the household. With the tiny space most of these give you (sometimes as little as sixty square feet), with no pass-through, no view into the living room, no light—it's a nightmare, especially for mothers with young children, because they're always around your feet. It's very bad. We solved that in Phipps West simply by opening up the kitchens to the dining area and the window beyond.

Lynda also considers features that provide the tenants more security. In Phipps West the buildings in each cluster were connected to each other at the corners, which resulted in some long and winding corridors. Lynda had the walls fitted with stainless steel panels that act as mirrors, allowing the tenants to see whether someone is lurking around the corner. The contractor who installed the steel initially refused to remove the protective paper coating, afraid that the panels would get scratched and ruined even before he was off the job. But Lynda was right. There are hundreds of feet of steel mirrors, and yet, at the time of this interview, sixteen years had gone by without a single scratch or any vandalism.

What's remarkable about this place is that it's sixteen years old and it looks brand new. We didn't have to repaint the hallways for nine years. In fact, we have painted the hallways exactly twice in sixteen years. It's unheard of. That's why I say I've proved all my theories that beau-

"When people feel good about where they live, they don't trash it."

ty is biologically important. When people feel good about where they live, they don't trash it.

Her views are based on the conviction that beauty performs a vital practical function. Beauty, in Lynda's mind, is the label that should be applied to things that provide sensory stimulation necessary and sufficient to the human organism. Deprivation of stimulation is as harmful as excessive stimulation. Both have been shown to interfere with children's growth and with healthy functioning once adulthood is reached.

Lynda believes art is necessary to human health, not just a luxury. She points out that a building's materials—its shape, colors, and site—all communicate meaning to the people who live in them. They trigger associations and present symbolic messages that affect the self-image of everyone who comes in contact with them. A building "tells" a person who enters it how that person is expected to use the building, what that person's status and place in the world is, and what that person's value to society is.

In fact, Lynda believes that it is impossible for

"It is impossible for buildings to not be symbolic; it is only possible for architects to be unaware of what their buildings are symbolizing."

buildings to not be symbolic, that it is only possible for architects to be unaware of what their buildings are symbolizing. When a building gives rise to associations degrading to the user's self-image, it does not enhance his or her life even though it may meet other physical needs. Public housing that tells its inhabitants they are worthless is not going to encourage them to strive for a better life.

Lynda became president of Phipps Houses in 1982, but even before that she was the main driving force in moving things along there. She created an organization comprised of several companies performing the various functions required to create a community. She made it Phipps's business to get the community built, make it work, and keep it going.

Lynda believes it is not enough to create a community. She is convinced that unless you put equal effort into keeping communities functioning, they will fail. The people who work in the community development arm of Phipps Houses have the function of building a social community inside the physical structures. They run the public spaces and help the tenants in various ways. In Phipps Plaza West there is a large elderly population, so there is a strong emphasis on programs for the elderly. But in Phipps Plaza South there is a large number of children, so the emphasis is on educational and recreational programs for children.

Recognizing that building management is every bit as important as design and construction, Phipps Houses also established a management company, Phipps Houses Services, Inc., which manages nearly 3,000 housing units accommodating approximately 9,000 people. It also manages buildings for other organizations (including Rockefeller University and New York Hospital), totaling more than 9,200 housing units.

I'm sure I wouldn't be involved in all of this if I weren't an architect and thinking architecturally. The architecture of communities is not just physical. It's also

"The architecture of communities is not just physical. It's also social."

social. And that's what's unusual about what we do. We have the whole package. There are a lot of people who do this kind of designing now, especially community-based organizations. But what is unusual about us is having the development and property management companies all together.

Phipps Houses has practically adopted the South Bronx in an effort to redevelop it. Such urban neighborhoods are often places where poverty, crime, drugs, and a harsh environment make living very difficult. While such conditions are endemic and difficult to change, the kind of housing that is developed in these areas can significantly affect people's ability to at least survive there.

They started with Lambert Houses, which was 731 apartments in six-story buildings spread over twelve acres. It serves very low-income tenants, in a neighborhood in which 30 percent of the buildings were abandoned in the 1970s and 1980s and in which drugs and violence are common. Although progressive in some ways, it was an incomplete prototype for the projects that followed. The buildings are large, and there were only three community development workers for the 731 units. However, they did go out of their way to avoid making the scale of the total project overwhelming. It was expensive not to build to maximum density, but Phipps held out for that. Also, most of the apartments have bay windows. The buildings were constructed as hollow rings in order to create small courtyards with grass and trees in the middle.

Unfortunately, that configuration turned out to have been a mistake. To make up for the extra cost of such an arrangement, continuous corridors were built that circled each floor. They could serve all the apartments on each level with a minimum of elevators that way. The result has been that the tenants tend to not get to know their neighbors. People passing in the hall could belong anywhere on the floor, or not belong in the building at all. The crime and vandalism rates are high. This was an early project in which the value of breaking down the project into small clusters of connected apartments had not yet been discovered.

Next came Mapes Court Apartments, which consisted of ninety-one apartments in two buildings. This time Phipps Houses created a playground and community garden out of an abandoned lot next door they convinced the city to donate. There is also a gazebo for

outdoor socializing, as well as large community space inside. The community development worker for Mapes Court is a young woman who herself grew up in Lambert Houses. She has helped the residents get their children medical examinations for school, she started a tenants organization, and she has helped some of the women enroll in GED programs and even college courses.

Among the last projects Lynda worked on, before her retirement in 1991, was a twenty-building rehab on the west side of Crotona Park that served homeless and very low-income residents. Called Crotona Park West, the 563-unit project began accepting tenants in 1992. This part of the South Bronx is a very rough neighborhood, where poverty is a crushing burden. Keeping the community support programs functioning will be crucial to the project's long-term success.

Just before Lynda retired, she said that, after years of acting on faith, she felt that they had finally begun to see some concrete results. She believes her theories are being proved.

We founded this community development corporation about eighteen years ago because this is what I thought should happen. But until now, we haven't seen it happening, and it's because we haven't had enough resources to make a meaningful dent. But with that combination, we are making a big dent. It's just astounding. We don't have all the answers to the questions this raises, but we're going to follow it. We're going to see if people actually get off welfare, if we have less kids into drugs, fewer people going to jail, etc. Because, basically, this proves our ideas that these people want the same things everybody else does. If you just give them the chance to learn and to grow, they'll take advantage of it.

Lynda now lives in Colorado and is beginning to write about developments in social housing based on her twenty-five years experience in the field.

Elizabeth Ayer

Elizabeth Ayer, born in 1897, was raised on a dairy farm in Olympia, Washington. She and her four older brothers helped her mother run the farm after her father died. Although she attended a poorly staffed one-room schoolhouse as a child, she went to college, entering the University of Washington in 1916 just before World War I. She became one of the first women to graduate from the architecture program, and was the first woman to be licensed as an architect in the state of Washington. She is also probably the first woman to become a principle in an architectural firm. In the course of her career, she designed many upscale residences in the Seattle area. She became a partner and then owner of the architectural firm she started working for in 1920. She worked as an architect for over fifty years and died in 1987 at the age of eighty-nine.

Washington's First Woman Architect

Elizabeth Ayer did not think of herself as a feminist, but she certainly believed that women are as capable as men of doing most kinds of work. She seems to have been more amused than irritated at the discomfort expressed by men who found it difficult to accept the presence of women in the field.

She loved her work, did it well, and had no regrets about the choices she made. When interviewed in 1985, Elizabeth was full of spunk and enthusiasm. She had never married, but she did not lack emotional support in her life and career. She was very close to her brothers and their families and enjoyed enduring friendships with several women she had known since high school.

In an interview with Nelda Patton, a grandniece who is compiling information for a book about Elizabeth, Ms. Patton recalled that Elizabeth was adept at figuring out what her clients really wanted even when they weren't sure themselves. Elizabeth always gave them more than they expected (and didn't charge high fees for her work). Patton attributed Elizabeth's ability to work so smoothly in a male-dominated field to her farm background; she was used to working long hours, and with four brothers, all older than she, Elizabeth had learned to get along with men.

In the years following the turn of the century, Washington state itself was young. Elizabeth went to school in a tiny one-room school house on the edge of virgin forest. Her father died when she was six years old. Her oldest brother, who was only thirteen, had to take over management of the farm and its sixty head of cattle. From seventh grade on, the Ayer children had to ride their bikes eight miles into town to continue their schooling (farm chores were done before and after school).

Elizabeth's mother kept the family together and encouraged them all to stretch their horizons.

The thing I liked was the big, old potbellied stove. My mother read to us every night. We had, of course, no radio or TV. She read all the old classics to us. We went through Dickens, Scott, George Elliot, Thackeray, and, of course, Mark Twain.

Elizabeth was one in a long line of career-minded women, following the example of several of the women in her family by remaining independent all her life. She had an aunt who was the secretary to the first governor of the state and to the state Supreme Court. One of her father's cousins was an editor for children's books and

school books at Macmillan. Another cousin was a Latin teacher. Her mother was an artist.

Also notable was Elizabeth's father's sister—a law graduate of Mount Holyoke who helped with finances and basically took over the role of father after Elizabeth's father died. Partly due to her aunt's example, Elizabeth realized that although many careers were dominated by men, it didn't mean those careers were closed to women who were persistent.

I went to college because I wanted to be on the go. I took just a general course, but I had the feeling that I'd have to make a living. And so I was considering what I could do. And the only two things that I had in my favor were art and math. My walks home from the campus took me by this building with Architecture *on the front of it. And I got to thinking that I could use both of them. And that was that.*

When Elizabeth entered the University of Washington, the architecture department was very small and brand new. It was housed in an old wooden

building that was formerly a construction shack. When she originally applied, Elizabeth was told she would be the only woman, and that was not permissible. She mentioned to an architecture instructor that she had actually thought of majoring in landscape architecture, but the university didn't offer it. His response was ostensibly very encouraging, but was actually a subtle attempt to steer her away from architecture.

He thought that was a fine idea. "Just wait," he said, "They'll be starting a landscape architecture course in a year or two." So I went down and asked the dean of fine arts when it was going to start. He said, "There's never been any talk about it."

I guess he was annoyed at the architecture department for giving me this advice, and wanted to sic me on them. Anyway, he told me I could apply to the architecture department: "It's a coeducational university. Why don't you take it?"

When she entered the program, the campus newspaper ran a big box right in the middle of the front page: "Architecture Is Not for Women!" It was clear that she and the one other woman who had dared to enroll in the department were not altogether welcome. The first day they walked into their classroom they found a single table elevated in the center of the room. It was to be their work table.

Fortunately, after the initial discouragement there was no further harassment. Elizabeth and her female classmate were generally treated as part of the gang. However, there were still obstacles. Students often pulled all-nighters at the drawing boards, but women were not allowed on the campus after dark unless they were in groups of at least two, and not at all after ten o'clock. Elizabeth managed to ignore the rule and worked all night anyway, like the other students. Another problem was no women's bathroom in the building, but eventually she managed to convince the dean of women to order that one be installed.

Elizabeth's professional experience started with summer work, for the firm of Edwin J. Ivey, about two years before she graduated. After graduation, she worked for Ivey full-time.

I have often thought of how fortunate I was. To begin with, I had this super teacher. And then I went into this office and worked for a man who loved his work with all his heart. His own drawings weren't all that good, but his houses were lovely. His manual skills were just, for him, an instrument. I was more at home on paper. I did *most of my thinking on paper. That was my way. He was more at home on the job, not paper. It was a very small office. He was in debt when I joined the firm. He had inherited the debts with the firm, so there wasn't any money. When business began to come in, we just worked longer hours. I loved it, too. I got a chance to do everything that was to be done in an office.*

During two interludes from working with Ivey, Elizabeth spent one year touring Europe and absorbing the architecture, and another year working at a couple of firms in New York City. Elizabeth enjoyed applying for work. She would go late in the afternoon, when the firms weren't so busy. Invariably she was able to talk to the principals, successful architects she had read about. She was thrilled to meet them in person and to be taken seriously by them.

While in New York, she worked for a leading residential office. The principal had two old houses he had turned into offices. They were quite busy and there was no office space for Elizabeth, so they set up a table for her in the principal's private office. He was very active with the American Institute of Architects; all of the leading architects of the time met there. Elizabeth was in seventh heaven. After a year of this, though, she returned to Seattle to be with her family and resumed her position with Edwin Ivey, eventually becoming his partner.

Over the years there were slow periods when money was tight, but Elizabeth and Ivey always managed to meet their payroll. In recounting the difficulties, Elizabeth remembered the personal challenges of meeting her own expectations, of struggling to be as competent as she could be. The hardest obstacle was coming in to work in the morning and finding an order on her desk to do something she had no idea how to do. But she had to do it, so she did. Each time that happened, of course, she acquired a new skill.

Her first assignment to supervise a job was a typical example of how she grew into her career. It was a large alteration job in the Bellevue section of Seattle, and the site was right on the water. Elizabeth had made the drawings and she had worked with the contractor in the office, so she was familiar with the work. But Ivey was in charge of the job, while she had always been in the wings. One day when Elizabeth came into the office there was a note on the table explaining that Ivey had to go out of town and instructing Elizabeth to go to the job site in his place. She was terrified. She took the streetcar to the shore then a ferry across the lake. The contractor met her on the other side and escorted her to the house.

She couldn't imagine herself, with her minimal experience, telling these men, who had worked with these projects all their lives, what to do. But as soon as she got there someone wanted to consult with her. And then somebody else needed to talk to her. Then it was the plumber, the electrician, and so on. Before she knew it, the contractor said, "If you're going to catch that ferry you'd better get going." And that was it. No one questioned her capabilities. No one was disrespectful. They had treated her as a professional, and she had been able to answer all their questions. She discovered that she knew what to do. It wasn't difficult at all. This experience helped her to gain self-confidence.

Elizabeth soon found that she got the same response nearly everywhere she worked, that, "As soon as the contractor knew that you knew your stuff, there

"I'm a rotten salesman. I never went for work. But it just came in. That's what I call good fortune."

was no problem." In the absence of a women's liberation movement, she may have been seen as an oddity, but she wasn't perceived as a threat. Concentrating on residential design was somewhat beneficial in this regard. The home was, and in many ways still is, considered a woman's domain. Establishing credibility as a designer of houses, rather than as a designer of commercial buildings, has always been easier for women.

Both Elizabeth and Ivey preferred residential design. Most of the houses she worked on were very expensive projects—mansions, estates, and even a "castle." Some have become famous landmarks in the Seattle area. Her taste was extremely eclectic, within the confines of what she considered to be traditional architectural styles. This was the time when Bauhaus was sweeping architecture, and the trend was toward a sleek, industrial look. But there was no wavering. Elizabeth found the modern style to be cold and barren, even "brutal." Clients who requested it were politely referred elsewhere.

Elizabeth's very successful partnership with Edwin Ivey came abruptly to an end in 1940, when Ivey was killed in an automobile accident. Elizabeth had been very close to him and his family. His sudden death was a blow. At first she didn't see how she would be able to manage the business without him. She eventually took on a partner, but got through those first years on her own very well. Her dedication was to the art of design; the business end had never been her forte. But she got along well with people, and that made a big difference both in being able to do good design work and in keeping the business together through the hard times.

I was very fortunate. I'm a rotten salesman. But it was a going office by the time Mr. Ivey was killed. I had been, of course, close to the clients and to the contractors and builders. They actually took over. They became my salesmen. I never went for work. I'm no good at it. But it just came in. That's what I call good fortune.

"I would usually ask for a scrapbook. You get a good idea of what their taste is that way."

Elizabeth had a knack for finding out what clients had in mind when they approached her for a design. Some customers are better able to articulate this internal vision than others, but almost all of them have, somewhere inside, a mental picture of what they want. The challenge is to discover what that picture looks like.

I would usually ask for a scrapbook, anything that they have kept that they liked (regardless of whether it had anything to do with the project they were planning). You get a good idea of what their taste is that way—the sort of things they like.

Elizabeth's basic strategy was to embrace her client's perspective. Over the years she collected an impressive library of clippings, sketches, and photographs of all the classical building types. When she obtained a commission she would decide with the clients which style they preferred and would then immerse herself in studying her files, absorbing every aspect of the chosen style until she felt she was practi-

cally living and breathing in the period and provenance. Only then would she begin to formulate her ideas for the house.

The first house Elizabeth designed on her own was the Linus H. French house, in West Seattle near Puget Sound. Ivey had contracted the job but then left for a trip to Europe, so Elizabeth took over. The French house is a three-story colonial-style house in what was then a sparsely populated area. West Seattle was connected to Seattle by a bridge that had just been completed when Elizabeth's client decided to move there.

French, a doctor and dentist who had worked for many years in Alaska, gave Elizabeth free rein in creating a house that would be both practical and fun to live in. He had sold the family's previous house almost on a whim, and moved his family suddenly to a rented house in what was then an up-and-coming neighborhood. They loved the view of Puget Sound and the mountains beyond so much that they decided to build their new home in the same neighborhood.

Linus French had plenty of money to invest in a home for his growing family. Elizabeth took the opportunity to put in all the features that she thought would make a house not only well-built and good looking but nourishing and satisfying to live in. Some of the progressive features Elizabeth incorporated included the low-pressure steam heating system, numerous electrical outlets in each room (the house had thirty circuits), several rooms with three-way light switches, and a central vacuum system. Such features were not common in residences in 1926.

The living room, dining room, and parlor were all connected to the front entrance hall, so each room was accessible without having to walk through the others. There was an open staircase with custom-turned balusters and a balcony overlooking the front entrance hall. The front entrance hall, with its arched doorway and grand staircase, was such an appealing space that several of Dr. French's daughters married there, as well as several friends and neighbors.

There were fireplaces on every level of the house, including the basement. The interior walls were plaster, decorated with elaborate hand-carved moldings. The moldings were custom designed, and the wood was seasoned for a year before being milled so that it would not shrink after installation. Even the wall treatment was special—a sand finish antiqued with a dark brown stain and wiped to a soft beige.

Impressive as the house was to adult eyes and taste, Elizabeth did not neglect the interests of the children who would also be living there. Suzanne French Black, one of Linus French's daughters, remembers it was a child's delight, with lots of nooks and crannies all over the house. Besides the intentionally playful features, there were a few unintentionally amusing features, such as the shaft for a dumb waiter (that was planned but never installed) where Suzanne and the other children often played.

One of Elizabeth's most spectacular projects was known as Schafer Castle. Schafer Castle started out as a summer house built by a logging and railroad tycoon Albert Schafer. Schafer, along with two brothers, had built one of the largest logging operations in the Northwest early in this century. They commissioned the house in the early twenties, at the peak of their financial empire.

The house, located along Hood Canal, is one of Seattle's more prominent architectural landmarks. It is very large, with turrets, arches, and a huge spiral staircase hugging a curved brick wall, giving it a castle-like appearance. The massive oak beams that dominate the living room were custom-designed and turned into spindles by a giant lathe in one of the Schafer mills. Adding to the romantic atmosphere in the living room was a leaded-glass window made with pieces of old bottle glass. The house was designed to accommodate large numbers of summer guests and had two bunk rooms, one for boys and one for girls. The back of the house opens directly onto the canal.

Although Elizabeth is most noted for the homes she designed in the Seattle area, her job list (which in her fifty years of practice exceeded 1,600) included houses in Yakima, Olympia, Everett, Leavenworth, Bellingham, Aberdeen, and Tacoma. When she retired in 1970, she made an effort to return her original draw-

ings to the owners of many of the houses she designed.

The people were just so delighted to get them, and even when it was somebody else living in the house. I had a lot of nice visits. There's one up in Bellingham, some people bought it a few years ago. They came down to see if I had anything on it. It was one that I hadn't delivered, so I still had it. I gave them the plans. When they went back they got an artist to make a drawing of the house. They had it framed and sent it down to me.

In her later years, Elizabeth also returned from time to time to look at some of the houses she designed a generation or more ago. There were a few she went out of her way to avoid seeing again, but those were exceptions. There were also some buildings that she outlived—several were torn down to make room for new projects, and a few were extensively remodeled.

Interestingly, Elizabeth never designed a house for herself. She lived for many years with her mother, an aunt, and one of her brothers in what started as a tiny three-room house (it had originally been a bootlegger's

"As I look back I think I've had a pretty good life."

cabin). Over the years Elizabeth designed improvements, and they added on and upgraded the house. Elizabeth really liked the house and she never felt the need to design a house of her own.

When Elizabeth Ayer entered the field of architecture, women architects were extremely rare. But if she saw herself as a pioneer in any sense, it was as much a part of a new category of professionals as it was a woman breaking into a male-dominated field. (She was the first woman and also only the fourth person to graduate in architecture from the University of Washington.) She said what she recalled about that era was the high quality of the training she received, not the struggle to be accepted as an equal.

Always modest about her achievements, Elizabeth attributed her success to luck rather than skill or ambi-

tion on her part. She did look back on her career of more than fifty years with a great deal of satisfaction. Though she was reluctant to acknowledge it, she knew that she had influenced the lives of many families and left some spectacular buildings that contribute to the charm and elegance of Seattle's architectural legacy.

"I have no regrets. There were times that were hard. But taken all in all, as I look back I think I've had a pretty good life."

Carolyn Geise

Seattle architect Carolyn Geise started her career in 1969, designing single-family homes. From 1973 to 1977, she worked with a partner, Jane Hastings. Since that time, she has had her own practice, Geise Associates in Architecture, Inc. Her work is almost equally divided between residential and commercial projects. Most of her commercial work is with psychiatric facilities, schools, community facilities, and transitional housing. She has focused on design techniques that allow such institutional settings to be as comfortable and homelike as possible. Her projects include the student union building renovation at the University of Washington, the Activity Center for the Seattle Children's Home, a residential treatment center at the Children's Psychiatric Hospital in Steilacoom, Washington, and dozens of private houses. In twenty-six years of practicing architecture, Carolyn has designed more than nine hundred individual projects.

Healing Environments

Carolyn Geise was born in Seattle and lived there until age eight, when her family moved to Olympia, Washington. She loved to sew and studied textiles and clothing in college, expecting to have a career in clothing design. However, her interests broadened as she discovered new ideas. She enjoyed linking different areas of study, and she developed her own major—a radical thing to do in 1954—an interdisciplinary course in textiles, clothing, art, and science. However, in her senior year she took an interior design class from a teacher who taught it almost as an architecture course—students were taken on tours of new buildings and new homes that young architects had designed, and they analyzed spaces: how they are used, how they relate to the outdoors, furniture layout, colors, and decoration.

This experience planted a seed in Carolyn's mind that sprouted about two years later. After graduating with a degree in home economics, she got a job with a sportswear manufacturer in Seattle as a "floor lady,"

> *"It was after I was in the architectural program that I discovered what an excellent education I'd received in home economics."*

supervising fifty power-sewing-machine operators. Carolyn soon realized that she wanted more freedom to develop her artistic ideas, to be able to follow a product from beginning to end, and to have more control over the end result. She thought that being an architect would give her all of these, so she decided to go back to school for another four years to get a degree in architecture.

It was after I was in the architectural program that I discovered what an excellent education I'd received in home economics. The approach in clothing design had been to analyze what the activity is that you're doing: what are the requirements of the clothing, what materials work to meet those requirements, and how they should be cut to accommodate the activity and the body and the individual piece. The approach is the same when you design a house.

Just a few months before Carolyn graduated, she decided to get married. For the next seven years, her career slowed down as she devoted most of her energy to her duties as wife and mother. In spite of the fact that she did continue her education and was working toward a career of her own, Carolyn was very traditional in her view of men's and women's roles, especially in marriage. She became very involved in supporting her husband's career as an artist, even though it meant holding back on her own need to grow and express herself. But it wasn't working; she began to grow restless and depressed.

A few weeks after she finally obtained her architectural license in 1969, Carolyn's husband shocked her by announcing he was leaving. To make matters worse, they had just sold their house in town and purchased one on the east side of Lake Washington. Although they hadn't moved, the deal was closing and they were in the middle of packing.

Carolyn was devastated. She had never considered that she might be forced to bring up a child alone. Gaining strength from her strong religious convictions, she struggled to convince herself that the world hadn't come to an end and that she could manage on her own. Although she was an architect, as yet she had no clients or job.

"I let another person set the direction of my life."

And the house I loved, the house in town that I was happy in, we had sold. And so I had to pack all the stuff and move to a house that I couldn't afford. The new house was on the other side of the toll bridge from Seattle, where my potential work was. There was no child care at that time; I'd have to cross the bridge two or three times a day. It was too much.

Carolyn decided to put the new house up for sale and look for something she could afford. She finally located a suitable house and turned the upstairs into an apartment she could rent for extra income. She set up an office in her house, got her first real client, and started working.

Carolyn threw herself into design with a passion. Her former husband had moved to the East Coast, but in time he returned to Seattle and they became friends. He was amazed at the transformation. "You know," he said, "you are just like you were when I first met you."

I had changed so much in the time I was married. I had become a different person. I took on his standards and adjusted to his lifestyle. I let another person set the direction of my life. As it drifted into areas that weren't good for me, I didn't take a stand for my own direction.

It wasn't so much *what* she did as it was the fact that she was neglecting her responsibilities to herself. Her dignity, her religious convictions, her self-esteem, and her effectiveness all suffered. These were symbolized for her by self-destructive habits she had acquired while married.

I smoked and drank. I didn't ever do that before, and I didn't after. When he moved out of the house, I consumed all the alcohol that was there, in one day. And I smoked all the cigarettes that were there. And I didn't touch another cigarette or drink since. It actually frightened me, to sit there and to drink up that liquor cabinet. I thought, boy, this isn't me. That's not what I want to do.

The idea of a husband walking out on me on two weeks' notice was a little bit of a comeuppance. That was when I began to realize that this is a different world than I envisioned.

It took Carolyn about two years to get back on her feet. But then her career flourished. She started out with residential work, later branching out into commercial projects. In both cases, her focus was on creating living space that is nurturing to its inhabitants. Much of her commercial work was with hospitals or mental health centers, generally long-term care facilities. In a sense they are also residential to the extent that people live in those buildings for a period of time. She eventually developed a reputation for creating sensitive designs for public facilities.

Carolyn's first psychiatric facility project was the Activity Center at the Seattle Children's Home, a private facility for emotionally disturbed children. She presented herself as an architect whose background would enable her to provide an environment for children that was not typically institutional. In spite of the crisp, modern look of the building, the atmosphere, arrangement, and spaces she created were constructive, soothing, and appropriate.

My architectural approach is that you take the site and you start from the access to the property, how a car comes up, what the orientation to the sun is, the directions of the view, the directions of the wind. And you start to put the spaces together that the activities on the site require in relation to all of those outer things. You've just got to start that way, from the very beginning. In a sense, the project develops from the inside out.

When Carolyn was first interviewed in 1985, she was designing a $4 million Child Study and Treatment Center for the state mental hospital in Steilacoom, which provided housing and therapy for disturbed children. The state mental hospital had been built on that site, originally Fort Steilacoom, the oldest settlement in Washington, around the turn of the century and was notoriously grim and depressing.

The project involves several individual residential units. They're calling them "cottages," but they're almost 11,000 square feet each. So trying to make them feel like cottages is quite a challenge.
They sit in a beautiful site, down here just off the highway, in a field of oak trees and grass. The oak trees are

"We tied the trees into our presentation. We used them as a model of the qualities of strength, of stability and serenity, that we felt should be expressed in the facilities."

three- and five-hundred years old. These great, huge native oaks and native prairie grasses. In fact, it's a historic landscape. It's classified as an historic district.

For the presentation, we took slides of the old mental hospital facilities there that really are just terribly, terribly oppressive. Almost like a jail. We took photographs of the site and the buildings and the trees.

As we looked around, the only thing constructive were the trees. So we took some good shots of the trees and some close-up shots of the trunks of the trees. It was fall and the trees were silhouetted against the sky. We tied the trees into our presentation. We used them as a model of the qualities of strength, of stability and serenity, that we

felt should be expressed in the facilities. We made that the focus of our presentation, that saving the trees and capitalizing on their inherent qualities in the building design was our goal. It did the job in terms of our sales pitch.

For commercial and residential projects, Carolyn places a great deal of emphasis on the flow of activities from one room to the next, how people use a space, and what that space must provide to meet their physical and emotional needs. In addition, she looks at how the house interacts with the environment.

One of Carolyn's recent residential projects is a 3,266-square-foot house perched on a hill overlooking Salmon Bay. The design challenge was to create a house that contained elements of New England architectural traditions, reminiscent of the client's childhood, within a generally northwest stylistic treatment. Carolyn took full advantage of the site's spectacular view of the bay by integrating several patios and a wraparound porch into the design.

A garage with a guest room and play area beneath it is connected to the main house with a wooden bridge. Inside, the living room, dining room, informal dining room, and entry all radiate from the central kitchen. The kitchen itself has no windows, but it has only one wall. The other three sides open over island countertops to views of the other rooms and through windows beyond. These rooms circle the kitchen with increasingly formal living spaces, starting with the breakfast

nook and continuing to the living room and front entryway.

Carolyn likes to put kitchens in the middle of a floor plan, because they are usually a hub of activity. Windows aren't needed if the room feels light and airy, making it a pleasant working space. In kitchens with islands, she orients work areas so they look through breakfast or family rooms to living rooms with large windows. From the kitchen, you can look over a dining table where people sit in chairs, to the living room where people sit lower on couches, to windows that can be low or even floor level. Such an arrangement also has the advantage of allowing these rooms to be connected socially, and people in the kitchen can work without turning their backs on people in adjacent rooms.

The second floor contains a master bedroom suite and a study. A lower level, which also has a view to the bay, has two children's bedrooms, a rec room, and utility rooms.

The bay view dictated the orientation of the house to the north. To offset this problem and make the inte-

rior sunny and create an open feeling, Lynda constructed a high-ceilinged extension on the living room at the southeast corner. On the lower level where that was not possible, the utilities, laundry, and stairwell were placed along the solid, hillside end of the house and the activity room in the center was given a high ceiling and grade-level access to the outdoors. Generous windows on the north, bay view side eliminated any basement feeling to the bedrooms.

In the twenty-three years Carolyn has been practicing architecture, her work expanded from single-family home commissions based on contacts generated by friends and family to multimillion dollar public facilities, as well as other commercial projects she acquires on the basis of her reputation as one of Seattle's finest architects. She spearheaded an effort to increase public awareness of handicapped-accessible design and to increase compliance with standards and regulations. Barrier-free architecture became a specialty of her firm. Over the years she has donated countless hours of design time to a variety of human service

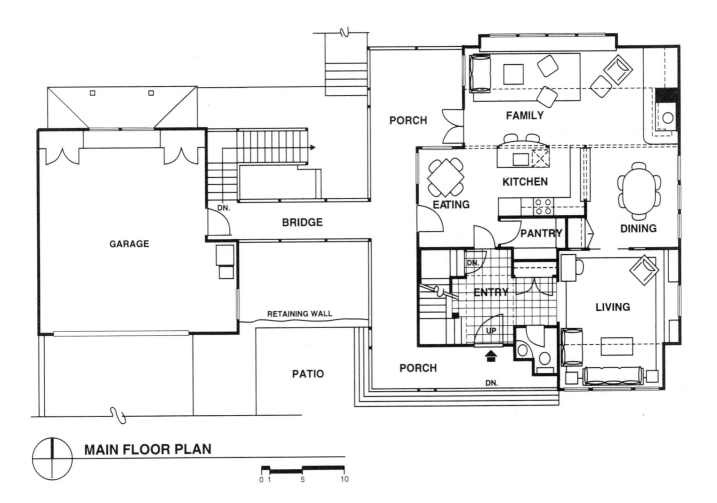

MAIN FLOOR PLAN

0 1   5   10

"In 1959, with only fifteen women licensed to practice in the state of Washington in its entire history, there weren't many role models."

agencies and educational projects. Carolyn's firm has been and may still be the largest woman-owned architectural firm in Seattle, and possibly in the state of Washington.

Carolyn reiterates that women have a difficult time becoming established in the field of architecture. In 1959, with only fifteen women licensed to practice in the state of Washington in its entire history, there weren't many role models, and there was little encouragement from any source. Building a practice was not easy at a time when bank policies restricted the amount of credit they would give to women-owned businesses.

Not only has Carolyn managed to succeed financially, but she has achieved significant recognition, even within the generally conservative professional organizations in which she has participated over the years. Her residential work has won her an American Institute of Architects (AIA) Home of the Month award and an award from the Washington State Historical Trust Commission. And in 1989, she became a fellow of the AIA, the only woman out of forty-four architects to be awarded the honor that year.

Carolyn believes female architects do have one advantage over their male counterparts—their ability to recognize unspoken needs and to see things through other people's eyes. One example is the presentation process, the means by which architects secure state jobs. The state agencies advertise in the paper that they are looking for architects for a particular job. An architect who is interested in bidding on the job must first send in a written proposal that states what his or her qualifications are and describes previous work done by that firm, the team who would be working on this particular project, and so on. From those responses, the state agency will choose four or five firms to interview. The interviews are usually only about half an hour long. A selection is based solely on the firm's qualifications as architects, with the fee to be negotiated later (based on standardized fee schedule guidelines). If they can't

agree on a fee, the state will go on to the second firm. It's a difficult, time-consuming, and expensive process for the prospective architects. They must try to convince the agency why they can do a better job than the other firms.

It takes a tremendous amount of work to get that organized. We do a lot of investigation of the project—trying to see what the owner needs and how we can meet those needs—and condense our past experience into examples of how we have met similar needs. We don't do a design. We never get into doing a design. Some people do. But I think it's jumping the gun. I also think that it locks you into a preconceived idea before you know what the factors are. That can be a problem. What we try and do is find out as much as we can about the site and about the program. Then we say, "From what we know about the program and site, we consider these factors important." Then we talk about those factors and about how we would handle them. It's a lot to do effectively in half an hour.

"The biggest need, I think, in architecture is to be sure we're hearing what the clients need and looking at the things society needs as well."

I was talking to an architect friend of mine the other day when he was bringing through a group of students on a tour of the office. We were talking about the presentation process. He commented to the students that our firm and another woman-owned firm that he knew were by far the most interested in the client, and that the presentations that our firms put on stood out way above the men's firms, because we spoke to the needs of the clients and had some understanding of their needs. It comes out, I think, in a focus on the work. The biggest need, I think, in architecture is to be sure we're hearing what the clients need and looking at the things society needs as well.

A "program" that details the client's job requirements is developed at the beginning of each design project.

Carolyn Geise **169**

The program is a listing of all the needs, spaces, and required relationships: two bedrooms, a kitchen with a view to the garden, a pantry close by, two ovens, a gas cooktop, some open shelves, etc. The program should also list the qualities you want the project to express, such as warm, light, comfortable, lived-in, sophisticated, etc.

Ideally, as a project progresses, it develops an identity and personality of its own. The architect's personal stamp becomes less noticeable than the functionality of the final product and its fit between the client and site.

Ten years from now the project will stand alone and speak for itself. No one will know if the budget was impossible, the client demanding, or if there were conflicting codes from multiple jurisdictions. The project will be there, hopefully serving the current needs with dignity and grace.

The genius of design is to take the specific program requirements, consider the features and constraints of the site, abide by the ever more restrictive building codes, watch the budget, and blend these elements into a cohesive whole that sings.

Carolyn does see the field of architecture changing. There is more attention to cities now, and more attention to how buildings fit into their surroundings and meet the needs of their communities as well as their occupants. Contextual architecture, as this is called, has always been a hallmark of Carolyn's work. She was never interested in making buildings into jewels that stood out, that look like sculptures or serve as objects in themselves. She has always viewed the build-

> *"The genius of design is to take the specific program requirements and blend these elements into a cohesive whole that sings."*

ing as a setting for human activity rather than the site as a setting for a building. Though women seem to have been more in tune with this thinking than men, it isn't a focus women architects monopolize, and Carolyn is glad to see it becoming more widespread.

Carolyn has an enormous amount of energy. She's been a competitive skier, an international class sailboat racer, and a mountain climber in her spare time. But she doesn't see herself as an ambitious or goal-oriented person. She says her success has derived primarily from a stubborn streak and from an abiding religious faith that has kept her on track and unwilling to quit in the face of adversity.

In spite of her modesty, Carolyn seems to have been adept at juggling the conflicting demands of her profession. She remarried in 1978, and this time she has managed to be wife, mother, *and* architect. She has kept her eye on the ball and her values intact throughout her career. In both residential and commercial work, she never loses sight of what she sees as the essential function of architecture.

Part Two

Part Two

Women's experiences in building, in doing something nontraditional, is by definition pioneering—staking out a claim in an area that is unfamiliar and probably uncomfortable. How are we expected to see ourselves when we do things we've been told women can't do or shouldn't do? Suddenly some of the most basic rules and habits we've grown up with no longer make sense. How do we get our bearings without instructions or compass points by which to orient ourselves? Do we imitate men? Do we perform men's work with a feminine style? Our backgrounds have not prepared most of us for exploration of such foreign territory. The skills necessary to succeed in nontraditional endeavors such as building will be picked up along the way or borrowed from some other experience and applied in a new context.

We do more, however, than merely explore new roles. As we make ourselves at home in houses we build ourselves, we take control of our physical surroundings, surroundings that affect how we live and who we become. The houses we live in influence our moods, our interactions with other people, many of our physical activities, and literally our view of the outside world. Designing our homes gives us a measure of control over our own destinies.

As women, we are largely invisible in this society, being neither seen clearly by others nor seeing ourselves clearly most of the time. Images of women are plentiful, but those images are mostly created by men—they are not self-images. Society mirrors men in countless ways: Most of our institutions were invented and are controlled by men. These institutions necessarily reflect men's experiences, perspectives, and goals. Such representation is a rare experience for women. We usually see ourselves as we are defined by others—a useful, but incomplete picture.

Architectural design is a form of expression that conveys our values, tastes, and identities. Taking control of the shape of our homes gives our self-image a physical reality, helping us see ourselves in a new perspective. My purpose in documenting women who build and design is not only to honor their audacity, determination, and imagination but also to hold up a mirror to activities we rarely see.

The following observations and reflections are drawn from my own experience and from listening to these women discuss the significance of this challenging work in their lives. Building and designing houses means different things to different people. Some of the women interviewed here felt a dramatic impact on their lives; others felt a more subtle effect. Some had regrets, and for many the cost was high. The different contexts facing these women tremendously affected their building experiences, as well as their view of themselves in relation to their houses and to other people.

Some women were just finishing building when I interviewed them; others had been living in their houses for years. Many of these women had well-considered ideas about their experiences, but just as many had not thought much about the meaning of what they had accomplished. A few had advice to offer women who are thinking of building or designing.

Whatever her experience, each of these women had something to say about where designing and building her home fit into her life. Common themes were frequently intertwined: increased self-confidence, a feeling of control over their lives, a sense of accomplishment, the social implications of housing design, and, often, an altered self-image.

The Politics of Housing

We have all been propagandized since the late 1930s and early 1940s to believe that the American dream of home ownership is the ideal for which we must all strive. Unfortunately, this arrangement has tended to isolate women as housewives and increase the separation of women's place (unpaid and home alone) from men's place (engaged in politics, business, and public life, but cut off from home and family).

Delores Hayden describes this shift in *The Grand Domestic Revolution*. She asserts that after World War II government and industry worked together to encourage suburban development, which increased consumption and reduced labor unrest. The idea was to disperse workers from the old tenement neighborhoods where well-established social networks supported political organizing. Women were marginalized even further from the paid workforce. Men in the suburbs found themselves in anonymous tract houses, the sole support of their now-nuclear families, with mortgage payments to meet every month. Car payments and installments on the many new labor-saving appliances were quick to follow. Going on strike took on new meaning in this context. With only one wage earner per family, political protest was much more risky.

The environmental, social, and political consequences of this transformation are monumental. In the span of one generation, vast amounts of once-productive land were swallowed up by suburban development. The decline of extended families living together or near one another has had enormous repercussions. Women found themselves increasingly dependent on a single individual (first their fathers, then their husbands) and restricted in their activities due to their relative exclusion from public and private decision-making. Times are changing, not necessarily for the better. With the breakdown of the nuclear family and more and more women without the support of husbands, this problem is becoming acute.

Women have sought various routes to independence in our male-dominated society. Some have made enough money to support themselves and satisfy their needs without having to submit to another person's control. Others have accepted the rules and played to win or have tried to change the system (from within or from without) to make it less oppressive. Women like Debrin and Oceanlight, or the members of Salmon Creek Farm and Silver Circle, found a solution closer to home—carving out a separate territory, creating a refuge or private domain where they defined their own independence. They are saying, Our communities haven't worked for us, so we're going to create ones that do.

Many women own property, even design and build their own homes, to reclaim stature and authority. Sometimes this works and sometimes it doesn't. The

"They are saying, Our communities haven't worked for us, so we're going to create ones that do."

hippie communes and land cooperatives that sprang up in the early 1970s were often expressions of youthful rebellion. Some, however, were attempts to revisit the fundamental question of how a community is put together and how individuals relate to it. The communes of the seventies, which challenged the dominant patterns of housing and community organization, were actually the most recent examples of a long history in the United States of utopian and alternative housing experiments. Some date back at least to the middle of the nineteenth century.

People have tried a number of different living arrangements in an attempt to obtain personal power and independence without giving up close relationships and shared resources. In many cases, this meant challenging the sanctity of the single-family house as the only legitimate model. Alternative communities were created in which groups of people shared living quarters, household chores, and decision-making. By manipulating the physical layout of the community, domestic arrangements could be totally reorganized.

> ## "I really played the game by the rules. And what did it get me? Backward! One step forward, two steps backward."

These changes spilled across nuclear family boundaries, influencing economic and social relations.

The most consciously political response that I heard in these interviews came from Gail Atkins and Gwen Demeter, the creators of Silver Circle. In establishing their commune, Gail and Gwen definitely considered it an escape from many of the limitations imposed on women. They were trying to create an alternative model of how people can live together. Their use of communal land and an environmentally low-impact approach was a direct response to their ecological and feminist perspectives. They wanted a place where women could have control over their own lives, live in harmony with nature, and realize their potential as human beings.

There was a strong economic factor behind all this. Gail described how the impetus for building Silver Circle came about: "I think the thing that really turned me around, in terms of my head, was I really played the game by the rules. And what did it get me? Backward! One step forward, two steps backward. I taught school for fifteen years, and I watched my purchasing power just shrinking. I was living just a titch above poverty. And I was at the top of the pay scale! Now I have a vision of an alternative way women can work together. I want it to be a way to have a good time and the energy to do some of the things you want to do in life. Not come to the end and realize you've given it all to The Man."

Gail and Gwen worked on their conditioning as consumers. They recognize that, like all of us, they've been taught that it's necessary to acquire a lot of impressive, or at least respectable, possessions to have status, and that status is necessary to feel successful. Gail and Gwen have tried to escape the vicious cycle of working more to spend more. They now buy things they need or really want and are sure will make their lives more pleasant. Gail says they're trying to move

"It's the negative aspects of the patriarchy, the oppressive aspects of the patriarchy that I want to change."

away from what she calls a deprivation mindset—interpreting feelings of dissatisfaction as a lack of material possessions. Such an outlook induces people to consume with an appetite that can never be satisfied. The buildings at Silver Circle are modest and unassuming, yet are deeply gratifying to Gail and Gwen because their home represents freedom from that compulsive cycle and therefore a personal triumph over a system they find offensive.

Their rebellion should not be misunderstood, however. They don't reject everything about our country's culture or politics. One of the most difficult parts of selective resistance is getting other people to appreciate the distinctions that are important to you. Gail tells of an argument she had with a friend who is a lawyer. Her friend said, "The difference is, you're radical. You want to abolish the system, but I want to work within the system." Gail replied, "No, I don't want to abolish it. I just wanna make it do what it says it's gonna do!" Gail is convinced that America's political system can be made to work. Our constitution and legal structure address issues of equality and human dignity, presenting a framework to address our problems.

Gail is concerned about a feminist movement getting bogged down in rhetoric. Rather than engage in endless railing against the patriarchy, Gail's approach is to look first at what effect a particular element in the system has on women, then decide what to do about it—as she explained, "It's the negative aspects of the patriarchy, the oppressive aspects of the patriarchy that I want to change. The injustices, and the part that just keeps people . . . on this treadmill. They just barely make their utilities, and they barely can buy their food, and they barely can do this, and they barely can do that. And that's most women!" Cooperative living fosters a strong sense of community with close ties among its members and provides an opportunity for women to tackle both the injustices of society and the sense of alienation that the disenfranchised feel.

Community values, and human values in general, can be expressed in architectural details, as well. The architects and developers I spoke with generally addressed these issues from an aesthetic and psychological perspective. I found that many women focus one way or another on the concept of harmony in architecture.

Sam Morse focuses on social harmony; her commitment to community values underlies every decision. She firmly believes that the countryside should be left rural. She doesn't think we should be using farmland to build tract houses. When that land is taken out of production, she wonders, where will we get the land needed to grow our food? Instead, we should be renovating the many well-built, structurally adequate, abandoned houses that already exist in our cities. They could provide needed housing stock, and their restoration would go a long way toward retrieving our cities from further deterioration. It's alarming how many vacant buildings there are. Why is there so much new construction when we already have so many underutilized buildings?

Sam works to improve blighted urban neighborhoods because she believes something should be done about the problem of homelessness. Where housing stock is available, whole neighborhoods can be revitalized. Public transportation is already in place. Schools and shopping centers are nearby. In a neighborhood like Philadelphia's Kensington district, everything is within walking distance. It's unnecessary, and not irreversible, for Kensington or any other neighborhood to suffer such abandonment.

Clearly Sam believes it's a human right to have a decent home. She sees the duty to do something about this as a community responsibility. Sam is also a big booster of the idea that if you're not part of the solution, you're part of the problem: "I think it says a lot for the moral decay of this country that there's no commitment to the citizens. We pay thousands of dollars in taxes, and people sleep on the street. It's just my thing, about vacant houses and people having a decent environment to live in. There's absolutely no reason at all for any environment to be crappy."

Lynda Simmons is also an inspiration as a community-oriented designer. She shares Sam's conviction that people shouldn't have to live in miserable conditions. She also believes that pleasant surroundings are not merely a kindness, but are necessary to human functioning. As she puts it, "Beauty is biologically

> *"The task of architecture is to support and enhance human lives, nothing else whatsoever."*

important. It's absolutely essential for human beings to be in a beautiful environment for their greatest flourishing. A lot of other things are required for human beings to flower; beauty is certainly not enough. But it is extremely important."

Architecture is critical in an urban setting, differing from the country, as it defines the community's whole environment. In New York City, where Lynda worked as a developer, much of the architecture is neither pleasant nor very nourishing. Like Sam, Lynda doesn't accept the prevailing notion that providing a pleasant environment for the poor as part of public housing policy is unrealistic.

Throughout her career, Lynda has held to a broad conception of the definition of design. She emphatically asserts that, "The task of architecture is to support and enhance human lives, nothing else whatsoever." She believes, "Every single space that a human being is in should be nourishing and beautiful. There's no reason that every single space, including the janitor's closet, can *not* be beautiful and nourishing." No matter how unappealing a space may seem to be, Lynda asserts there's always something you can do to improve it. She believes each component of a building should and can promote the inhabitants' feeling that they can develop and grow and feel more vital—that they want to be *alive*.

Lynda has had to overcome strict cost limitations to achieve her goals. Just thinking that beauty is important does not make it a reality in New York. Lynda has successfully found ways to manipulate costs to afford those considerations in her projects. In spite of some of her innovative successes, however, she has had to fight to get her ideas accepted. There is still tremendous resistance to the suggestion that beauty might make economic and social sense in the long run.

For one thing, planning isn't usually done with long-term goals in mind. Further, in large projects like apartment complexes costing millions of dollars of public money, the political considerations become extremely burdensome. Architects and developers find it very difficult to move beyond certain basic assumptions. Any sophisticated analysis of a project's social implications (embodied resources, social and psychological implications of design choices, race, class, gender, and other issues of use and access) will founder long before the first brick is laid.

Many planners and developers don't want to consider these issues. Cost, schedules, and public resistance to offering "extras" to the poor meet with great resistance. There seems to be general hostility toward the poor in this country, with a lot of resentment over tax money used to provide services to low-income people.

Instead, policy makers focus primarily on just grinding out public housing. As Lynda describes it, there is not much commitment to the needs of the people who will live in these buildings: "For many architects, the job is a job. It's a way to pay the salaries and take some profit home. For the housing agencies, it's numbers, so they can show the mayor that they met their quotas. For the mayor, it's, I did so many units of housing. This is how it happens all the time."

Lynda's work affected hundreds if not thousands of people. However, most architects, developers, and designers operate on a much smaller scale and with more modest goals in terms of effecting social change. Yet even small, purely aesthetic considerations can express an underlying commitment to human welfare.

Sandy Seth and Kristina Wilson's elegant houses are perfect examples. Originally Sandy's main reason for building was the joy of doing it. She enjoyed the satisfaction of having created something whole, real, and lasting. She found it rewarding to create something "big." She initially built a house with a couple of friends. Their construction work in the Taos area, however, gradually gave her a much broader understanding of what they were doing.

Sandy and the women she worked with came to realize that what they loved was in danger of extinction. So part of their reason for continuing in the building business and writing a book about adobe architecture was to encourage the continuance of traditional adobe construction in the Southwest. At the time Sandy and her friends Kristina and Valerie were building in the Taos area, a trend was developing toward more modern, mostly frame construction. This trend has continued in recent years, so fewer and fewer structures are built in the old way.

Contemporary adobe construction is a product of the blending of three separate cultures and many generations of architectural tradition. The inherent charm in that history is part of its appeal to Sandy, Kristina, and Valerie. The intertwining cultures and history lends character to adobe houses. They also consider the spe-

cific building material. Nowadays, even where the adobe "look" is retained, it is often done with a thin veneer of stucco over cinder block construction, not with real adobe. This distinction is important to them, not so much as an issue of aesthetic or cultural purity, but for the extent to which it affects how houses "feel." These three women take the impact of their houses on the lives of the residents seriously.

Sandy and her friends admire true adobe architecture because of its gentle, natural character. The appearance of buildings from the outside and how they age over time is also important. Adobe houses don't compete with the landscape but are made of and become part of it. Sandy believes adobe buildings provide richness and peace to those who live in them. She finds adobe "a strong, emotional material which connects one, not only with the earth but also with the past. It is an act, almost, of creating something living."

That people are affected by their surroundings is an observable fact. Just exactly how this works and how it can be manipulated in the details of design is less clear. How can one calculate the effect on people of a room's shape, a window's location, the construction materials used, the placement of a building on its site, the overall dimensions and interior feel of the house, and so on? How can we accommodate different personal desires and expectations about how a house should look?

Rosa Lane is a designer who also cares about these questions. A recent graduate of architecture school, she is eager to make homes and public buildings more responsive to the needs of people who use them. She would like to see building design become less of a trophy for the architects and developers. Her notion of what buildings are all about has grown more sophisticated over the years as her connection to buildings and design has taken such different turns.

Rosa first saw buildings only as objects. She now sees them as part of a social dynamic. She shares Lynda's belief that buildings should support human activity and, like Sandy Seth, she looks at design from a more personal and individual perspective. In addition to beauty, Rosa looks for stimulation and challenge as ingredients of a healthy environment. She says, for example, that a well-designed building provides interaction and surprise as well as rest and comfort. The building should give people choices and should allow them to live their lives with as few restrictions as possible.

"Buildings should be congruent with the environment and with culture itself."

To Rosa, an example of a poorly designed building is one in which a person entering is immediately lost down a long corridor or overwhelmed by its large size or intimidating entryway. Before even using the building, they are hampered by the impact of the structure itself. An office building with predictable cubicles of space, all lined up in neat rows and contained in a huge square box, is another example of poor design— nonconducive to creative, inspired, or efficient work or to the workers' general well-being.

With 80 percent of our lives spent indoors, our architectural environment has a tremendous impact on our lives. Like Lynda, Rosa believes the goal of architecture is to design buildings that enhance rather than diminish our individual well-being as well as the health of the community. Buildings should be "congruent with the environment and with culture itself." Her dream of reopening Hardscrabble Hill reflects the continuing frustration many women feel about the slow pace of change in housing design and an eagerness to be included in decisions affecting where and how women can live.

Internal Affairs

Building a house can raise a variety of emotional and philosophical issues. Some of the women interviewed spoke of deep insights emerging as a result of going through the ordeal or adventure of building. Designing and building a home may stimulate questions about what "home" means. For some, the house which contains us is a metaphor for the place we belong. When we discover the intimate details of how a house is structured and build one of our own, we change the meaning that both "house" and "home" have had for us all our lives.

Control meant different things to these women. Sometimes this aspect of the building experience came out only gradually or indirectly. One of the ways I tried to explore this area was to ask about their dreams. I have a recurring house dream that has intrigued me for years, and I wondered if other women did, too.

My house dreams are usually exploratory. I find myself in an abandoned or empty space that I have just discovered and that I am contemplating living in. Sometimes I'm in rooms in my parents house, way up in the attic, that I didn't know were there before. In other dreams, I'm in a different house, and I am as concerned with how much I will like the outside and the surrounding yard as I am with evaluating the inside rooms. I think of these dream houses as a metaphor that I am exploring neglected parts of myself. The

dreaming mind may be uncovering or inventing new possibilities or probing the boundaries and limitations of current patterns. Since houses are both "home" and "container," these dreams are useful images and tools for psychological analysis, whether real or not.

Many, though not all, of the women interviewed reported having dreams about houses. Often, they were houses the women had grown up in, not houses they were building or hoped to build. Some dreams were of frustration or of loss and confusion. One woman dreamed of houses made of glass, a kind of crystal palace filled with light. Oceanlight's dreams are exploratory like mine. Many of her house dreams are about staircases. She described them this way: "I think they're about moving around inside myself. Different parts of myself. I go up. I go down. I look for things. I forget where I am. I try to get somewhere. Sometimes I get there and sometimes I don't."

Sandy Seth reported dreams of an old house she lived in as a young child. It was a rambling, multilevel structure with things going on at each level. In her dream, she is aware of parts of the house she never fully understood at the time. The house was torn down years ago, so there's no way of comparing her memories with her adult understanding of spaces, particularly as it has changed as a result of designing and building. She mourns the loss of that house and wonders about its

> *"I really think that on a physical, emotional, and spiritual level we build our nest. Just in a physical sense, I have arranged my home to suit who I am."*

place in her imagination. She feels it might be "the basis for this continual need that I have to re-create and to build."

Thoughts like this make us wonder when we acquire the urge to build. Is it when we first become aware of the spaces we live in? Is this why playing house (or in the case of boys, building forts) is so common? At what point do we notice spaces as not merely stages for action, but as entities that have the power to shape action? When do we first want to manipulate these spaces? Why do houses and the various spaces that contain us matter more to some people than to others?

Building one's own house can do more than confer a sense of power or safety. It can also satisfy a fundamental emotional need. The urge to make a home, to settle into a place, and to personalize it seems to originate at a deeper level than control over the external world. Some of these women used a nest metaphor. Gail Atkins used it to describe how she feels about her house: "I really think that on a physical, emotional, and spiritual level we build our nest. Just in a physical sense, I have arranged my home to suit who I am."

Valerie Graves also mentioned a nest when she described Kristina's house as the product of successive building spurts. "Something about spring brings out this building urge. Every spring, everybody wants to add on a room. It's crazy. Like birds or something, the urge to make a nest. Kristina's house is a fabulous example of how wonderful it can be when you just add on. It's an unplanned, spontaneous, very old-feeling house. This friend of mine from the Taos Pueblo told me they call her The Swallow."

Some of the women I interviewed talked about wrestling with the meaning that building and designing held for them. Sometimes this required resolving conflicting emotions. Others wanted to build but felt

pulled in different directions, blocking action. Rosa Lane, for example, enjoyed carpentry but also saw herself as a poet. However, she couldn't get herself into the right frame of mind for writing poetry when she was building the cabins at Hardscrabble Hill. While she was building, Rosa said, "the aesthetic side of me, or the part that was itching for metaphor, would . . . kind of wizzle up." One day a friend described her as an "architectural muse." She liked that idea and searched for a way to turn it into action. Becoming an architect seemed like the perfect solution, since it is, at its best, the fusion of building and imagination.

> *"By far the most critical requirement for them is perseverance."*

Different personality traits come into play when building a house. This is especially true for amateur builders. By far the most critical requirement for them is perseverance. Some would call it stubbornness, or determination, or single-mindedness. Given the magnitude of such an undertaking, there will be a lot of hard work and frustrating setbacks throughout the project. If women lack the technical training and physical skills many men have, they can compensate with an ability to lock onto a goal and not let go. These women usually described this as an attribute that they brought to their work, not something they learned. Indecision can be crippling, but once it is overcome, women have found that shear dogged determination can get them through when all other resources have been exhausted.

Almost every woman interviewed declared they did not know what they were getting into when they started. In almost all cases, their projects took more time, money, and hard work than they had anticipated. Getting through the stress when money got tight and energy flagged was as much a part of the accomplishment as the creation of the house itself.

Having gone through this process once, some women elected to go through it again. Sandy Seth described, not entirely tongue-in-cheek, how she managed to keep taking on larger and larger projects: "I think the main ingredient in my ability to do it over and over like that is based on this terrible memory that I have. This really bad memory. I do not remember what it was like when I was having to do the roof [on an 1,800-square-foot house]. It was like roofing an ocean. And I was putting down the tar, and I was putting down the paper and the insulation. Over and over, blackness upon blackness upon blackness. And then what did I do but launch right into another house. Because I did not remember how bad it was roofing in that ocean up there."

The days and weeks that seemed to drag on forever are often compressed when we look back on the building experience. It's natural for our unpleasant memories to fade with time. Sandy says there will always be one or two pieces that are just left out of her memory of a project. It might be the roofing on one job, cement work on another. Or it might be the endless hauling of heavy adobe bricks in the blistering summer heat. Although she thinks there's something slightly wrong with forgetting the difficult work, she believes it does enable us to persist and to survive.

Carolyn Geise also speaks of perseverance and survival, but in her case being self-sufficient was not something she chose to do. She had no sense of her own capabilities, either as a young woman or in the early years of her career. She survived because she "had to," as many divorced women must. The need to earn money to support her son comfortably was her incentive to take her career seriously.

Carolyn transformed herself from a dependent, self-effacing person into a confident, accomplished architect and business owner. She may have initiated this out of necessity, but she found the strength to do it within herself. She was clear that ambition had nothing to do with it. Given a choice, she would have picked an easier path. However, she persisted in building her self-confidence and a successful career: "I've always been persistent. Persistence is my biggest thing. It hasn't been because I'm goal-oriented, though. Because I do *not* know how to set goals. And that's been the most frustrating thing for me. When I was growing up, your goal was always to find a husband and settle down and have a family. I mean, that *was* the goal. And so, all the work I did before was sort of just something to do until I was married."

While confident of her capabilities now, Carolyn is still somewhat self-deprecating when recounting her progress and is reluctant to take credit for it. She prayed extensively during the period following her divorce and insists that luck and her deep religious faith were what enabled her to pull herself together. "And then it just all worked out from there. I'm really grateful I had the push. Because I don't think—I mean, there's no question that I wouldn't be where I am today without having had some real pushes. Because I wasn't oriented to pursuing goals and didn't have the courage to do it."

Building represents a certain control over the external world. The experience of building sets an example that many people carry over to other parts of their lives. For both men and women, there are a vast number of things that are out of their control. We live in a world that is alienating and often threatening. Our lives are filled with circumstances and events over which we have little say. As women, we are not raised to build or design houses, but we are certainly raised to believe that our homes are important and central to our lives. So taking control of our houses is partially taking control of our lives.

Dale McCormick saw building as a way of healing and nurturing herself at a time when she needed to do that. For her, the issue was not of gaining control but of changing its focus. Her need for control in her life changed when she built her own house and took stock of her emotional needs. "When I decided to build my house, I think that was a metaphor for taking care of myself. Not a metaphor. It was a big way of taking care of myself, in a way that I had never done before." It was a pivotal point in her life. At the same time she was building her house, she experienced a huge personal growth spurt. For one year, her entire focus was on building and personal development.

In retrospect, Dale saw that control was a big issue for her. The way she has lived could be characterized as constantly trying to master the physical world. She identified this as an ACOA (Adult Children of Alcoholics) trait. She first learned how to do routine maintenance on her truck. She then learned carpentry, started her own business, and eventually built her own house. This was all to gain competence so that her physical environment was never out of her control. Only then did she realize that it was important, not just to "accomplish" things or to be the Responsible Child, but to look inside,

> *"When I decided to build my house, I think that was a metaphor for taking care of myself."*

search for her feelings, and learn how to feel them again.

Dale's self-image was altered during the time she built her two houses. However, she was reluctant to ascribe it all to the self-confidence she gained by building. Many changes took place in her life during that period. It was at that point that she decided to run for the state senate. Politics had been a lifelong goal for Dale. Her high-school yearbook predicted that she would be the first "lady vice president." Though she does not aspire to the vice presidency, she has harbored political ambitions for many years. Even so, she didn't feel ready to launch her political campaign until after building two houses.

In fact, Dale realized that she had been stalling for some time before she finally took the plunge in 1990. Evidently she was putting up more internal resistance to her political debut than she was encountering from other people; her friends were actually encouraging and were impressed by her success. People often ask her how she did it. She asks herself, "Is it the accomplishment—taking in that I had accomplished such a big thing as that? As building a house so that I could have the self-esteem—we're talking about self-esteem here—to think that I could serve thirty-five thousand people well in the Senate?"

Confidence

The issue of self-confidence often comes up for women who do nontraditional work. It is not surprising, then, that it's an issue for women builders. As women, we do not grow up with the expectation that housebuilding is something we can do. In order to do it, we have to change our self-image somewhere along the way. Some women gain confidence first and then build. But many start their building projects in spite of profound insecurities. They gain confidence little by little as they go. But it isn't easy and it isn't automatic. Rosa Lane had a lot of confidence in herself from an early age. However, she learned when building and running Hardscrabble Hill that many women lack confidence in themselves and are seriously handicapped as a result. She referred to it as the "missing ingredient" for most women.

Although Rosa's father always had tremendous confidence in her, her mother sent the opposite message. She thinks her mother didn't have much confidence in herself, particularly to do things that were new and different. That insecurity was projected onto Rosa and undermined the self-confidence she was developing when she helped her father around the house and with his fishing. Remembering what it was like when she was a child has made Rosa think about how women learn. "Those of us who don't have confidence in ourselves then do not have confidence in other women. Some of this I saw when I was building Hardscrabble Hill and discovered other women, even in the local women's community, not having confidence that we could do it. And that lack of confidence makes us much more vulnerable to criticism. I see the fearing to take a risk as the biggest culprit to women's sense of power and our ability to do things."

Dale McCormick pointed out another aspect of carpentry and building. "Carpentry is problem solving continually. And you cannot solve problems if you are berating yourself for causing them. You know, like, 'I'm too weak,' or, 'I'm too stupid. How come I didn't know that?' You know, you go to pull out a nail and it doesn't come, and you say, 'I'm too weak.' Well, that is not the problem. The answer is not inside anywhere. The answer is in the work."

Perhaps because we haven't been encouraged to believe we can do things like carpentry, it's easy for us to blame ourselves for every failure. At the same time that we are trying to prove we aren't limited by stereotypical female behavior, we are ready, just under the surface, to give up the uncomfortable alternative. Even being able to distinguish between the discomfort of an

> *"The biggest hurdle in building is taking that first step into the unknown."*

unfamiliar role and the frustration of being blocked at a task is often difficult. Rather than face the difficulty, we often collapse at the first obstacle and conclude that we are not up to it.

Dale has invented a mental gimmick for dealing with this. She goes into what she calls her "carpentry alpha state." It's a very calm level of problem solving which suppresses the sense of panic or the impulse to throw a tantrum. She takes control of her reactions. Then she figures out what is causing the problem. She looks at the work, not at herself. She looks at the nail or turns the board over, considering whether the nail is bent over on the back or is cement-coated. Once she has determined the cause of the problem, she calmly and logically decides what to do about it. For Dale, it's not so much a matter of being good at analyzing a problem as it is getting into the right frame of mind.

Women blame themselves for external problems and become discouraged with their tasks. Many women describe feelings of inadequacy when they make a mistake or run into an obstacle at work. Men are given different strategies to deal with obstacles, such as blaming a tool, some material, or someone else for a problem. Trying to prove you can do "men's work" when others are saying you can't is harder when a voice inside you says, "You're no good. You can't do this!" Learning to turn the board over and investigating the problem is critical.

For many women, the biggest hurdle in building is taking that first step into the unknown. Daring to try something new, especially when you feel very insecure, is very difficult without encouragement. Those of us who teach carpentry to women know that lack of confidence is often much more of a handicap than the lack of any specific technical skill related to building. Discovering that they can handle things they thought were beyond their control sometimes comes as a revelation to many women.

My students often say, "Wow! This is really *simple!*" or, "Is *that* all there is to it?" and especially, "Even *I* could do *that.*" Carpentry and building are unfamiliar to most women. They assume it must be very complicated and difficult. They don't know the names of the tools they'll have to use, let alone how to use them—an intimidating prospect. When women do learn basic carpentry and work on a housebuilding project, they discover the tasks are no more difficult than the tasks of any new endeavor. Women speak of the experience of building as taking the mystique away from "men's work" for them. This discovery has a profound impact on some women, changing their self-image in important ways. As Oceanlight puts it, "I feel more of a match for men and the world, knowing I can do things that people think only men do." Men often take traditional knowledge for granted. Those who are handy with tools already know how simple the simple skills are. But such specialized knowledge is mysterious to a novice.

Debrin Cox, just by fixing up the tiny tool shed she initially lived in, was excited because she had never done anything like that before. She was thrilled to discover how much she could do. Even though she didn't build her cabin right away, she had a sense of progress. However, she discovered that her feelings of competence increased in fits and starts. It was not an intellectual process. The confidence grew out of her experience of actually doing the work: "The pictures in the books and all the line drawings of how to build structures don't quite take it into my body for me," she said.

Picking up a tool and starting to use it triggers the surge of confidence that moves women forward. There's just nothing like it. Being told you can do something is not the same as feeling it with your own muscles and seeing it with your own eyes. And anyone who can operate a sewing machine can operate a jigsaw. After making that first cut with a saw, it's like a veil has lifted—now they *know*.

The awesome size of a housebuilding project is a large stumbling block for many women's self-confidence as well. A very large task isn't necessarily more difficult in any of its parts than a small one, but the magnitude and the mystery of something as complicated as a house is intimidating. For many women the shear size of construction is a major deterrent. Any endeavor, whether it's building or something else, usually gets easier further along in the project. Those first steps may be tentative, but for every job there comes a point when you have to throw yourself into it and

"*Being told you can do something is not the same as feeling it with your own muscles and seeing it with your own eyes.*"

either sink or swim. Then our successes encourage us to take a chance the next time.

The next big lesson is learning to not give up. The first obstacle, the first major frustration can wipe out some of this new confidence. Those old messages spinning around in our heads are hard to obliterate completely. So we find we have to relearn confidence. Debrin's first spurt of carpentry wasn't enough to carry her through the whole building process. In spite of the power of the experience, many women find their self-confidence slips away and has to be regained. Debrin reached a point where she realized both how much she knew and how much she didn't know. There was more to it than she first thought as she renovated her little shed. But there wasn't so much to it that she couldn't build a whole cabin with a little help and a lot of time.

Rosa Lane believes common sense and motivation are the basic skills of building. With those skills, you can teach yourself the rest and you won't go far wrong. In learning to construct buildings, Rosa says, we draw on an intuitive understanding of structure that comes from knowing our own bodies. In order to walk, we must be square, level, and plumb. Our bodies are structures subject to the same principles of gravity, torque, leverage, and weatherproofing as a house. In a sense, our body is a house in which we dwell. We start with that knowledge and add to it as we learn the specifics of house construction.

What's wonderful, and confidence-building, about construction is that it is so solid. Every woman I've talked to who has built a house or who works in the building trades has commented on how "concrete" building is. Once you've built something, it is external to you. It's out there as objective proof of your accomplishment. It's solid and permanent. It even takes on a life of its own. Women prone to belittling their own accomplishments, or making excuses for their success because they have a hard time seeing themselves as competent people, discover that building a house can turn that around.

The incredible aspect of building a house is that the reality and magnitude of what you've done is visible immediately. You can see what you've accomplished at the end of each day in a very dramatic and visual way. There's a wall today where there was empty space yesterday, a roof today where there was only sky, a door where there was a hole in the wall. Things may go wrong along the way and the house may or may not be there a hundred years from now, but it's likely to last a very long time. This is a sharp contrast to the work many women do in traditionally female jobs. A building doesn't "go away." It isn't filed and forgotten. It doesn't pass unnoticed in a stream of similar products. It isn't lost in the shuffle of bureaucracy or belittled as frivolous or unnecessary by people with greater power or authority. Whatever ideas you may have about what you're doing, the solid reality of it is undeniable.

Take-Home Pay

When women list the rewards of building and designing, the most frequently mentioned are the sense of control, the increase or renewed self-confidence, the exhilarating challenges, and the satisfaction of standing back and seeing such tangible proof of their capabilities.

As girls, many of us were taught not to be physical in general. Yet handling building materials is central to the satisfaction of building. It's not just the idea of building that makes it fun. The actual labor, though strenuous, satisfies a deep human need for physical connectedness with the world. Outside of sports, this represents a rare opportunity for women to be physically exuberant.

Many women expressed a desire to be immersed in a totally engrossing and worthwhile activity, finding the overwhelming aspect of building attractive. This is ambitious for women. We are taught from an early age to think in terms of making small things—needlework, crafts, cooking, painting, gardening, and so on. A house is a very large object as well as a large undertaking. Women often want to rebel and break out of the limitations of "small," to strive for freedom from confinement and for a sense of accomplishment. House-building also entails opportunities to make choices and be in control of a long series of related events. Being responsible for so many decisions, often under pressure, can be very gratifying and enriching.

Ambition is, however, considered somewhat

> *"Women often want to rebel and break out of the limitations of 'small,' to strive for freedom from confinement and for a sense of accomplishment."*

unfeminine. Many of us feel the need to downplay our accomplishments, so it's very rewarding when our activities generate praise from the people around us. Several women described their experiences as validating. A change in how they perceived themselves was sometimes matched by a change in how they were evaluated by other people. Building a house is a very conspicuous activity. You can accomplish a lot at your job or in the privacy of your own home without attracting attention, but building a house is something everyone can see. Far from stimulating criticism, though, it often results in a boost in status. Women sometimes find they are taken more seriously by friends and neighbors. People are impressed by the feat that amateur building

> *"Being responsible for so many decisions can be very gratifying."*

"I'm a more substantial woman than I was when I started."

represents. It's not only a big project, it's also a mature and responsible one. It earns respect. Some women said their families didn't support them strongly. Several said their families didn't understand why they wanted to build, but overall, when their houses were finished most found their accomplishments impressed the people around them.

Pat Liddle said it felt particularly good to have strangers stop by to watch her while she was building. It helped her to keep going, knowing that people took notice of what she was doing. Even when it was all done and she was living in the house, she still got a charge out of occasionally surprising people. When she was hired for her current job as an insurance adjuster, the branch manager wanted to meet her because he had never met a woman carpenter before. That felt good, too: "It's funny. You know, you tell people that you built your own house, they think you mean you hired somebody to build your house. You say, 'I built my house,' and they'll say, 'That's nice.' They don't get it right away. Then you talk a little bit and they realize what you mean, and they'll say, 'Oh, *you* built your house!' Then they get it. Then they understand it."

The recognition you receive for building a house goes beyond the glow of pleasure you feel when someone praises what you have done. Having once built, you know you could do it again. You know you are capable of organizing a large project. You now have equity in valuable property. Owning a house you have built is very different from owning a house you have bought. You not only hold legal title to it, you understand every inch of it inside and out. You can diagnose and repair anything that goes wrong with it because you put it together in the first place. You know that you can add onto it or remodel it. You know the house's strengths and its weaknesses. You know why every part of it is the way it is. This gives you a powerful degree of control over your environment, as well as pride. There are no mysteries at home to intimidate you. The mystique of constructing houses is gone. There is also a very real financial security that comes with owning property. You may end up thinking of your house not only as your nest but also your nest egg. As Dale McCormick

describes it: "I'm a more substantial woman than I was when I started. And I mean substantial in the world. I'm more economically independent because I did that."

Interviewing women at various stages of building and designing served as a reminder that each step is unique. In retelling their stories it is easy to lump the entire experience into one big event. But the reality is not experienced that way. The beginning, middle, and end of each project require different energy and strategies. The obstacles that confront a builder at different phases of the work cannot be handled by the same response.

When Debrin Cox and Oceanlight were first interviewed, none of the cabins they had planned had been built. At first, it seemed there wasn't much to talk about. But after listening to them, it became clear that the beginning stages of a building venture, particularly when the builder is stuck at that stage, is a story itself. Lost momentum is a universal problem, no matter what the undertaking. How people handle it, what it means to them, how they redirect their energies to unblock the process, is valuable information.

Debrin spoke eloquently about the need to pay as much attention to those first halting steps as to finishing the project. The letdown after the initial excitement of a new venture begins to wear off when the end is nowhere in sight. It's a very difficult stage to get through. Debrin used to assume that people with carpentry skills had no problem with that initial period. But she learned that it's hard for everyone to get over that hump. Lacking skill and confidence simply made it even more difficult for her and Oceanlight. When they became stuck in the early phase, they were at a loss as to how to proceed. Living in cramped and uncomfortable conditions also slowed them down. They needed to build in order to be more comfortable, but they needed to be more comfortable in order to build.

When she turned for inspiration to books about people who built their own houses, Debrin felt that they were able to separate themselves from the other parts of their lives in order to do the building. If not, they were able to hire other people to do the work. Debrin could not figure out how you could hold a job, run your life, and still have time to build a house.

Then Debrin received a flyer in the mail from an owner-builder school. It contained an interview with an elderly couple who had built their own house. There was a picture of the woman hauling brush through the woods to clear the building site at the very beginning. Debrin stared and stared at the picture. She said, "Yes!! That's what we need to see. It's not enough to see a house under construction once the framing is up or the headers are going in. There is so much more that has to happen before you even get that far. How important those beginning steps are, that we don't give validation to. You don't see any finished product. You don't really see much progress. I look at that wood pile as progress. But when you want to be cuddling up in your cabin, it's hard to remember that this is getting us there."

In addition to the general ego boost that building produces, there are some less dramatic but important skills that are acquired or honed by the work. Problem-solving techniques, patience, common sense, physical strength, and spatial perspective were among those mentioned by the women interviewed. It's difficult to sort out what they brought to the building process and what they took away from it. They may have discovered skills they didn't know they had until they found themselves applying them to building. The demands of building sometimes forced them to develop new skills.

"I look at that wood pile as progress. But when you want to be cuddling up in your cabin, it's hard to remember that this is getting us there."

Dale McCormick, for instance, believes carpentry taught her patience. She thinks that carpentry demands it—that you learn patience when building because you have to. It's true that rushing things often results in mistakes. The maxim, "measure twice and cut once" is a very good one. All carpenters learn that a mistake on paper is much easier to fix than one that's already built. Having to rip out a whole wall or stop work to replace the last piece of lumber you just miscut is a pretty good motivator for learning patience. The physical dangers involved in construction work also eventually temper rash behavior.

For Rosa Lane, an important benefit gained from building was the way it reinforced common sense. The foundation of her experience was laid in childhood with the make-do approach to problem solving she learned. Since the family couldn't afford to hire a plumber or an electrician, they had to trust their own abilities to figure things out. She mentioned that in doing carpentry, you often have to come up with quick responses. Catching something that is about to fall or seeing that something isn't going to work requires spontaneous, common-sense action. This ability is honed with experience. Common sense—generalizing from what you *do* know in order to solve the problem—is a starting point when learning a new trade. Creativity combined with common sense add up to resourcefulness, an important survival skill.

Building her house completely changed how Valerie Graves viewed her ability to tackle any kind of large undertaking. It was actually her divorce that led to the challenge of building her house. She was told she couldn't build her own house, and that made her so mad she decided to do it to prove that she could. Although it took a tremendous amount of backbreaking labor, it turned out to be a very healing experience. She said, "All my anger drained away as I worked

"On some deep level it [building] gave me a real true sense of myself as capable."

toward completion." She didn't anticipate this but is glad for the insight it gave her. Now she thinks she could do almost anything if she put the same effort and energy into it that she put into building her house.

Most of the women said the confidence they gained from building expanded to include feeling self-sufficient in general. They felt they had acquired a skill they could always fall back on. No matter how bad the economy or where their lives took them, they would always be able to take care of themselves and their home. They could even earn a living as carpenters if necessary. Gail Atkins summed up the feelings of those women who did not grow up with a strong self-image: "On some deep level it [building] gave me a real true sense of myself as capable. I think that's something I missed in childhood, because I definitely had an overly critical mother. I think that sent me into adulthood with a real inferiority complex. Being able to build this house and do what I've done here on this farm has pretty much obliterated that."

For some of these women, there was yet another dimension to the feeling of inner strength. Not only did they get something from their contact with building, but they left something behind. A part of themselves was incorporated in the houses they built. Ronnie Sandler commented on the sense of connectedness she felt for her house: "I love my house. It's very much who I am. I really feel like I am in this house, that my essence is in this house." Gail Atkins described how meaningful that connection can be: "I like the shape of this space. There's something important to me about this high ceiling, the way your spirits are drawn upward by this shape. And I have pieces of furniture around me that mean something to me. And this is . . . I love this house. My heart and my soul are in this place."

"My heart and my soul are in this place."

Collaboration

Several of the women profiled built and designed projects in collaboration with other people. For some, the shared venture was joyful and exciting. For others, the collaborative process made the work more complicated and introduced an element of stress that was greater, perhaps, than the stress of managing alone. In any case, it is a different kind of stress. It's a different experience when it is shared.

Decision-making can be confusing and complicated for one person working alone. It is even more complicated when it becomes a kind of public process and must be coordinated with other people's requirements. It is especially difficult when the people who work together don't see eye-to-eye. When unequal levels of time, money, and skills are contributed, there must be a mechanism that leaves each partner satisfied with a fair distribution. The pace and quality of work, the long-range goals, the hundreds of little decisions that must be made daily when building a house all require teamwork. This is a social skill quite apart from the technical skills needed to construct a building.

Housebuilding is notorious for breaking up marriages. Whether the marriages break down under the stress of building or whether the stress of maintaining an already fragile relationship makes building an excessively painful process is not always clear. Building, or any other significant upheaval, can be the event that tips the balance in a relationship. There is no doubt that building a house is a major disruption of people's routines.

However, there's good news, too. A joint venture can yield unexpected rewards. New insights may be sparked by the friction of conflicting personalities or by the pleasures of a powerful shared experience.

When women build together they bring their own unique strategies and responses. There is a serious shortage of role models to give us information about what to expect. Though our circumstances are varied,

"Collaboration requires relinquishing some measure of independence and control."

we know that other women have been through this before. But our history books, our television programs, our movies, our teachers, our cultural storytellers fail to tell us much about how women accomplish joint activities. Until there is more information available, women must create their own opportunities to share with each other what it means to work together, design together, and build together.

The most obvious reason for joint efforts is to share the burden. The bigger and riskier the task, the more reassuring it is to have someone else to count on. A second reason for collaborative ventures is the pleasure of intensified companionship. A person who observes or shares our experiences becomes a witness to our life, understanding our victories and appreciating the nuances of our pain. We are *known*, we are not invisible, and our interpretation of reality is tacitly confirmed.

When collaboration works, it's extremely gratifying. The sense of shared adventure, of working shoulder-to-shoulder with your partners, the stimulation of other ideas put to a common purpose—all of these make collaboration appealing. However, it doesn't always work so well—partners might disagree or personalities might clash. Collaboration requires relinquishing some measure of independence and control.

Gender is an issue in collaborative efforts. Some women saw their cooperative building projects as experiments in changing how they worked with other people. Feminist ideology was the basis for several working arrangements. The formation of a team was viewed as purely expedient for some. What these women expected and how events actually played themselves out were often very different.

Debrin Cox and Oceanlight's arrangement depended on cooperation on many levels. In addition to joint decisions about the design and placement of their cabins, they negotiated and maintained the shared

main house, the use of the land, and living arrangements by consensus.

Debrin described their decision-making process as very structured. They held regular house meetings during which they could each express their feelings, needs, resentments, hopes, and fears in a safe environment. They learned a lot through this process, but it never became easy. It was cumbersome and time consuming to express their ideas and feelings about every decision. The alternative, however, was a hierarchy of power they were unwilling to accept. They don't regret their choice, but they recognize that it takes skill and practice to make it work. The experience of going through three housebuilding projects simultaneously has changed Debrin's attitude about consensus as a basis for group decisions. She is more aware of its limitations and its cost in time and emotional commitment.

Now that the cabins have all been built, Debrin's attitude is very positive. However, when I first interviewed her in 1985, she was not having a whole lot of fun. She said, "I know I have expectations that it's supposed to be this glorious time of my life. I mean, holy shit, I'm finally building a house! I'm building a house with other women. It's supposed to be wonderful. But . . . I mean, what part of it's been wonderful? Yeah, it's work, but it's got to be fun, too. This has just been real frustrating."

Oceanlight's mood has also changed since she built her cabin. Her ideas about how to design her cabin were influenced by the experience of trying to work through conflicts with her partners in the early stages of the project. She began to think in terms of providing herself with more privacy and more separateness from her partners. She saw that their time with one another would be improved if it was balanced by time to be alone. She said, "I really like living with other people, despite all this stuff. I like coming home and things are different from when I left. There's a note on the table, or there are groceries in the refrigerator. But I do need a lot of my own space. I want to have a setup in my own cabin where I can at least fix my own breakfast, so I can get up in the morning and not have to interact with people before I leave for the day."

It was not an easy goal to fulfill. Oceanlight saw the group dynamic as precarious at times. The radical feminist model of consensus for planning and decision making was useful, but it was exhausting. They used this model to deal with both personal conflicts and the purely external building-related decisions that had to

"I know I have expectations that it's supposed to be this glorious time of my life."

be made. Consensus decision making is not common practice in this society, and they had little previous experience with it.

Eventually, Debrin, Oceanlight, and their partner, Kim, resolved their differences and agreed on when, where, and how the cabins should be built. Oceanlight was able to leave her land and move to New Mexico with a sense of closure and fulfillment. Having moved back into her cabin after that absence makes the building experience a bittersweet memory of a remote and different time.

Carol Yee, Michelle Giffin, and Christine Acebo also had their share of differing opinions while building the Connecticut triplex. Carol and Michelle had the most difficulty, and their friendship was on shaky ground for awhile. But both of them expressed confidence that they would be able to restore goodwill eventually.

Christine reports mixed feelings about the arrangement. She is comfortable with it, but it is not what she would have chosen if she'd had more options at the time. Her reservations are somewhat different than Carol's or Michelle's. Christine was the least

inspired by the idea of building her own house and is the least invested in it emotionally. She needed a place to live and couldn't afford to buy one. She'd rather have lived alone, or at least with only one other person. However, the sacrifice of mobility and privacy represented by the triplex seemed worth the value of owning her own place and getting a house tailored to her taste. She did what she could to ensure as much privacy as possible and argued for the features of the house that were important to her.

Social skills are just as important as technical skills. When disagreements aren't resolved, there's a cost. An enormous amount of energy is used in fighting these battles. While they are going on, people often lose their perspective. At the time, it seems important to get your own way—after all, this is going to be your home for years and years. The triplex project is fairly typical in that each woman suffered some disappointments even though they have managed to feel generally positive about it overall. They all had to adjust their expectations to fit circumstances none of them had experienced before.

> *"They looked at conflict as a steppingstone to change. Conflict is stimulating. It challenges our assumptions and prods us into creative thinking."*

Interestingly enough, Christine says she has gradually become much better about handling conflict. But it has been through therapy, not through the evolution of their group process. From Christine's perspective, building the house was just another thing to get through in life. She wouldn't say that it was any more of a learning experience than others in her life.

The building partnership went much more smoothly for Sandy Seth and Kristina Wilson. For one thing, they weren't living together. Also, their personalities, values, and ideas about how things should be done were more compatible. In fact, they don't seem to have had any friction at all. They were stimulated by each other's suggestions, found comfortable ways to divide up the various tasks, and generally enjoyed each other's company.

The key to all this, as far as Sandy is concerned, is the fact that they were working to please only themselves. They were doing it to have fun. It was an adventure for them. They never got themselves into a frame of mind where they felt trapped. There was nobody to tell them what to do. Each of them had somewhere else to live—they weren't waiting to move in, nor did they have to live in the middle of a construction site. So they neither had to follow orders nor live with their mistakes. There was no one to be disappointed. Since they were building a house on speculation, the house would be sold to someone who wanted what they saw.

Although spec building is risky, Sandy says she prefers it to having a client. She isn't the least bit interested in working for someone else. The joy for her came in being able to give free rein to her creative imagination and to work at her own pace, in her own style, using the materials she preferred. Since Sandy and Kristina got along so well, I could understand why they would want to keep it that way. Sandy said, "I guess it's incredibly selfish to want to be a loner like that. I haven't wanted to

hire a crew or even to teach other women as apprentices. I just wanted to do my own thing."

Rosa Lane's experience of working with other people was also largely pleasant. The three-way partnership that established and ran Hardscrabble Hill lasted for seven years. Each of the partners came from different backgrounds and contributed a different mix of skills, talents, and work styles. Rosa says that they seemed to complement each other very well and felt they were all part of a team. This isn't to say there wasn't ever frustration and conflict, but they established a process that worked for them. Though it was very intense at times, they never allowed resentments to build. Whenever there was a problem they stopped what they were doing and attended to it immediately. Giving immediate attention to complaints, careful listening, and remembering to acknowledge the larger picture were the three main ingredients in their success. During development of Hardscrabble Hill, they came to view each other's frustration as an opportunity to "revision" their work or their goals. They looked at conflict as a steppingstone to change. Conflict is stimulating. It challenges our assumptions and prods us into creative thinking.

Pat Liddle's experience provides yet another perspective on collaboration. She did most of the actual work on her house alone. However, her friend Clint came by to help her some of the time and to give her advice when she ran into problems. Since he knew much more about building than she did, his role was almost that of a supervisor. For the most part, this arrangement worked very well. Knowing she had someone to lean on gave Pat the confidence to attempt to build her own house. But conflicts did arise, and the ambiguity over who was in charge sometimes made it difficult to resolve them. Tensions arose when Pat questioned his judgment. She wanted to finish the house, but she wanted it done right. Being stubborn and independent, Pat needed to have everything explained to her. Sometimes she could get Clint to justify his directions. Sometimes there was yelling and screaming. It was usually Pat who took on the responsibility of repairing any damage and smoothing things over. When she didn't have the energy for it, they'd end up having an argument.

Another problem for Pat was that Clint wasn't around all the time. Sometimes he would leave for a week at a time to go visit relatives or attend to his own business. At the time this was extremely frustrating for her. In retrospect, Pat sees the value in it. She discovered that she could manage things on her own. When she ran into a problem or was faced with a task she didn't

"Asking questions was the key to working with other people."

know how to do, she had no one to lean on. The situation forced her to rely on her own intelligence and common sense and to be resourceful. It's easier to have someone around to tell you what to do, but Pat discovered that you learn more when you have to figure it out yourself: "The nice thing about not having him around was that I didn't turn to him. If there was something I didn't know how to do or didn't think I knew how to do, I said, 'Now, wait a minute. I bet I can figure this out.' Because when somebody's there, you just automatically go and ask. You don't even *think* about the fact that you could do this if you wanted to." Besides boosting her self-confidence, Pat also found that asking questions was the key to working with other people. Knowing she could manage on her own made Pat both more patient and more confident being part of a team.

The Question of Men

The question of men—or of men building versus women building—is really three questions: What does it feel like for women to do work that is publicly defined as men's work? Do men and women work differently; do they have different work styles, attitudes, strategies, and ways of relating to the materials or tools at hand? Do women design different types of structures than men?

The women I interviewed had very different attitudes toward the gender issues raised by engaging in nontraditional work. It's a complicated issue and frequently plagued with misunderstanding. Many, but not all, of them would probably be considered feminists. However, that label itself means different things to different people. Each woman I spoke to was at a different point along her own individual path of sorting out these things for herself. One's perspective changes over time, and not always in sync with those around you. Many women have experienced the frustration of being perceived by other people very differently from how they view themselves.

Building and designing houses contains some obvious pitfalls in the gendered terrain of our lives. This is particularly true for women who become professional carpenters. Dale McCormick pointed to the impulse for women to try and fit in: "When you're working with the boys, I think you want to be 'one of the boys' inasmuch as you want to be accepted. You don't want to have the constant stress of being weird and different and harassed."

Even so, Dale was aware she wanted to do things differently from the way men did them. She didn't think people should be as cruel to each other, for instance, as construction workers seemed to be. She didn't want to have to be as macho as they were "as to step into icy water one day up to your knees and not go home and change your clothes, just continue working in ten-degree weather."

When she was in the union, the issue of gender was a big one for Dale. She used to say she had "sex-gender identification problems," meaning she felt uneasy about both her sexual identity and her gender role. She says she never thought of herself as a woman but as a person. When she first worked as a carpenter, wearing men's clothes all the time, she felt she was in the garb of a "nonfemale-type person." It made her remaining ambivalence about her femininity even more confusing.

It takes a lot of courage to believe your own per-ceptions in a society that denies so much of your value as a woman to begin with. Many of us feel the stress of this conflict and are profoundly uncomfortable. The popularization of the women's movement in the early 1970s gave many support and a vocabulary to deal with all this. But it remains a very personal and lonely battle.

Dale, like others in this predicament, longed for moments when she could feel normal. Doing carpentry and construction intensified the childhood confusion over male versus female behavior. She felt that doing "men's work" did not allow her female side to grow, because she believed that being female in the construction world was to admit defeat. If women can't do it, then success meant not acting like a woman.

In some ways, working in male-identified jobs forces us to confront these gender issues more honestly and directly than women who, though uncomfortable with society's dictates, hide behind conventional appearance and behavior.

"They're setting the standard. And if you're just learning, how do you know? Their standard is the only standard that you know."

Dale, like many other women, finds this extremely frustrating: "You're never going to be one of the boys. I just tried—I can't say that I learned to not try to be one of the boys. Because it's just hard not to buy into that having to prove yourself stuff. They're setting the standard. And if you're just learning, how do you know? Their standard is the only standard that you know."

It's very tempting to think you *have* to be accepted by male coworkers, even when you know you never will be, no matter how strong or how competent you are. Some men simply do not want women to cross that line and invade their territory. It isn't a matter of meeting their standards in order to get their acceptance. The sexual harassment and disparagement that women encounter in construction work may be partly based on men's underlying fear that their sexual identity is challenged by this female invasion and that their economic security is threatened by women's increased access to the better paying jobs men now monopolize. However, much of it may come from a fear of change. Women in men's roles upset some very basic assumptions, and that scares some people. When the gender roles are thrown wide open, many men—and a lot of women, too—are made uneasy by this change in accepted and familiar lifestyles. Women who are professional builders and architects, of course, run into an unaccepting attitude more often than women who build houses for themselves, forcing them to examine their own work-related definitions of femininity and of themselves.

Nevertheless, resistance from men is not universal. Some women ease themselves into the male world of construction jobs without a great deal of soul searching. Both personality and circumstances play a role in this. Some job sites are absolute bastions of macho culture. Others are more open to integration.

Jane Dexter's work experience was very different from Dale's. She also had a nontraditional job at a fair-

ly young age. But her coworkers were more accommodating, and the environment was not especially competitive. When she first started working in the sawmill, Jane worried a bit about it not being feminine work. Then she became engrossed in what she was doing and stopped worrying. Some of the loggers were a little sarcastic in the beginning. But it was a small company with a relatively stable crew, and the men were not constantly proving themselves to each other. Once they got to know Jane and saw that she was work-oriented, they came to accept her. She gets along well with her male coworkers. Now she rarely thinks about the nontraditional aspect of what she is doing.

Jane does see a difference between the way women and men work. She thinks that as a woman she is more concerned with people's feelings, about not being fair, or with offending someone. To fit in and succeed in her business, she has to fight the tendency to be self-effacing.

Jane, who has worked with men in various building situations, said, "I think that guys are much more aggressive and, perhaps, more wasteful." She also noted that because women, on average, aren't as strong as men, they tend to move materials differently. That's not to say they can't do the work. They just do it differently. Women use their hips and lower bodies more than their shoulders in moving heavy objects. Where

strength is an issue, women rely more on leverage, finesse, and planning ahead. How women share tasks is also affected by their physical and social differences from men.

Of all the women I interviewed, Sam Morse worked in some of the toughest positions for a woman in construction. She is not happy about how women are treated and how little acceptance they encounter even after years of working in the trades. She has definite opinions about the difference between men and women in their approach to construction and design. She finds much more commitment to human values from the women she meets than from the men she has dealt with.

"I think that guys are much more aggressive and, perhaps, more wasteful."

"I get their respect, but I always have to start out fighting the stereotype."

Sam claims that, although men say women aren't conceptual, it's the other way around. She thinks it's men who don't look at the whole picture. When they see a good site, they only consider what's quick or easy or profitable to build there. They don't look at what's appropriate for the neighborhood. Sam always considers what's already in place. She looks at how a new project will spill over into the surrounding area, how it will work, what impact it will have on the community. Nothing exists in a vacuum, there is an interaction between all of a neighborhood's elements.

Sam likes the power she has now. She likes going out in the field and having men turn to *her* for expertise. She makes a lot of decisions. But construction is very much a male world. She misses the presence of women at work. As a strong and committed feminist, Sam feels frustrated in her isolation. She doesn't want to be one of the boys. She wants there to be more women in construction. She doesn't accept that it should be a male domain, and she bristles at the fact that she has to accommodate their attitudes: "The irony is that I deal with nothing but men. It's my cross to bear. All day, every day. Boys, boys, boys. I get their respect, but I always have to start out fighting the stereotype."

When she works with men for the first time, Sam says they "circle the wagons." The first day on a new job the men all gather at the work site. They pull out the blueprints and look at them together. They form a tight circle around the table with Sam on the outside. Then they start talking about the job, treating Sam as though she were invisible.

Sam says nothing at first. She doesn't try to muscle her way in. She lets them "talk their boy talk, do their bonding." Instead, she looks for a ladder. There's usually one somewhere on the site. She ignores the men, walks over to the ladder, and climbs right up. Then she begins a conversation with the demolition crew, or the roofer, or the carpenters. The fact that she climbed a ladder changes everything. Sam says that when she comes down the ladder the circle magically opens. It almost never fails. It may sound silly, but some men

"She rarely sees women in the field; they're just not given the chance."

need to "see" her confidence and her familiarity with the work before they allow her any credibility.

As irritating as it is for Sam to have to prove herself to each new set of male construction workers, it's even more aggravating to see how many women are kept out of construction altogether. Sam particularly resents so many contractors avoiding government mandates for hiring women on federally funded construction projects. She rarely sees women in the field; they're just not given the chance. Maybe once a year a woman will turn up on a crew. Then it's as a laborer, and only at the apprentice level. Contractors are expected to make a "good faith effort" to employ women and minorities having no legal hiring quotas to meet. Many contractors come up with feeble excuses that most (male) supervisors will accept. Not Sam.

On the positive side, there are women in administrative positions in community development work who handle the finances and monitor the programs. These women are sometimes in positions of power. Unfortunately, they are usually in positions of authority at a higher level than the project manager. This puts women like Sam in a kind of limbo in which they have no female peers.

When Lynda Simmons started her architectural career, she was always the only woman in the room. That was okay with her. She was smart and she worked hard. She thought for awhile that she wasn't being discriminated against. She believes that women who do very good work are able to move farther than women who do run-of-the-mill work, but there are definitely limitations. There were meetings that she wasn't invited to because the men were going to swear, or they just didn't want to break up the all-male atmosphere.

Lynda says that in real estate in New York, particularly at the higher levels, women are not allowed in at all. In New York, real estate is very much a family business. Passed on from father to son or to male cousins and so on. Lynda once tried to get on a waterfront commission that a group of commercial developers had formed among themselves to make recommendations to the city. She had done a number of large projects by this time, $30- and $40-million-dollar jobs. She was

president of her organization. She wanted to be on this commission. So through the housing commissioner and another influential man, she let it be known that she wanted to be appointed. The word came back—they didn't want her on the commission, period.

While many women feel isolated in nontraditional jobs, Elizabeth Ayer never felt lonely or discriminated against as a woman architect. Even though she was a pioneer in the field, she didn't report feeling alienated. She had friends and family outside of work and got all the support she needed from them. She got along well with the men in her profession and didn't see it as a struggle in terms of gender. It was a struggle to succeed, to gain the self-confidence and knowledge to carry on the business by herself, but she seemed relatively content in her chosen career and never expressed resentment about its domination by men. In fact, she seems to have enjoyed being the only woman in her class. She said, "It was fun to me in college to watch professors change. Where they'd never had a woman in a class before. They would be sort of embarrassed and not know what to do about it. But then, by degrees, I'd just become one of the class."

Elizabeth saw architecture as a good choice for women of her era. It is a profession with several allied fields that women could enter if their main interest was blocked. But she did think it is a hard field for women to enter, leave to raise a family, then return to later. Technological changes are occurring at such a rapid rate that a few years away from it would be crippling to a career. It wasn't surprising to her that there weren't many women in architecture when she entered the field. It did surprise her to see so many women in it in 1985, because it is a difficult and competitive profession in general.

Architecture and construction work are two different things, however. Lynda Simmons's example clearly demonstrates that an office job is not easy when it violates the gender labor division. But hands-on carpentry and building has been particularly difficult for women to break into.

Karen Terry has worked with men, and by herself, in various roles over the years. She has been carpenter, contractor, designer, developer, and client. She finds the men aggressive and construction unfriendly to women. It's a tough business, and she doesn't think there are very many women who can handle it. Women have sought employment with her, but she said many of them don't have a realistic image of what the work will be like. "I don't think women should be in construction. A lot of women have asked me for work, but, see,

"Construction is really violent. Just the whole process. Tearing up the ground and moving all this heavy stuff from one place to another, cutting things up and hammering."

this is real heavy work, this adobe stuff. It's not like stick framing. I don't know—it's just that men are stronger and more experienced. So I've never looked for women to work with me."

Many women don't appreciate what's involved in construction work. They may be restless and dissatisfied with a sedentary office job and would like to do

something with their hands. But they don't realize that, although carpentry is a skilled craft, the work is hard and long and often tedious. Karen doesn't think most women, particularly middle-class women, are prepared to work that hard. And the working-class women she knows are not at all eager to embrace a nontraditional role. Karen herself finds some aspects of construction distasteful. She says, "Construction is really violent. Just the whole process. Tearing up the ground and moving all this heavy stuff from one place to another, cutting things up and hammering—you know, so many things can go wrong."

Karen's the only woman I interviewed who pointed out the aggressiveness inherent in the nature of construction. She echoed many, however, in characterizing the construction business as stressful. In Santa Fe, as elsewhere, most self-employed contractors go out of business in their first year. But Karen stuck it out. Whenever she thought about giving up her business and doing something more conventional, more "appropriate" for women, she just wasn't willing to let go. She has learned to do what makes sense to her, even if it doesn't fit in any convenient pigeonhole. She said, "I realize that most people look for a job that already exists. I figured it's better to make up your own—and it's possible. I've made up lots of different jobs. It's harder work, but really, there's nothing else I want to do at this time." She told me that every time she gets sidetracked by something else that takes her away from building, it seems less rewarding and she returns to doing her own work. "Maybe I just don't fit in at other places, so I have to make a place for myself."

Several women said they thought women approach design very differently from men. There is a perception that women bring a different set of values and priorities to the work. Specifically, women seem to place less emphasis on virtuosity or display and more on the comfort and peace of mind of people who will live or work in the building. True or not, this may change as men's architectural traditions continue to evolve and as more women work in these fields.

Sam Morse has great faith in women and believes they will eventually change the face of construction work and design. She asserts that most of what passes for architecture these days is ugly. It's cold and barren and neglects human needs, and it lacks personality. She says you could go to New York City and look at ten new skyscrapers and not be able to tell the difference, because they all look basically the same. Sam has a theory about how these buildings get designed: "My theory is that they're all penises and each generation of boys feels his penis has to be bigger than his father's. If you look, the 1880 penises had little embellishments, maybe they had a curve or two. You know, they weren't these solid metal missiles!"

Sam is convinced that women would design buildings very differently—and better. "Maybe I've got rose-colored glasses, but I think if a woman built a sky-scraper, the sucker would be different. Maybe on every tenth level it'll be open to the air. And there'll be an indoor park that's a block long. Or . . . who knows? Maybe they'll be round and hollow in the center, have a huge atrium, you know."

Most women learn to build and design from men, so for the most part they are reproducing what men do.

They may or may not have questioned which of their design ideas are their own and which are derived from the established practices of the men now in control of the profession. Sandy Seth hopes that when women start to look at these learned assumptions, we will see some differences as women strike out in new directions. The standard construction design elements, based on the sizes of readily available lumber and sheet goods, for example, might give way to "more natural, nurtur-

> *"Maybe I've got rose colored glasses, but I think if a woman built a skyscraper, the sucker would be different."*

ing shapes" if women had more to say about how houses are designed. Valerie Graves suggested that women already design differently from men because women don't always "know the rules" and are therefore free to break them. Gwen Demeter thought women tend toward more customized and creative, though perhaps more timid, designs.

Like Jane Dexter and Dale McCormick, Debrin Cox noticed differences in men's and women's work styles and their design styles. She believes women are sensitive to the body and are quick to help each other out. They are less burdened by the macho mentality, which requires men to suffer pain and take unnecessary risks. When working as a masseuse she noted that fewer injuries happen to women than to men in the trades.

Dale McCormick was less ready to assert that design differences exist or that the differences we see should really be viewed as male or female in origin. "My style of designing was influenced by men. But maybe the reason I wanted to adopt it was because it felt very natural to me. I think it's a very female style. Well, it's hard to say what is female. The process of designing that I like is about fitting spaces around people instead of people into spaces. And some men do that, too, while some women do the opposite. So it's hard to say."

My own impression is that men and women design differently, their approaches to design reflecting their upbringing and life experiences. Women often emphasize feelings of well-being and harmony in a building, rather than a structure's visual impact. These differences are not drastic, however, as women building and designing today have learned their trade from men. As more women become architects and gain comfort in their field, their designs are bound to reflect their circumstances and priorities.

Rather than viewing women's work as opposed to men's, it can be seen as an added dimension to designing and building, combining the two perspectives and enabling us to see our environment with a more sophisticated understanding. The practice of architecture will undoubtedly be enriched by women's contributions.

Taking Stock

Perspectives about building change over time. The women interviewed looked back on the adventures of their youth with the perspective of more responsible, experienced middle-aged adults. Some of the women said their building and designing changed how they looked at things other than building. Others saw their buildings in a different light as time went on. Lynda Simmons has grown a bit cynical, Carol Yee is not as reckless as she used to be, Ronnie Sandler and Pat Liddle are settling into homes that feel more permanent than they'd anticipated, and Elizabeth Ayer and Leona Walden looked back on their accomplishments with satisfaction.

It is still very difficult for women to find the opportunity to build or design on their own or in their own way. Those of us who entered the building trades in the 1970s thought that by now there would be lots of women carpenters, electricians, plumbers, and so on. It hasn't happened. We thought we were paving the way for large numbers of women to follow us. But there are hardly more women in construction now than there were in 1978 (about 2 percent of the workforce). In the white collar professions, women have made great strides. In the craft occupations, however, men still monopolize the work.

It's always hard to get people to change the way they operate. Lynda Simmons started out thinking that she could accomplish great things in the world if she worked hard and was responsible and imaginative. She has had some remarkable achievements, but she now believes there's a limit, particularly in the present climate, that she didn't see at first. As a developer in public housing she has reached a plateau. It's been gratifying to see her theories born out by the response of the tenants in the buildings she has designed and had built. However, she is somewhat pessimistic about the future when she steps back to look at the broader picture. As Lynda sees it, not very many people who are in positions of power are thinking about how to make life better for the people who live in these buildings. Lynda says she no longer has illusions about how the world works: "When I was younger, I thought most people were really working to make the world a better place. If you just showed them how to do it, then it would get done. Well, of course, that's not true. I was very naive."

Carol Yee's outlook has become more subdued over time. When she was building her cabin in Vermont, she was partying every chance she could get and having a great time. She also worked very, very hard. She thought all things were possible if you just kept at it long enough and hard enough. Now she's lost some of that starry-eyed optimism. She's begun to realize the folly of taking so many risks and of doing everything the hard way. She looks back on those early years with a mixture of amusement and relief.

"When I was younger, I thought most people were really working to make the world a better place."

When Carol was building her cabin in Vermont, it was rare for women to be doing something like that. She had a constant string of visitors, women who had heard of her and wanted to see her cabin with their own eyes. Carol didn't know what to do with them. They would come up and look at her "with their eyeballs popping out of their heads." They were in awe of what she was doing. Now it's different. Now a lot of women *can* imagine themselves building a house, at least in theory. But in those days it was amazing.

Looking back on what she did, Carol says, "I don't want that kind of existence any more. I would never want to do that again. But I'll say this: I would never, ever, want to forget the fun we had and the experience it was for a lot of people."

> "I would never want to do that again. But I'll say this: I would never, ever, want to forget the fun we had and the experience it was for a lot of people."

When asked if she felt sad about losing something she had worked so hard for and put so much of herself into, Carol said a lot of people have asked her that. Women who had come up from the city to help build were hurt that she could sell her cabin. How could she get rid of this place that had meant so much to *them*? Even if they had been there only one weekend, the spectacle of all these women working together to make a homestead in the wilderness was an inspiration to them. At the time, Carol became frustrated and impatient with all the adoration she was generating. She knew that most of those women could do the same thing in similar circumstances. Nevertheless, they just stood around staring in fascination and disbelief. Carol says, "That was touching to me, what they said when I sold it. It meant a lot to an awful lot of women in those days. And I didn't realize that until after it was all over."

Carol's second house, the triplex, was a very different kind of undertaking. She didn't build it all by herself. There weren't the work parties of excited women feeling like they just discovered something marvelous. Carol herself had changed. She had quit drinking and settled down, and she got started in the cabinetmaking business. The first building to go up on the triplex land was a workshop. When she built it, her main concern was to build it quickly so she could get her business established in Connecticut.

Carol said that if she could have afforded to hire someone to do all the work of building the triplex she would have. She doesn't enjoy construction work. She doesn't like the stress and heavy lifting. She sees building as a chore. She has no plans to do any more building on her own. Her attitude is: "You do it once and you get a big thrill; you're proud of it. You have a nice home to live in; it's there when you want it." She thinks that ought to be enough.

When she was younger, she said, everything seemed *so* important. But now Carol is a little more serene. She has reached a stage in her life where adventures such as housebuilding don't seem as necessary to her as they once did. She doesn't regret having built the cabin and done all the other wild and crazy things she's done. In fact a lot of it was really fun. However, she thinks she's been very lucky in her life. She describes herself as essentially optimistic, always the one to dive in without looking to see if the pool has any water in it. There have been some near disasters, but so far she's come away from all of it without much damage. In spite of that, she says, "All the things I've done . . . I just wish I could have done twice as much. I wish I could have done a million other things."

Dale McCormick experienced a similar shift in her attitude about building between her first house and her second. Having built a house once, she knew how much time and effort it was really going to take. If she had her way, she would have bought a house instead of building again. It wasn't only the construction she didn't want to face. She knew that the planning and design work, the supervising, and the general disruption it entails were all going to be a burden.

Dale's partner, Betsy, was more enthusiastic, but she eventually came to understand the magnitude of the task they had undertaken and joined Dale's viewpoint. By then it was too late, though. They had already started the process. Mainly it was the land that charmed them into it. They really wanted that spot. There wasn't a house on it, so they had to build one.

Once Dale accepted the reality of another housebuilding project, she went at it with the same energy and thoroughness that she brings to everything she does. She doesn't regret having built this house. It has just about every feature she wanted. She's proud of it and finds living in it a pleasure.

Building *is* hard work. However, people get caught up in big and dramatic undertakings. The hardships are offset by the excitement and intensity of the work. When I look back on the winter that my husband and I spent virtually living outdoors while building our house, working every daylight hour, scraping ice off the lumber pile each morning, I'm amazed that we were able to stand it. Seeing progress each day kept us going through the hardest times.

Leona Walden built four houses for herself. She doesn't view having built four different homes as a tortuous path to finally having a house that is just right. Each endeavor was appropriate to that particular time in her life. Looking back, she says it's wonderful to "just watch your life unfold." In summing up, she said, "I'd say it was exciting and challenging and required a certain amount of perseverance. Mostly it was very satisfying. It seemed like every nail you drove added something."

It made Leona feel secure to have a house around her and a place for her daughter. But she hesitated to

"It seemed like every nail you drove added something."

use the word "proud" in describing her accomplishment. She says many people have been impressed with what she's done, yet somehow their reaction to her doesn't quite gibe with how she sees herself. Like Carol Yee, Leona found herself an object of awe. She says people treat her like some sort of superwoman but that she doesn't feel like one. She feels like an ordinary person. She knows that what she did, other people could do. She is disconcerted to find people making such a fuss over her. As far as she's concerned, each time she came up against some obstacle in her life, she just did what she had to do. Building houses was no exception.

Few women expressed serious regrets about what they had done. No one said they wished they hadn't built at all. Gail Atkins says she wishes she had known more about construction before she built her house. However, each of the buildings she and Gwen have built has been easier than the last, because they learned from their earlier successes and mistakes. She also spoke of the impact building her own house had on her life overall. "Building has affected me personally in that it has given me a real sense of myself. As an adult. As a nest builder. It has been a very, almost spiritual experience for me. Boy does that sound corny. But it's true." To Gail, it was almost miraculous that the buildings at Silver Circle were completed and that they're going to build an addition.

A key factor to success for Gail and Gwen was learning to work well with other people. Gail was deeply moved by accomplishments owed to emphasizing cooperation over competition. Her problem-solving strategies have also changed as a result of this experience. In addition to building the structures at Silver Circle, she has helped friends over the years with their building projects. She has learned to appreciate the value of different work styles and ways to approach a problem. She believes that working on building projects has made her more willing to listen to all points of view and to think through a project more carefully. She also learned how to pace herself, to work at a rate her body can handle.

Gail also says the help and moral support of her friends and family were crucial to their being able to get through the hard times. At first this didn't seem so important, but as the project at Silver Circle wore on, it became more and more valuable to have people to lean on. Oddly enough, it was this experience that made Gail feel much more self-reliant. In the context of working with other women, Gail found herself blossoming into a more complete version of herself.

The sweat-equity factor was one of the main reasons most of the women gave for building their own homes. Substituting labor for cash and minimizing the debt burden is the only way many of us can afford to own our own homes.

Because so little money was spent on their place, Gail and Gwen have no mortgage payments at all. With low maintenance costs and extensive vegetable gardens, Gail could even afford to lose her job and continue to live comfortably for quite awhile. As several women said, there's comfort in knowing that, no matter what happens, you won't end up a bag lady. Surprisingly these obviously capable women felt a great uncertainty about life. This may be the legacy of women's dependency-oriented upbringing or possibly a sign of current eco-

"The understanding that comes from building is a transferable realization to anything else that you do in life."

nomic realities. However, women identified a very fundamental level of self-sufficiency as a part of the payoff of building that would have a lasting impact on them.

Pat Liddle has lived in her house for a long time now and is very comfortable with it. She says it feels good to be living in a house she built for herself. There were only a few things she'd do differently if she had it to do over again. There are a few things that never got done, some parts that are unfinished. She never put the closet in the upstairs bedroom. The lumber is all neatly stacked and waiting. It's been waiting for ten years, but she'll get around to it someday. She added on a garage a couple of years ago, which gives her a place to keep her table saw so she can continue to work on the house.

There just never seems to be an end to the list of details that are left to do when you move into a house before it's completely finished. That list hanging over your head can be depressing. It's unfinished business. But I don't know anybody who built her own house and refrained from moving in until absolutely everything was done. What's worse is that by the time you've checked the last item off your list, you've already started to add new items as the house begins to require maintenance. When Pat stands back to really look at her house, she sees the things that need to be fixed. She'll look up at the eaves and remember that she never caulked the space between the shingles and the facia board, so now the wasps are making nests in that space and she has to get up there with a ladder and do something about it some day. Like most of us, she sees the tiny faults and mistakes that a visitor wouldn't notice. But she does stop to admire her handiwork once in a while.

Pat was able to cash in on her building experience not only in landing a job in a related field but also in many other aspects of her life. As she put it, "Building this house gave me a better sense of self than I had prior. During that process you end up realizing you can do things that you didn't know that you could do. The understanding that comes from building is a transferable realization to anything else that you do in life."

Without the ability to adjust, life (and work) gets very difficult. Flexibility is right up there with perseverance as a necessary and powerful asset to successful building. The redwood cabins certainly wouldn't have been completed were it not for a hefty dose of both attributes. Debrin and Oceanlight are both glad they didn't give up. Oceanlight only regrets that she wasn't able to enjoy living in her new cabin for very long after it was completed. She still thinks leaving it was the right thing for her to do at that time. She didn't realize how hard it would be to get the cabins built, and she wishes she had had more money to work with. But she wouldn't let lack of money stop her. Having more money would have made things easier, and the cabins would have been built sooner.

Oceanlight took about two and a half years to build her cabin. She lived in it during much of that time, so her life was disrupted for a long time. The toughest time was toward the end. The finishing details are always frustrating, because there is little visible change as work drags on. By then, everyone is short-tempered and impatient. The sense of adventure has gradually turned into a grim determination to get the job over with. But the connection that Oceanlight felt to her cabin after moving away wouldn't have been as strong if she hadn't built her home herself.

Oceanlight has also come to understand how many things work by extrapolating from what she went through in getting the cabin completed. She knows that things always take longer than you think they will and involve more details along the way than you're aware of at the beginning. She understands "the difference between what the mind can plan and the body can do."

Debrin thought she knew when she started how big a job building would be. Everyone she knew who had any experience with building told her that it would take more money and time than expected. So she made what she thought was a realistic allowance for that, and it *still* took more. Another surprise for Debrin was discerning her own capabilities. She was surprised at how little she really knew about construction. She had always considered herself handy. Now, after seeing the

skill it takes to build, she realizes she was handy by being "crafty, artsy, and self-assured." So her first adjustment was a downward revision of her sense of her building prowess.

As she started working on the construction of her cabin, Debrin surprised herself again by how much she was able to figure out and how many new skills she picked up. The intensity of that growth plus the pace of the work once it was underway made the project her "main focus mentally, financially, emotionally, and physically." For Debrin, the whole experience was "like a rite of passage . . . a birth."

Toward the end, Debrin became less attached to the details of the work. She now understands which aspects really matter in the long run and which tasks can be done less meticulously. She regrets spending as much time as she did in the early stages trying to get everything exactly right. She also regrets having missed so many weekends over those six years. She could have been spending that time with friends, lying on the beach, riding her bicycle, or dancing.

Now that the buildings are complete, Debrin finally feels free to think about traveling, exploring something new, or starting new work. She feels open to these possibilities because she has a home. She says the fruits of her labor are starting to "ripen very sweetly." Even planting bulbs in her garden and knowing she won't have to move and leave them behind is gratifying to her. If she does leave to travel or to live somewhere else for awhile, she always has a home to return to—and the bulbs will be there waiting.

Some of the women who built primarily because

> *"I think you always make over your house in your own image to some extent. But to build your house and to really be a part of it, it's even more in your image."*

they needed a place to live said that before the experience they would have been just as satisfied buying a finished house. Few said the same afterward, though. Ronnie Sandler said the difference was enormous, "like night and day." She discovered a whole new world of meaning and connectedness by building onto the house she originally bought. She said if her house was finished and she came along and bought it, it wouldn't be the same. "I think you always make over your house in your own image to some extent. But to build your house and to really be a part of it, it's even more in your image."

Ronnie loves the attention she gets from friends who visit her and see her house for the first time. She gets to see her house through their eyes. They always oooh and aaah at the fine work she did. They love the beautiful hardwood trim. They compliment her on the stairs and the windows. It brings back all the memories of building. She doesn't think she could ever give up her house. She might move away for some reason, but she wouldn't sell the house. It's important to her to know that it belongs to her wherever she is and that she can always come back to it.

However, a house is not something you can take away with you. The things Ronnie likes about her house are not very portable. She couldn't just rip out the trim and use it in another house; it was such hard work. (Ronnie doubts if she would ever trim out a house in cherry again.) She couldn't take her view with her. Nor could she take the history of the house—neither her own history with it nor the history of the house before she bought it. She couldn't take the spirit of all the women who pitched in to help her build her second floor. To be able to live with all these things that are precious to her, she has to stay with her house. So Ronnie is rooted there in that spot, in that house, in her home. Which is, after all, what she has wanted since she was a teenager.

The architects have a different perspective of building and design. Their reflections focus on a string of projects through the course of their careers. Elizabeth Ayer's fondest memories of her long career are of the design work itself. She loved to plan and to draw. That part of it was "just pure, unadulterated fun" for her. She got along well with her clients and seemed to have a knack for being able to see what they wanted. She thought of herself as a professional, but she didn't see herself as a businesswoman even after she took over when her partner died. That was a rough period, financially. With typical modesty, she credited others for her success, saying her former clients helped her keep the business going by being her "salesmen."

Elizabeth must have been very good at her work, because she was often called back by the same clients to remodel or design additions to the houses. She even designed houses for the children of some of her earliest customers. Her enjoyment of those projects, even in the telling many years after the fact, was contagious. It wasn't hard for me to see how she could generate enthusiasm and cooperation from the people she worked with. When I met her she was eighty-seven years old and living in a retirement home, but she was the liveliest person in the place. Modest to the end, Elizabeth offered this as a summation: "I'm no genius. I think we did good work, and I think I had wonderful training. But it was due a great deal to just good luck. I loved it, so that, of course, helped."

"Looking back I really don't know how I dared to attempt such a huge undertaking. I guess I didn't stop to think about what I was getting into."

It is somewhat frustrating to hear so many women sound meek when they evaluate their work. It should be acknowledged as a real feat to swim against the current. Most women in America today work outside the home. However, the glass ceiling has kept us pretty much confined to the lower ranks. Many of us want to be players. We want respect. We want responsibility. We want to make decisions. Building and designing has provided the mechanism for me to achieve some of those things.

It means a lot to me to drive by houses I've built and to have the satisfaction of seeing the permanence of what I've done. Creating or altering another person's surroundings is an interesting way to relate to people, and affecting other people's lives has been important to me. Living in my own house is a continuing richness of experience I can't compare to anything else. If I hadn't built, I'd never have known about this. It's strange and wonderful to be reminded on a gut level of the whole process of assembly—the building emerging gradually out of thin air, by my own hands.

The physical connectedness with the world is a wonderful element in building. It's instinctively gratifying to handle and manipulate things. The purely operational nature of building is a huge part of its enduring appeal. To build is to be controlling, creative, sensual, productive, and dignified all at the same time. What could be better?

The answer to that, of course, is that it could be easier. Unfortunately, it can be, as it was for me, quite an ordeal. And I did not build my house all by myself. Collaborating with my husband was tough in many respects. The stresses and strains of building under difficult conditions have reverberated through our lives for years. Though painful at the time, some of those conflicts drove us to examine and redefine ourselves and our relationship. This process led to some impor-

tant and wonderful changes for us. And in spite of the hardship, the year we built our house was a great shared adventure that created a bond between us and gave us our own legacy.

I don't regret having built my own house. All in all, I'm glad I did. However, I'm not sure I'd care do it again now, nor would I have done it then if I had known what it was going to be like. Looking back, I really don't know how I dared to attempt such a huge undertaking. I guess I didn't stop to think about what I was getting into.

Our house is a container in the sense that we live inside it. Since we put it all together, however, something of ourselves is woven into the very structure of that container, animating it in a way. It is almost like living with a third person. Our house is certainly a presence that hovers over us, speaks to us, comforts us, and still provokes us in unexpected ways.

Building and designing for other people and now teaching other women to build is a natural extension of and a delightful way to enlarge the dimensions of my homebuilding experience. It is difficult to sum up the changes in my life caused by becoming a builder. One thing I do know is that my contact with housebuilding has profoundly influenced the way I see things. Building also raised certain issues for me and other women I've spoken to that provide a context for analyzing a variety of social concerns. Architects, sociologists, and feminists have commented on the built environment's influence on individuals and communities for some time. However, the importance of women actually building and designing houses—what we take from it or put into it, and where that leaves us—is something we've only begun to explore.

Advice

Lynda Simmons

Never put limits on yourself. You'll meet them in the real world soon enough. You have to do what you want to do. You have to live. You have to enjoy life.

I think that the surest way to find out what you're meant to do is to watch what you really enjoy doing. You'll do a lot more for yourself and the world if you really enjoy it.

I think that women, myself included, have a very hard time knowing who we really are. We've absorbed so many influences from other people. It takes years to probe and feel out who we really are. Introspection, meditation, therapy, talking to friends, whatever it takes. Watching what you like to do and what you enjoy and what makes you feel good. That's how you figure out who you are and what you should do.

Jane Dexter

Don't cut any corners or don't shortchange yourself for fear of it being too big, or too heavy, or too awesome. You can get around any one of those obstacles and still do what you want to do. If you really want to do it, and you have something in mind, don't let anybody talk you out of it just because you're a woman, because they say you can't lift it, or it's too big, or you're biting off more than you can chew. You can always find a way to do it.

I have to talk to myself a lot. I say to myself: trust your judgment. It's proved itself okay before. Trust it. And go for it. Listen to it. Don't listen to the other side putting doubt in your mind. Take a deep breath, look carefully at what you're doing, and carry on.

Be careful, as far as physical things. You don't have to prove anything. Even if, for a moment, you don't see a way of accomplishing something, don't panic. Because you can find out. Either it will come to you in the night, or you'll read a book, or you'll talk to a friend, or . . . there are ways of learning what you don't know. You don't have to know it tonight. It doesn't mean you're dumb because you don't know.

Dale McCormick

I would advise a person to take a whole year in the design process. Because it's the most fun, and it's very creative. And it's worth it.

You've got to budget your time and your money for building the house. I have had many friends who have had trouble with that. And that can just ruin this process. Either because you run out of money and therefore don't have a house, literally. Or you're rushed and have to get

> *"If you really want to do it, and you have something in mind, don't let anybody talk you out of it just because you're a woman."*

in, and therefore live with a plywood floor for the rest of your life, because in order to put down a floor, you have to move out.

I also think that your relationship, if you're building this with someone else, should be on solid ground. And it should not be something that "saves" the relationship.

Debrin Cox

Hire people with skill, don't try to train yourself to build while doing your own house. Be an assistant but not the main carpenter, and start with as much money as possible.

Karen Terry

Plan carefully. Get some help from professionals. Be realistic about your costs—your labor isn't worth as much as you think.

Dawn Hofberg

Make a "dream plan," or a fifteen-year plan first—then begin with what you can afford. Having a long-range vision to begin with is easier. Also, do it right the first time, or do it over instead of letting it go. If you make small mistakes in the beginning, they'll catch up to you.

Ronnie Sandler

It always takes twice as long and costs twice as much money as you ever expected.

If you're in a relationship and plan on building a house, look at it very closely and look at the pitfalls. I've seen a lot of people break up over building. You should know how you work together and have some idea of what you're doing.

Another thing that's interesting is that by the time you get proficient at doing something, you're on to the next stage and you're not doing it anymore. Once you finally understand how to frame, you're not framing anymore. Now you're learning how to put up drywall. Then you finally figure out how to put the drywall up, and now

> *"There are a lot of women now who are building houses. And working with women is very, very different from working with men."*

you're taping. So it's a constant battle of learning how to do stuff.

Gwen Demeter

I think a lot of women idealize or romanticize the process. They see the finished product, but not the hours, years, and sore muscles that went into it. When I'm down, I sometimes feel it was too great an expenditure of energy. But I know it was no more than most jobs people work at for years to pay off lengthy mortgages. Daily, I'm thankful I don't have one of those!

Christine Acebo

If you can get the money any other way, buy it. Building yourself is too much trouble.

Gail Atkins

Go work with some people who are building a house or who are doing some building project, because there's some basic joining techniques and some basic techniques of using tools that are real good to learn. There are a lot of women now who are building houses. And working with women is very, very different from working with men.

Carol Yee

You need to understand how much it is going to cost. You should have some *idea* of what you're getting into. I don't think anybody would look at the cedar shakes on my cabin and say, "Oh, man, I got to make my own cedar shakes!" I would definitely talk them out of things like that.

I would still say there's no reason in the world why you can't do everything yourself. I would try to point out to them what it was like to do that, though. Let them know how horrible and how long and how . . . forever it takes. It would depend on the person, what their time schedule is, what they are thinking, how realistic they are, how crazy they are. That element comes into it. To do what I did, you have to be a little crazy.

Leona Walden

I think one of the biggest problems women have, when they have men working for them, is that some men can't take directions from a woman. So it's necessary to find a man who's willing to cooperate with you and to deal with you as a person rather than as a woman. If you can find a woman builder, that's even better, that's even easier.

What advice would I give other women who want to build a house? Go for it. Do it. Because it's possible. It's just step by step. It's exhilarating and satisfying—it's a wonderful process. Any woman who wants to do it, I thoroughly recommend it.

> *"Do it because it's possible. It's just step by step. It's exhilarating and satisfying. Any woman who wants to do it, I thoroughly recommend it."*

Glossary

2-by-. A term used to describe the size of lumber; framing lumber is usually two inches thick by four, six, eight, ten, twelve, or more inches wide, and any length up to twenty-four feet (for example, a 2-by-4 is a board with a nominal dimension of two inches by four inches in cross-section). The actual measurement is less due to shrinkage from drying the lumber and loss from milling the lumber to a smooth surface.

3-4-5 Proportional triangle. A triangle with two adjacent sides equal to three feet and four feet having a 90 degree angle resulting in the third side equalling five feet; corresponding triangles have the same proportions, for example, six, eight, and ten feet.

Active solar energy system. Uses an additional source of energy, such as fans or a circulating pump, to store and distribute solar heat.

Adobe. Building material made from clay, sand, and water and is formed into bricks that are hardened by baking.

A-frame. A steeply-pitched, peaked-roof house.

Apprentice. The first level of a training program that instructs workers while they earn wages in a labor union or other state-approved program.

Backhoe. An earthmoving machine with a narrow bucket attached to the end of a long arm that can bend and rotate; used primarily for digging trenches and holes.

Baseboard. Wood trim attached to the bottom of an interior wall; used to protect the wall surface and to conceal the gap between the wall and the floor.

Beam. A horizontal framing member, usually wood, that supports joists, walls, rafters, and other parts of a structure.

Bearing wall. A wall that supports the weight of the walls, floors, or roof structures above it.

Bird's mouth. A notch cut at the bottom of a rafter allowing it to sit securely on the top plate.

Board foot. A unit of cubic measure indicating the volume of a board; equivalent to a board one-inch thick, one-foot wide, and one-foot long.

Butt joint. The simplest connection between two pieces of material; the connection is held in place by glue, nails, or other fastening devices, and the two pieces do not interlock.

California barn-style. A style of building meant to imitate traditional California barns, characterized by a center section with a peaked roof flanked by side sections with lower shed roofs.

Casement window. A window hinged on one side like a door.

Casing. Wooden trim boards placed on the surface of a wall around the openings of windows and doors.

Cathedral ceiling. A very high ceiling, usually including the space below the roof, which would otherwise be attic space.

Caulk. A waterproof compound with many uses, such as sealing cracks against water, air, and sound.

Cinder block. A masonry block made primarily of cement and sand (originally cinder blocks were made of cement and coal cinders); also called concrete block.

Clapboard (pronounced CLA-board). Horizontal wooden siding in which the individual boards overlap and are thicker at the bottom edge than at the top.

Clerestory (pronounced CLEAR-story). A row of windows at the top of a building below the eaves and above a second, lower roof structure.

Combination square. A tool with two fixed angle guides, one at 90 degrees and one at 45 degrees, used to mark lumber for saw cuts.

Crawl space. The space beneath a house with no basement or, alternatively, an attic that is too low to allow a person to stand upright.

Creosote. Hard, enamel-like residue

deposited on a chimney flue by the condensation of smoke as it cools; it's a serious fire hazard when ignited. In liquid form, it is sometimes used to seal wood in order to prevent moisture penetration and rot.

Cross-bracing. Bracing applied to a structure to resist forces in directions other than the primary stress for which the structure is designed (for example, joists are designed to resist vertical pressure in supporting floor loads but are also cross-braced to resist bending and twisting sideways).

Divided lites. Small, individual panes of glass in a window separated by a gridwork of thin wooden frame pieces called *muntins*.

Dormer. A structure protruding from a roof in order to expand the living space of the top floor, usually to accommodate one or more windows.

Double-hung window. A two-part window that opens by sliding the lower half up.

Drawshave. A knife used to carve and shape the surface of a flat or round wooden object.

Drywall. The interior wall or ceiling surface material most commonly used in houses; made of gypsum and fiberglass sandwiched between two layers of paper. Also called wallboard, gypsum wallboard, plasterboard, or Sheetrock (a brand name).

Dug well. A well dug by hand, or by a machine such as a backhoe, usually 10 to 20 feet deep (as opposed to a drilled well, which may be hundreds of feet deep).

Eaves. The bottom edge of a roof parallel to the ridge which extends beyond the exterior side wall of a building; also called the overhang. *See also* rake.

Fascia (pronounced FAY-sha). A wide trim board attached to the ends of rafters to form the face of the eave and rake.

Ferroconcrete. Concrete reinforced with steel.

Finish. The final stages of construction; the final layer of material which remains exposed to view; and the nails, tools, and so on used in performing finish work (for example, finish floor, finish nails, finish carpenter).

Fixed glass. A window that does not open.

Flashing. A strip of sheet metal applied around openings in a roof to seal the gap between the shingles and the walls, chimney, skylights, and so on.

Flue tiles. Ceramic lining for a chimney to prevent the spread of fire from the chimney to the rest of the house.

Footing. A wide, shallow base, usually made of concrete, below a foundation wall, post, pier, or column; it spreads the building's weight over a larger area of ground surface to prevent sinking or settling of the foundation or post.

Framing. (a) Erecting the basic structural components of a building; (b) the basic structural portion of the total building (essentially, the skeleton of a building); and (c) tools used in building (for example, a framing square).

Froe. A short-handled splitting tool with a wide, flat blade set at a right angle to the handle.

Fronting. Facing a certain direction or object (as in fronting on Main Street).

Furring strips. Narrow wooden strips fastened over a rough surface, usually to make it even or as a base for nailing. Used to level a floor or to plumb a wall before applying new flooring or wallboard, or to create a space for insulation or electrical wiring.

Gable. The upper triangular portion of the end wall of a peaked-roof house.

Gambrel roof. A roof with two surfaces on either side of the peak, or ridge, the lower of which is more steeply pitched than the upper.

Hacienda. A large house.

Hammer beam. A beam structure in which the braces that reinforce the connection between the posts and beams are made of a combination of

diagonal and right-angled members.

Header. A horizontal member over an opening; used to carry the weight of floors, walls, or a roof above it.

Heat sink. Material used to store solar or other forms of heat energy; usually masonry, but sometimes wood, concrete, tile, or containers of water.

Jamb. The exposed layer of wood lining the top and side frames of a window or doorway opening; it is the width of the studs plus the thickness of the wallboard on both sides of the wall.

Joist. The parallel framing members of a floor or ceiling, usually placed at 16-inch or 24-inch intervals and installed parallel to the rafters.

Journeyman. A graduate of an apprenticeship program, or an equivalently trained union worker.

Lath (pronounced LATH). Thin, narrow strips of wood, usually nailed to wall or ceiling framing to provide a base for a plaster surface.

Lathe (pronounced LAYTH). A machine that spins a piece of wood along its long axis so that it can be carved (for example, a table leg, a spindle, a baluster).

Latilla (pronounced la-TEE-ya). A small pole used as lath in ceilings, or one of a series of poles in a fence.

Linear foot. A unit of measurement referring to the combined length of a board or several boards (for example, 160 linear feet of boards could represent 20 boards each 8 feet long or 10 boards each 16 feet long). When buying lumber, the price may be quoted by the foot, but this could mean either the board foot or the linear foot—two very different numbers.

Lintel. A stone, concrete, or wooden header over a door or window which remains exposed to view.

Masonry. The work done by a mason; construction using blocks of stone, brick, concrete, and so on.

Mill. To cut or shape rough lumber into the finished size.

Molding. Trim lumber with a specific, usually curved, profile.

Mortise and tenon. A method of joining two pieces of wood in which a square hole (the mortise) is drilled into one piece, and a square tongue (the tenon) is shaped on the end of the other; the two parts are fitted together and either glued or pegged to hold them in place.

Nailers. Pieces of wood added to framing to fill in gaps where drywall or other material requires a solid backing into which it can be nailed.

Nonbearing wall. A wall which does not carry the load of structural members above it and serves only to separate spaces within a building; also referred to as a partition wall.

Off-grid. Independent of utility company energy source (for example, solar powered).

On center. The spacing of parallel framing members. If studs are said to be 16 inches on center, then they are at 16-inch intervals (measuring from the center of one stud to the center of the next).

Partition wall. *See* nonbearing wall.

Party wall. A shared wall connecting two residential units in a building or several units in a long row of attached houses.

Passive solar energy system. Collects and distributes heat derived from solar energy without any additional energy source (such as fans, electric pumps, or other mechanical devices requiring energy not derived from the solar collectors).

Peaked roof. A roof with two equal sloping surfaces, one on either side of the ridge or peak; sometimes called a gable roof.

Peñasco (pronounced pen-YAHS-co). A style of cabinetwork characterized by vertical slats cut in a zigzag or sawtooth pattern, named after the town in which the style originated.

Photovoltaic cells. Cells containing electrons that are excited by sunlight, thereby producing electrical energy.

Pitch. The incline of a roof expressed as a fraction: the total distance a roof rises, divided by the span between the supporting walls (for example, if the rise is 4 feet and the span is 24 feet, it would be expressed as a 1/6 pitch). *See also* slope.

Plaster. A paste, hard and brittle when dry, consisting of lime, sand, and water that is troweled onto a flat surface, typically as a finish surface on walls and ceilings.

Plate. The top and bottom framing members of a stud wall.

Plumb. Exactly vertical.

Plywood. A structural material consisting of several layers of wood glued together with the grain of adjacent layers at right angles to each other.

Portal (pronounced por-TALL). A porch or large, roofed outside space adjacent to a house.

Post and beam. A construction method in which a framework of large, horizontal beams rest on widely spaced vertical posts; typical of barns and very old houses.

Pressure treated. Wood impregnated with chemical pesticides and fungicides via a mechanical process using extreme pressure to force the chemicals beneath the surface of the wood.

Rafters. The parallel supporting framing members of a roof.

Rake. The edge of that section of roof that extends beyond the end, or gable, walls of a building; *See also* eave.

Ram pump. A device for pumping water that uses hydraulic energy as its power source.

Rigid insulation. A stiff board, made of foam, fiberglass, or other material, used as building insulation.

Rough opening. A space created during the framing of a wall, floor, or roof to accommodate a door, window, stairwell, skylight, and so on, and made large enough to allow for finish framing such as a jamb, sill, lintel, or other accessory component.

Rough-sawn. Lumber roughly cut to size in a sawmill (as opposed to "dressed" or dimensioned lumber that has been milled to a smooth surface of uniform dimensions); also called rough cut.

Saltbox. A roof with two unequal sloping surfaces, in which the rear slope is longer and slightly steeper.

Scale drawing. A drawing depicting elements in exact proportion to their actual size; usually expressed by a conversion equation (for example, 1/4" = 1' means that one-quarter inch on the drawing represents one foot in actual length).

Sheathing. The exterior covering over wall studs or roof rafters; originally wooden boards but now commonly made of plywood or synthetic composition material. It reduces air and moisture penetration, enhances resistance to diagonal stress, and provides a nailing base for siding or roofing material.

Shed roof. A roof with a single sloping surface.

Sheet metal. Building material in the form of thin sheets of metal, usually steel or aluminum.

Shims. Thin, wedge-shaped pieces of wood or other material used to level or align parts of an object or structure.

Shiplap. A siding pattern in which the edges of adjacent boards have half their thickness removed so the boards can overlap and still lie flat against the wall.

Sidewall. A wall of a building parallel to the ridge.

Siding. The exterior surface material of a wall, usually wooden boards, shingles, or synthetic materials such as aluminum or vinyl.

Sill. A beam placed on the foundation on which the walls of a house rest; also the horizontal finish member laid across the bottom of a door or window opening.

Skid. In logging, to drag logs across the ground.

Slope. The steepness of a roof expressed as a ratio of vertical rise over 12 inches of horizontal distance (for example, a roof that rises 5 inches in height over a distance of 12 inches is considered a 5 in 12 roof). *See also* pitch.

Soffit. The exposed surface of any boxed-in area; usually the bottom surface of the eaves or rake, but also applies to the boxed-in space over kitchen cabinets, for example.

Spec house. A house built on speculation; the builder has no buyer at the time of construction but hopes to sell the house after it is finished.

Stair riser. The vertical surface of an enclosed stairway that covers the gap between treads.

Stair tread. The horizontal surface of a step.

Stress-skin panels. Prefabricated wall or ceiling panels that contain a thick layer of foam insulation, sheathing, and (often) drywall.

Stringer. The large boards that carry the weight of a stairway, usually on either side; often under the middle of the treads.

Structural. A building component that is essential to the physical integrity of a building (as opposed to partition walls, soffits, trim, moldings, wainscoting, and other decorative elements).

Stucco. Wall covering made of plaster, cement, or a synthetic substitute and often containing sand particles to increase texture; generally applied with a trowel to exterior walls in lieu of siding.

Studs. The vertical pieces of wood in a framed wall to which sheathing, paneling, or lath is attached.

Stud wall construction. A construction method employing walls framed with studs (as opposed to post and beam, concrete block, brick, and so on); also called stick frame construction.

Subcontractor. A tradesperson hired on contract, rather than paid by the hour, by the contractor who, in turn, has been hired by the client on contract.

Subfloor. Sheathing covering floor joists; usually made of boards or plywood on which the finish floor material is laid.

Sweat equity. Equity, or ownership in a property created by the owner's labor during construction.

Table saw. A circular saw mounted in a stationary base with a flat surface on which pieces of lumber are guided through the saw blade.

Taping. Covering the gaps between sheets of drywall with a thin strip of paper plastered over with joint compound (a wet mixture of calcium carbonate, gypsum, talc, clay, water, and other substances that hardens when dry).

Thermopane. A type of window in which two layers of glass are separated by a thin air space; the air is removed by vacuum and sealed in the factory, producing a window with a higher insulation value than one or two layers of ordinary glass.

Thermosiphon. A method of transporting water whereby water rises as it is heated, inducing a siphoning action (for example, circulating water through a system with a solar heating panel without using an electric pump).

Tierra bayita. A kind of clay, typically lighter than other clays used to make adobe.

Timber frame. Post-and-beam construction.

Toenail. To drive a nail diagonally through one piece of wood into another; used when the second piece of wood cannot be reached by nailing straight through the first one.

Tongue and groove. A joint made of two pieces of wood in which the edge of one is grooved in the middle, and the other has a matching protrusion, or tongue, along its length.

Trim. Wood moldings, casing, or other finish wood strips used to cover gaps and as decorative accents.

Trombe wall (pronounced TROME). A solar heat-collection structure made by placing a solid wall behind a glass wall separated by an air space; solar radiation passing through the glass is absorbed by the solid wall material and gradually reemits the energy in the airspace as radiant heat, which is then drawn through the house in ducts or other circulation methods.

Truss. An assembly of small connected parts in a system of triangles that forms a strong, lightweight framing member; generally refers to prefabricated roof supports used in place of rafters. Also applies to a framework that functions in place of a joist, beam, or other load-bearing framing member.

Vapor barrier. A material, usually plastic, applied to obstruct the passage of air and, especially, water vapor.

Veneer mill. A sawmill specializing in the finest grades of lumber that is peeled off a log around its circumference to produce large, continuous sheets of very thin wood (veneer); these are often glued to a thicker wooden base resulting in high-quality plywood which is used for cabinetry and other decorative purposes.

Viga (pronounced VEE-ga). A round log used as a horizontal ceiling or roof beam.

Wainscoting (pronounced WAINS-coating). Decorative wood paneling covering part of a wall, usually the lower half.

Yurt. A portable domed tent stretched over a lattice framework, originating in northern Asia and Siberia; now used to refer to any circular hut or cabin with vertical walls and a conical or domed roof.

Selected Bibliography

The books and articles listed here are mostly by, for, or about women and architecture, housebuilding, construction trades, and the specific issues of gender, community, and design, which are discussed in this book.

Guides and Manuals

Adams, Florence. *The Woman's Build-It and Fix-It Handbook.* Chatsworth, CA: Major Books, 1973.

Armstrong, Leslie. *The Little House.* New York: Macmillan, 1979.

Curran, June. *Drawing Home Plans: A Simplified Drafting System for Planning and Design.* Bakersfield, CA: Brooks Pub. Co., 1979.

————. *Profile Your Lifestyle: Questions to Ask Yourself Before Building, Buying, or Remodeling.* Bakersfield, CA: Brooks Pub. Co., 1979.

DiDonno, Lupe, and Phyllis Sperling. *How to Design & Build Your Own House.* New York: Knopf, 1978.

First Fetch Your Hammer. Optima:Women and Manual Trades Collective, 1988.

Frank, Ruth F. *Something New Under the Sun: Building Connecticut's First Solar Home.* Andover, MA: Brick House Pub. Co., 1980.

Gibbons, Gail. *How a House Is Built.* New York: Holiday House, 1990.

Herrick, Lyn. *Anything He Can Fix, I Can Fix Better: A Comprehensive Guide for Home and Auto Repair.* Valle Crucis, NC: Quality Living, 1990.

Holloway, Dennis, and Maureen McIntyre. *The Owner-Builder Experience: How to Design and Build Your Own Home.* Emmaus, PA: Rodale Press, 1986.

Keller, Suzanne, ed. *Building for Women.* Lexington, MA: Lexington Books, 1981.

Kern, Barbara, and Ken Kern. *The Owner-Built Homestead.* New York: Scribner, 1977.

Kicklighter, Clois E., and Joan C. Kicklighter. *Residential Housing.* South Holland, IL: Goodheart-Willcox, 1986.

McAlester, Virginia, and Lee McAlester. *A Field Guide to American Houses.* New York: Knopf, 1984.

McCormick, Dale. *Against the Grain: A Carpentry Manual for Women.* Iowa City, Iowa: Iowa City Women's Press, 1977; San Francisco: Spinsters/Aunt Lute Book Co., 1986.

————. *Housemending: Home Repair for the Rest of Us.* New York: E.P. Dutton, 1987.

Mills, Sonya. *Handywoman.* London: Corgi, 1985.

O'Neill, Barbara Powell, and Richard W. O'Neill. *The Unhandy Man's Guide to Home Repairs: A Complete Guide to Home Maintenance, Improvements, and Remodeling, for Men and Women, Handy or Not.* New York: Macmillan, 1966.

Owen, David. *The Walls Around Us: The Thinking Person's Guide to How a House Works.* New York: Random House, 1991.

Panchyk, Katherine. *Solar Interiors: Energy-efficient Spaces Designed for Comfort.* New York: Van Nostrand Reinhold, 1984.

Philbin, Tom, and Steve R. Ettlinger. *The Complete Illustrated Guide to Everything Sold in Hardware Stores.* New York: Macmillan, 1988.

Rifkind, Carole. *A Field Guide to American Architecture.* New York: New American Library, 1980.

River. *Dwelling.* Illustrated by Leona Walden. Albion, CA: Freestone Pub. Co., 1983.

Seth, Sandra, and Laurel Seth. *Adobe! Homes and Interiors of Taos, Santa Fe, and the Southwest.* Illustrations by Valerie Graves. Stamford, CT: Architectural Book Publishers, Co, 1980.

Stageberg, James, and Susan Allen Toth. *A House of One's Own: An Architect's Guide to Designing the House of Your Dreams.* New York: Potter, 1991.

Tatum, Rita. *The Alternative House: A Complete Guide to Building and Buying.* Los Angeles: Reed Books, 1978.

Tetrault, Jeanne, ed. *The Woman's Carpentry Book: Building Your Home from the Ground Up.* Garden City, NY: Anchor Press/Doubleday, 1980.

Thomas, Sherry, and Jeanne Tetrault. *Country Women: A Handbook for the New Farmer.* Illustrated by Leona Walden. Garden City, NY: Anchor Press, 1976.

Twitchell, Mary. *Solar Projects for Under Five Hundred Dollars.* Pownal, VT: Storey Communications, 1985.

Vale, Brenda, and Robert Vale. *The Autonomous House: Design and Planning for Self-Sufficiency.* New York: Universe Books, 1975.

Venolia, Carol. *Healing Environments: Your Guide to Indoor Well-Being.* Berkeley: Celestial Arts, 1988.

Wade, Alex, and Neal Ewenstein. *30 Energy-Efficient Houses . . . You Can Build.* Emmaus, PA: Rodale Press, 1977.

Wahlfeldt, Bette Galman. *Wood Frame Housebuilding: An Illustrated Guide.* Blue Ridge Summit, PA: TAB, 1988.

Wells, Karen Muller. *Building Solar: How the Professional Builder Is Making Solar Construction Work.* New York: Van Nostrand Reinhold, 1984.

Williams, Elizabeth, and Robert Williams. *Rough Carpentry Illustrated.* Blue Ridge Summit, PA: TAB, 1990.

Women in the Trades

Martin, Molly, ed. *Hard Hatted Women: Stories of Struggle and Success in the Trades.* Seattle: Seal Press, 1988.

O'Connor, Patricia. *Hitting the Nail on the Head.* San Diego: Nugget Press, 1989.

Schroedel, Jean Reith, ed *Alone in a Crowd: Women in the Trades Tell Their Stories.* Philadelphia: Temple University Press, 1985.

Walshok, Mary Lindenstein. *Blue-Collar Women: Pioneers on the Male Frontier.* Garden City, NY: Anchor Books, 1981.

Westley, Laurie A. *A Territorial Issue: A Study of Women in the Construction Trades.* Washington, D.C.: Wider Opportunities for Women, 1982.

Women in Architecture

Anderson, Dorothy May. *Women, Design, and the Cambridge School.* West Lafayette, IN: PDA Publishers Corp., 1980.

Berkeley, Ellen Perry, ed., and Matilda McQuaid, assoc. ed. *Architecture: A Place for Women.* Washington, D.C.: Smithsonian Institution Press, 1989.

Cole, Doris. *From Tipi to Skyscraper: A History of Women in Architecture.* Boston: i press, inc., 1973.

Lorenz, Clare. *Women in Architecture: A Contemporary Perspective.* London: Trefoil, 1990.

"Making Room: Women and Architecture." *Heresies Magazine,* vol. 3, no. 3 (Winter 1981).

Martin, Rochelle, Wendy Chamberlin, and Sarah Haselschwardt. "Women as Architects: Have We Come a Long Way?" *Women and Environments,* vol. 7, no. 2 (Spring 1985): 18-20.

McQuiston, Liz. *Women in Design: A Contemporary View.* New York: Rizzoli, 1988.

Torre, Susana, ed. *Women in American Architecture: A Historic and Contemporary Perspective.* New York: Whitney Library of Design, 1977.

Wekerle, Gerda R., Rebecca Peterson, and David Morley, eds. *New Space for Women.* Boulder: Westview Press, 1980.

Gender, Community, and Design

Attfield, Judy, and Pat Kirkham, eds. *A View from the Interior: Feminism, Women, and Design.* London: Women's Press, 1989.

Birch, Eugenie Fadner, ed. *The Unsheltered Woman: Women and Housing in the '80s.* New Brunswick, NJ: Center for Urban Policy Research, Rutgers University, 1985.

Brion, Marion, and Anthea Tinker. *Women in Housing: Access and Influence.* London: Housing Centre Trust, 1980.

Duff, Carolyn S. *When Women Work Together: Using Our Strengths to Overcome Our Challenges.* Berkeley: Conari Press, 1993.

Ellis, William Russell, and Dana Cuff, eds. *Architect's People.* New York: Oxford University Press, 1989.

Gray, Virginia, and Alan Macrae. *Mud, Space & Spirit: Handmade Adobes.* Santa Barbara, CA: Capra Press, 1976.

Hassel, Mary Joyce, and Frieda D. Peatross. "Exploring Connections Between Women's Changing Roles and House Forms." *Environment and Behavior,* January 1990, vol. 22, no. 1: 3.

Hayden, Dolores. *The Grand Domestic Revolution: A History of Feminist Designs for American Homes, Neighborhoods, and Cities.* Cambridge, MA: MIT Press, 1981.

————. *Redesigning the American Dream: The Future of Housing, Work, and Family Life.* New York: W.W. Norton, 1984.

Leavitt, Jacqueline. "A New American House." *Women and Environments,* vol. 7, no. 1 (Winter 1985): 14-16.

Matrix Book Group. *Making Space: Women and the Man-Made Environment.* London: Pluto Press, 1984.

Mazey, Mary Ellen, and David R. Lee. *Her Space, Her Place: A Geography of Women.* Washington, D.C.: Association of American Geographers, 1983.

Roberts, Marion. *Living in a Man-Made World: Gender Assumptions in Modern Housing Design.* New York: Routledge, 1991.

Rosenberry, Sara, and Chester Hartman, eds. *Housing Issues of the Nineties.* New York: Praeger, 1989.

Snyder, Tim. "A House of Her Own." *Harrowsmith Country Life,* November/December 1990: 54-56, 73-77.

Spain, Daphne. *Gendered Spaces.* Chapel Hill, NC: University of North Carolina Press, 1992.

Sprague, Joan Forrester. *More Than Housing: Lifeboats for Women and Children.* Boston: Butterworth Architecture, 1991.

Turner, John F.C. *Housing by People: Towards Autonomy in Building Environments.* London: Marion Boyars Pub. Ltd., 1976.

Verloo, Mieke. "Shaping Women's Lives." *Women and Environments,* vol. 11, no. 3/4 (Spring/Summer 1989): 16-20.

Wampler, Jan. *All Their Own: People and the Places They Build.* Cambridge, MA: Schenkman Pub. Co., 1977.

Weinstein, Carol Simon, and Thomas G. David, eds. *Spaces for Children: The Built Environment and Child Development.* New York: Plenum Press, 1987.

Weisman, Leslie Kanes. *Discrimination by Design: A Feminist Critique of the Man-Made Environment.* Urbana, IL: University of Illinois Press, 1992.

Wekerle, Gerda R. *Women's Housing Projects in Eight Canadian Cities.* Toronto: Canada Mortgage and Housing Corporation, 1988.

Intentional Communities

Brandwein, Nancy, Jill MacNeice, and Peter Spiers. *The Group House Handbook.* Washington, D.C.: Acropolis Books, 1982.

Fromm, Dorit. *Collaborative Communities: Cohousing, Central Living and Other New Forms of Housing with Shared Facilities.* New York: Van Nostrand Reinhold, 1991.

"Sitka Housing Co-operative: Women House Themselves." *Women and Environments,* Spring 1988: 19-23.

Bibliographies

Atkinson, Steven D. *Solar Home Planning: A Bibliography and a Guide.* Metuchen, NJ: Scarecrow Press, 1988.

Coatsworth, Patricia A., ed. *Women and Urban Planning: A Bibliography.* Chicago: CPL Bibliographies, 1981.

Doumato, Lamia. *Architecture and Women: A Bibliography Documenting Women Architects, Landscape Architects, Designers, Architectural Critics, and Writers and Women in Related Fields Working in the U.S.* New York: Garland Pub., 1988.

Huls, Mary Ellen. *Expansible Houses: A Bibliography.* Monticello, IL: Vance Bibliographies, 1987.

Inman, Marjorie. *Psychological Aspects of Housing and the Built-Environment: A Bibliography.* Monticello, IL: Vance Bibliographies, 1987.

McCullough, Rita I., ed. *Sources: An Annotated Bibliography of Women's Issues.* Manchester, CT: KIT, 1991.

Rosenfelt, Deborah Silverton, ed. *Strong Women: An Annotated Bibliography of Literature for the High School Classroom.* Old Westbury, NY: Feminist Press, 1976.

Poetry, Fiction, and Biographies

Doro, Sue. *Blue Collar Goodbyes.* Watsonville, CA: Papier-Mache Press, 1992.

———. *Heart, Home and Hard Hats: The Non-Traditional Work and Words of a Woman Machinist and Mother.* Minneapolis: Midwest Villages and Voices, 1986.

Eisenberg, Susan. *It's a Good Thing I'm Not Macho: A Cycle of Poems.* Boston: Whetstone Press, 1984.

Garvy, Helen. *I Built Myself a House: A Step-by-step Guide to Building a Simple Country Cabin with Post and Beam Construction.* Illustrated by Susan Freeman. San Francisco: Shire Press, 1975.

Gratten, Virginia L. *Mary Colter, Builder Upon the Red Earth.* Flagstaff, AZ: Northland Press, 1980.

LaBastille, Ann. *Woodswoman.* New York: E.P. Dutton, 1976.

Rich, Louise Dickenson. *We Took to the Woods.* New York: Grosset and Dunlap, 1942.

Richardson, Marilyn, and Janice H. Mikesell, eds. *Women, Houses & Homes: An Anthology of Prose, Poetry, and Photography.* Brookings, SD: UNIpress, 1988.

Stokes, Ann. *A Studio of One's Own.* Tallahassee, FL: Naiad Press, 1985.

Books for Children

Allinson, Beverley, and Judith Lawrence. *Myra Builds a House.* Toronto: DC Heath, 1975.

Homan, Dianne. *In Christina's Toolbox.* Chapel Hill, NC: Lollipop Power, 1981.

Lillegard, Dee. *I Can Be a Carpenter.* Chicago: Children's Press, 1986.

Mitchell, Vanessa. *Homes Then and Now.* Milwaukee: Gareth Stevens Pub., 1985.

Walker, Les. *Carpentry for Children.* Woodstock, NY: Overlook Press, 1982.

———. *Housebuilding for Children.* London: Architectural Press, 1977.

Journals

Communities. Rutledge, MO.

Country Women: A Feminist Country Survival Manual and a Creative Journal. Albion, CA: Country Women.

Tradeswomen Magazine. San Francisco: Tradeswomen, Inc.

Women and Environments. Toronto: Center for Urban Community Studies.

About the Author

Janice Goldfrank was born in Chicago and raised in St. Paul. After receiving her BA in art history from the University of Rochester, she went into the custom woodworking business. In 1979, though neither had experience in construction, she and her husband built their own home and woodworking shop. Ms. Goldfrank then started an all-woman carpentry company and established her own general contracting business, Octagon Custom Builders, Inc. in 1989. She is currently the program director of Training for the Trades, a nontraditional job training program for women. She lives with her husband, Edward, in Austerlitz, New York.

Quality Books from Papier-Mache Press

At Papier-Mache Press, it is our goal to identify and successfully present important social issues through enduring works of beauty, grace, and strength. Through our work we hope to encourage empathy and respect among diverse communities, creating a bridge of understanding between the mainstream audience and those who might not otherwise be heard.

We appreciate you, our customer, and strive to earn your continued support. We also value the role of the bookseller in achieving our goals. We are especially grateful to the many independent booksellers whose presence ensures a continuing diversity of opinion, information, and literature in our communities. We encourage you to support these bookstores with your patronage.

We publish many fine books about women's experiences. We also produce lovely posters and T-shirts that complement our anthologies. Please ask your local bookstore which Papier-Mache items they carry. To receive our complete catalog, send your request to Papier-Mache Press, 135 Aviation Way, #14, Watsonville, CA 95076, or call our toll-free number, 800-927-5913.